The Questions
of Moral Philosophy

The Questions
of Moral Philosophy

Michael Shenefelt

Humanity
Books

an imprint of Prometheus Books
59 John Glenn Drive, Amherst, New York 14228-2197

Published 1999 by Humanity Books, an imprint of Prometheus Books

03 02 01 00 99   5 4 3 2 1

Library of Congress Cataloging-in-Publication Data

The questions of moral philosophy / by Michael Shenefelt.
      p.   cm.
    Includes bibliographical references and index.
    ISBN 1–57392–637–X (paper)
    ISBN 1–57392–638–8 (cloth)
    1. Moral philosophy. I. Shenefelt, Michael.

Printed in the United States of America on acid-free paper

CIP data pending

To Ben

Contents

Preface

I INTEND THE following pages as neither a survey of philosophy nor a commentary, but an appreciation—a sort of stroll through the gardens of the discipline, where I hope to point out some of the more interesting sights. I have therefore made no attempt to canvass all topics that might come up in a course on moral and political thought (important though they are), nor have I tried to describe all the latest theories of living philosophers. Instead, my only purpose is to entertain, by walking with the reader down philosophy's royal road. I offer this excursion to anyone who has never had formal training in the field, but especially to the young, who may find philosophy both pleasing and inspiring.

Acknowledgments

I AM INDEBTED to two colleagues, Ronald Rainey and Phil Washburn, for many helpful criticisms, and to my wife Maria for her tireless efforts to steer me in the direction of plain English.

1.

Why Be Moral?

WHY DOES ANYONE bother to do the right thing? Do we do the right thing because it is right, or merely because we fear the consequences of doing wrong? This question now arises every day, but it is also quite old. Plato's brother Glaucon disputes it with the philosopher Socrates in one of Plato's dialogues, composed almost twenty-four centuries ago in ancient Athens; Glaucon says people do right only because they lack the power to do evil. And to buttress this view, Glaucon tells the story of Gyges' Ring.

Gyges was a shepherd in Lydia, in Asia Minor, and one day, while he tended his flock, there was an earthquake. When the earthquake subsided, however, Gyges recovered his footing and saw that the earth had been fractured nearby, leaving a gigantic chasm. He approached the chasm and looked down, then saw at the bottom of it a giant horse, made of bronze, that had apparently been buried ages before. Gyges gazed for a while, then mustered his courage to descend for a closer look.

When he reached the horse itself, he saw that it was many times larger than a man and that it was fitted with doors, which were ajar. He shifted his view till he could look within, then saw within it a corpse, the corpse of a giant, entirely naked, but for a golden ring on its finger. Gyges was a poor man; he crawled through the doors and took the ring. Then he climbed back to the surface, and no sooner did he reach it than another earthquake, apparently an aftershock, closed the chasm behind him. Gyges at first said nothing of the incident (perhaps he feared that it would appear as sacrilege), but he nevertheless wore the ring and had it with him later in the month when he attended a meeting of other shepherds. Exactly why the shepherds of Lydia found it necessary to hold meetings, Glaucon never explains, but evidently the subject of discussion was

11

infinitely boring, and in his boredom Gyges began to play with the ring. He turned the crown of the ring inward, toward his palm, and then discovered that the other shepherds spoke as if he had left the room. When he turned the crown outward, however, they spoke as if he had returned. And thus he discovered that he had obtained a ring of invisibility.

Gyges resolved not to let this opportunity slip by. He got himself chosen to be among the group of shepherds who would report to the king of Lydia during the next month. But when the time came and he had arrived at the capital, he turned the ring inward again, made himself invisible, and stole into the apartments of the queen. Then he appeared to her, seduced her, got her help in murdering the king, and became the tyrant of Lydia. And so with the ring of invisibility still in his possession, he enjoyed the fruits of tyranny to a ripe old age.

The story is of course quite fanciful, just the sort of fable in which the ancient Greeks delighted, but it nevertheless contains a real point. Why is it, after all, that people obey the rules? Glaucon says only because there are no such rings.

Where Glaucon leaves off, his other brother Adeimantus then joins the discussion with Socrates to buttress the claim that people are moral only because they are weak. Socrates opposes the assertions of both young men, who seem, after all, only to be playing devil's advocate, but he is willing to hear them out. According to Adeimantus, a man or woman of apparent virtue is really moral only because he or she lacks the power of a Gyges to avoid punishments and obtain pleasures without fear. We value morality merely as a means, says Adeimantus, a means to getting what we want, not as an end in itself. But not only the cynical say this; so do the poets, so do the priests. Look at what religion teaches, says Adeimantus, and you find exactly the same view.

The priests (meaning the pagan priests of ancient Greece) preach that when the just die they go to a vast table in the sky where they eat ambrosia and drink wine with the gods, as if the reward of virtue were to be drunk at a banquet through all eternity. The unjust, on the other hand, are plunged head first into the mud of the underworld or made to transport water in sieves or set to performing other impossible tasks forever as punishment for their wickedness. Why are we told these tales? Because, says Adeimantus, not even the priests and poets, who invent these stories, will trust us to do the right thing simply because it is right. No, they suppose we need to be threatened into it or bribed into it, if not with the rewards and punishments of this world, then with the rewards and punishments of the next. Parents often teach morality to their children in the same way. They tell their children to do right not *because* it is right, but because it pays, either in this life or in heaven. Thus, poets, priests, and parents often appeal to all that is lowest and basest in us—not to our noblest motives but to impulses that are actually selfish and cowardly.

The subsequent history of ethics is in many ways a commentary on Glaucon's view (which appears, by the way, in Book 2 of Plato's *Republic*). If morality pays, how does it pay? Or should we say instead that the truly honest person does the right thing whether or not it pays? Will it suffice to say that an honest person aims at *inner* rewards, the rewards of personal satisfaction? Or is this, too, a subtle confusion? That is, if we say that an honest person aims at satisfying his inner self, at achieving inner harmony and finding spiritual contentment, haven't we still put the emphasis on the wrong point? Instead, shouldn't we say, perhaps, that the truly honest person tries to do right *regardless* of whether it brings him spiritual contentment? And while we are at it, we might also ask, Is it even possible to find spiritual contentment if my only aim in life is to achieve my own contentment? (The English philosopher John Stuart Mill raised much the same question in his autobiography when he looked back on his own nervous breakdown. He remarks, "Those only are happy who have their minds fixed on some object other than their own happiness.")[1] Many able thinkers and writers have joined battle over these difficulties, but of all the answers through the ages, perhaps the most profound and puzzling comes from the German philosopher Immanuel Kant.

Kant (1724–1804) is remembered today as a man of strict habits (townsfolk are said to have set their clocks by his comings and goings) and bewildering terminology (he uses expressions like "the transcendental deduction," "the noumenal world," "the manifold of representations in space and time," "the analytic of concepts," and "the organon of pure reason"). And he spent his whole life in just one town—the city of Konigsberg in East Prussia. His works are exceedingly abstract and dwell on one of the most difficult of all philosophical domains, the field of metaphysics, yet he begins his answer to Glaucon in the simplest way. He begins with a basic distinction from everyday life, that there is an indelible difference between doing a thing because we *want* to and doing it because we *ought* to. This is how he distinguishes between doing a thing because it pays and doing it because it is right.

If I do a thing because it is *right*, says Kant, then whether I *want* to do it is beside the point. The whole idea of acting from conscience is different from acting for my mere satisfaction. It is certainly different from trying to make myself feel better or trying to achieve my own contentment. We often overlook this distinction (and we can also make too much of it), but it remains fundamental. Strictly speaking, the question posed to us by conscience is *not* about feeling better or being contented. Attend for a moment to the demands of conscience, says the Kantian, and observe what conscience requires. Does conscience beckon us to calculate which course of action will ultimately make us *feel* better? Or does it beckon us to calculate which course of action is morally right? Notice that the two questions *are* different. It is one thing to ask, "Will this

---

1. *Autobiography of John Stuart Mill*, Columbia Paperback Edition (New York: Columbia University Press, 1960), 100.

make me feel better?" It is quite another thing to ask, "Is it right?" Lest it seem that these two questions are *not* different, notice that I can always say to myself, "Ah, yes, this will certainly make me *feel* better, but is it right?" Yet this sort of internal scrutiny would make no sense at all if the two questions were originally identical. When I ask myself, in a moment of introspection, "Is doing what makes me feel better necessarily right?" I am not speaking mere nonsense; I am not asking, "Is making myself feel better the same as making myself feel better?" No, I am posing an intelligible question, which would be impossible if the two ideas (feeling better and doing right) were the same. To ask about the *feeling* of a deed, or about the contentment of it, is quite distinct from asking about its rightness. Yet what conscience demands above all is that we do right and that we strive for it without prejudice. Thus, the question of feeling better, though undoubtedly important, is beside the point.

If conscience has a voice, then Kant supposes this voice to be different from any other desire. Conscience speaks (as it were) in the language of a drill sergeant: "I don't give a damn what you *want* to do; I am telling you what you *must* do." Kant supposes that anyone who has ever felt the tug of moral obligation is acquainted with this voice. The awareness of "ought" is different in kind from the mere awareness of wanting. Kant calls this awareness of "ought" the "sense of duty"; he calls the mere awareness of wanting "inclination."

Kant propounds these views in a deeply ponderous book, *The Groundwork of the Metaphysics of Morals*, and many of the book's critics are quick to deny that the distinction between duty and inclination is real. The critics argue, with much justice, that no one would do his duty were he not already "inclined" to it. Hence, duty is just another form of inclination. If I have done what I ought (say the critics), then surely there is some sense in which I "wanted" to do so. But consider for a moment the real force of this objection. Its real force, I suspect, is only to stress a likeness between two things (between duty and inclination), whereas Kant is at pains to stress a difference.

Many things are in some ways alike and in some ways unlike, but on the whole, Kant's purpose is to bring out how they are unlike. Though "wanting" can be defined in such broad terms that it includes even the desire to be moral, the Kantian is still anxious to say that there is a crucial difference between wanting to do right and wanting, say, to have ice cream. Conscientiousness is a frame of mind quite different from mere hunger or appetite. And Kant's aim is to bring out this difference. If he then assigns different words to these attitudes, it is because he is still dealing, he thinks, with a basic difference in things. Put another way, the key point is not how duty is *like* other inclinations but how it stands apart.

Indeed, in Kant's view, the whole essence of duty is the feeling that we are commanded *regardless* of our wants. Recall, again, the drill sergeant: "I don't give a damn what you *want* to do; I am telling you what you *must* do." The sense of duty is the feeling that your mere wants, which are personal, are suddenly subordinated to something higher. To be sure, duty and inclination do not necessarily conflict. I often find my duty both pleasing and profitable to me, and so I have numerous motives for doing it. Duty can be enjoyable. Nevertheless, duty and inclination, though often in harmony, are still distinct. To act from duty is to act in the conviction that one's mere wants are beside the point.

Kant expresses this idea (in his rather ponderous way) by saying that conscience commands categorically. Because commands are usually expressed in what grammarians call the "imperative mood" (as in "Shut the door!" or "Be quiet!"), Kant says the voice of duty is a "categorical imperative." This takes some explaining, and one way to see his meaning more clearly is to consider for a moment two different uses of an imperative sentence.

"Beat two egg whites!" says a cookbook. But this imperative from a cookbook is addressed only to those who are interested in something particular—baking a cake. "Sell short!" says a stockbroker. But the stockbroker's imperative is again addressed only to those interested in something particular—making money. Kant calls these imperatives "hypothetical," because they are issued only on the hypothesis that the person being addressed wishes to satisfy a particular desire, such as the desire for a cake or the desire to make money. Such imperatives might be rewritten in the "if-then" form (what logicians call a "hypothetical" statement), thus: "If you want to make money, then sell short; otherwise, do whatever you damn well please!"

The voice of conscience commands differently. Conscience does not address a particular desire. It is unconcerned with your particular desire for a cake or your particular desire for money. Instead, its whole tone implies that your mere desires have been subordinated; it commands regardless of your desires. Its command is "categorical" in the sense that the command is unqualified; there is no implicit "if" clause inquiring into whether you have any particular desire other than the desire to be moral. Conscience omits these ifs, ands, and buts.

In some ways, Kant's doctrine resembles that of another rather ponderous writer, the founder of psychoanalysis, Sigmund Freud. Freud locates conscience in what he calls the "superego" and says it originates in the internalized judgments of one's parents. Yet Freud also takes for granted that the demands of the superego are indeed distinguishable from those of the body and the external world. Put another way, Freud, like Kant, assumes that the distinction between duty and inclination is already reasonably clear. The demands of conscience have a different tone from those of the stomach or of one's friends. To be sure, according to Freud, the internal demands of conscience were once external, having originated in our parents' praises or punishments. Still, in Freud's view, the process of internalization involves a change in tone, a change in voice, a change in authority. And it is precisely this change in authority that Kant means to capture. Wherever conscience comes from, the idea of it, once formed, is quite distinct from other mental phenomena (or so Kant supposes), and what he means to capture is this distinction. Thus, though Kant and Freud may differ on

other points (on the objectivity of moral judgments, perhaps), their main difference with regard to the voice of conscience is not really one of doctrine but of
purpose. Freud's purpose is to discover the *origins* of conscience: Where does it
come from, and what affects it? Kant's purpose, on the other hand, is to determine the *definition* of conscience: What do we mean by "conscience" in the first
place? As Kant himself puts it, his aim is to "develop the concept."[2]

In Kant's view, conscience is a kind of imposition on oneself, and it is sometimes quite onerous, yet it is still an imposition *by* oneself and not by someone
else. What matters for Kant is not whether *other* people believe your conduct
worth performing but whether you believe it in your own mind, and it is this
aspect of his philosophy that makes him most like a modern existentialist. He is
concerned above all with sincerity of purpose. Still, it is also important to see
that, for Kant, the voice of conscience is no mere whim. It is much more. The
subordination imposed by conscience, though imposed *by* oneself, is still a subordination *to* something higher. This, too, requires some explaining.

In Kant's view, the subordination demanded by conscience is a subordination to moral principle. Recall once more his point about "wanting," that to act
from duty is to act in the conviction that your mere wants are beside the point.
But in that event, the mere wants of anyone else in the same situation would
also be beside the point. *All* moral agents, faced with the same situation, would
be equally obligated. Some such meaning is apparently intended in his famous
formulation of the categorical imperative—that to act from duty is to "act on a
maxim that you can at the same time will to be a universal law." Kant's appeal
to universal law has generated numerous disputes among interpreters and critics,
and it is an old and troubling question whether universal moral rules can be for-
mulated for anything but trivial cases. Still, his basic point seems plain enough.
When you act from conscience, you act in the conviction that your duty goes
beyond your merely personal passions; there is something quite general about it.
It becomes for you a "matter of principle." And it is thus quite different from the
sort of motivation that Glaucon and Adeimantus have in mind. You impose on
yourself a commitment to moral principle even if you can't say exactly what this
principle is. You can easily have this feeling, believing your duty to be commanded by some sort of universal moral rule, even if you can't state with precision just what the rule is, and even if no one else can state it either. The belief
in such a rule can still be present even if no one can quite define it.

This much understood, it is now, perhaps, not too hard to see how a Kantian
answers another old and troubling question, slightly different from the one ini-
tially posed by Glaucon and Adeimantus, but closely related—the question,

---

2. *The Groundwork of the Metaphysics of Morals*, Section 1, 396. Most of my quotations are
from Lewis White Beck's translation, published by Macmillan as *Foundations of the Metaphysics of
Morals*, 2nd ed. (New York: Macmillan, 1989). All citations of the work refer to the reference numbers that are used by scholars and that appear in brackets in this and similar editions.

Why be moral? A Kantian answers this further question by attacking it as confused. What, after all, does it mean?

If it means "Why is path A the morally right path, rather than path B?" then perhaps reasons are available as to why A is indeed the right path. But the question can also mean something quite different. It can mean, "Why should I care whether or not my actions are morally right?" or "Why should I be conscientious?" And in that event, says the Kantian, it seems to betray a confusion of ideas. What it really means is, "How will conscientiousness be profitable to me?" But if a person needs further reasons why conscientiousness will indeed be profitable to him, then he is not being conscientious from the start. The whole idea of conscientiousness is to act *without* regard to profit. Anyone who needs further reasons why morality would be a good thing, is already looking to have the desire to be moral supplanted by some other desire. He wants to be moral only as a *means* to satisfying something else, and in wishing this, he has already forgotten what true morality is. The whole essence of conscience is to forgo this kind of calculation in the first place. He has turned a deaf ear to morality's "categorical imperative," and he listens instead for a merely hypothetical one. Long before Kant, the Roman orator Cicero made essentially this same point in a letter to his friend Atticus in the first century B.C.: "In saying that a man ought to be good to escape evil, and not because it is by nature the right thing to do, they do not perceive that they are speaking of a cunning man, and not of a good one."[3] In a word, to ask "Why be moral?" is to lose sight of what real morality is.

But where, then, does this leave Plato's old story of Gyges' Ring?

The answer is fairly simple. The real force of Glaucon's remarks in that old story of Plato's is not to propound an intelligible version of the question "Why be moral?"—which is often our first reaction to the tale. Rather, their real force, whatever Plato's original intention, is to propound a *distinction*—the distinction between a truly conscientious person and a merely self-interested one. As Cicero says, there is still a difference between a good man and a cunning one. Yet this is not quite the whole of the matter. We can still ask which of the two, the good person or the cunning one, has the better life.

It is one thing to say that the two sorts of motivation are different, the motive of conscience and the motive of self-interest. But it is quite another thing to say which of the two makes a life genuinely better. And the question of which life is better is still important, because the two sorts of motivation often conflict. More broadly, though the story of Gyges' Ring succeeds in distinguishing the motive of duty from the motive of inclination, it does not really answer the age-old question, What is the good life? Nor does it explain why people sometimes choose to be conscientious, but sometimes utterly renounce it. This, too, is a problem worth thinking about.

---

3. *Letters to Atticus*, Book 7, no. 2, 4.

2.

What Is the Good Life?

THE ANCIENT HISTORIAN Herodotus says that when the wise man Solon gave laws to the Athenians in 592 B.C., he decided to travel, ostensibly to see the world but really to avoid having to change the laws he had made. So Solon went east, and among the places he visited was the court of Croesus the Lydian, who was ruler of Sardis and the richest man in the world. Croesus knew Solon by reputation already, but when Solon arrived, Croesus avoided him for four days. Instead, Croesus had his servants show Solon the magnificent capital and its vast treasuries. Then he finally summoned Solon into his presence, and with a twinkle in his eye, he asked who, of all the people Solon had met, was the happiest man. Solon replied immediately, "Tellus of Athens."

Croesus was not pleased. Who, he wanted to know, was Tellus of Athens? So Solon explained that Tellus had had fine children, had lived to see his children's children, had flourished at a time when his country was prosperous, and had finally died gloriously in battle, where he had done more than anyone else to rout the enemy. Yes, Solon insisted, Tellus of Athens.

Croesus soon recovered his good humor and with a renewed twinkle he asked, Who was the second happiest man? Solon replied immediately, "Cleobis and Bito." Solon said Cleobis and Bito were brothers whose mother had wanted to be carried to the temple in an oxcart, but when the oxen refused to come in from the field, the two brothers put the yoke on their own necks and pulled their mother five miles in the cart to the temple. The townspeople marveled at the deed, and the mother marveled, too, and afterward she prayed that the gods would bestow some great blessing on her sons. Cleobis and Bito then feasted, entered the temple, and fell asleep, never to wake again. The gods had apparently answered the mother's prayer and had taken her sons' souls to heaven. Yes, Solon insisted, Cleobis and Bito.

19

Croesus now lost all patience with this strange Greek and demanded to know why he, Croesus, by virtue of his wealth and power, shouldn't be counted the happiest man in the world. Solon replied that a life is like a story, and that you can't tell a good one from a bad one until you hear the end. Solon counseled, "Count no man happy until he is dead." Croesus appealed to his riches, but Solon said even a treasury of gold is worthless if it fails to come also with a treasury of luck. Croesus invoked his dominion over many lands, but Solon answered, "The power above us is full of jealousy and fond of troubling our lot. . . . Oftentimes God gives men a gleam of happiness and then plunges them into ruin." Croesus at last dismissed Solon with a wave of his hand and for some years never thought of him again.

It was not long afterward that Croesus conceived the grand ambition of his life, to conquer the Persian kingdom of Cyrus, which was still farther eastward, but first he sent to the Oracle of Apollo at Delphi, in Greece, to know whether such an attack would succeed. The Oracle replied, if Croesus attacked Cyrus, a mighty kingdom would be destroyed. Croesus, delighted, attacked immediately. But he was immediately overwhelmed. (The Oracle remarked later that he should have asked which kingdom was intended; it was his own.) The soldiers of Cyrus seized Croesus at his defeat and tied him to a stake to be burned, but just as the flames were about to reach him, Croesus, who had been deathly silent, finally uttered just these words: "O Solon, Solon, Solon." Cyrus heard the utterance and commanded that Croesus be brought to him, but his soldiers would have been much too late to retrieve Croesus from the flames, were it not for the timely intervention (so it is said) of a rain cloud.

Croesus would at first say nothing to Cyrus, but after much prodding, he at last explained that he had once met a wise man, named Solon, who had told him to count no man happy until he is dead. Then Cyrus spared Croesus, and ever afterward Cyrus could find no wiser counselor in all Persia than this fallen despot, whose sufferings had made him a better man. This, at least, is how Herodotus tells the tale,[1] and though most historians now think the whole thing impossible, because the dates of Solon's travels do not match the dates of Croesus's reign, it is perhaps still useful as a warning on one of the Greeks' persistent themes: the dangers of arrogance.

The story of Solon and Croesus charmed the ancients, yet it is not hard to see that the story also contains a serious limitation. The story succeeds not by telling us what the good life *is* but by telling us what it is *not*. The good life, according to Solon, is neither vast wealth nor momentary prosperity. But in that case, What is it? Most answers now in circulation, no matter how much in vogue, are actually quite ancient.

Among the more austere answers, for example, is Stoicism—a doctrine that emerged as a distinct school about three centuries after Solon and that still sur-

---

1. In Book 1 of his *Histories*, 29–33, 46–91.

vives today. The Stoics say the good life consists of just two things: virtue and a positive attitude (or what they used to call "action and assent"). So long as you do the right thing and preserve a tranquil state of mind, this is a life worth living. It then makes no difference whether you suffer pain, defeat, opprobrium, or death. Versions of this noble and perhaps grim philosophy have appeared in all historical periods and probably in most cultures. Plato flirted with it, and it prompted Aristotle to remark that no one would call a suffering but just man happy "unless he were defending a paradox."[2] But the chief objection to Stoicism has always been its apparent inconsistency.

Protecting other people against unnecessary suffering is part of right conduct, a point that Stoics typically admit. Yet their creed also seems to assert that mere suffering does not matter. All that matters is action and attitude. So long as you think positively, mere suffering is irrelevant. Why, then, strive to alleviate the suffering of anyone else? The English philosopher Bertrand Russell slyly characterized the Stoic doctrine thus: "Certain things are vulgarly considered goods, but this is a mistake; what *is* good is a will directed toward securing these false goods for other people."[3]

Another way to put the problem is to say that the basic thrust of Stoicism is to discount physical torments and physical pleasures, but if this is so, why concern yourself with the physical well-being of anyone else? The Renaissance statesman Thomas More propounded a similar objection in his little classic *Utopia*, an objection that he phrased as a dilemma: either pleasure is indeed good, or it isn't; if it isn't, then why help anyone else to get it? But if it *is* good, then we can hardly be blamed for seeking a little for ourselves.

The more common view, to the contrary, is that the good life is a collection of multifarious elements—a composite. Right conduct is part of the good life, according to this composite view, but so is pleasure. And so the good life is a mixture of *different* things, none of which is reducible to the others. Perhaps the best defense of this composite view comes from Plato, who advanced it by proposing a small experiment involving an oyster. Plato's experiment of the oyster was originally intended to combat yet another theory (the theory that *pleasure* alone constitutes the good life, which is the doctrine now called "hedonism"), but his experiment can also be turned against the Stoic.

Suppose, says Plato, you were an oyster at the bottom of the sea, and suppose you could have the full complement of an oyster's pleasures (indeed, you would be bathed in bliss), but without memory, without knowledge, without acquaintances, and without discernible action. You would perform no noble or heroic deeds. You would have no work before you except digestion. Still, by hypothesis, you *would* have intense and continuous pleasure. Now, if you could

---

2. *Nicomachean Ethics*, Book 1, chap. 5, 1096a2.

3. Bertrand Russell, *A History of Western Philosophy* (New York: Simon and Schuster, 1945), chap. 28, 268–69.

indeed have such a life, would you really call it "good"? Oysters no doubt have a place in the world, but would you think human life improved if all the world's people could be reduced to the state of such oysters? Everything else being equal, wouldn't you prefer instead that your pleasure be *accompanied*, say, with knowledge and courage? As Aristotle expresses this point, "Pleasure *with* intelligence is better than pleasure alone."[4] You might envy the oyster's bliss, but hardly anyone would call this the *whole* of the good life.

The oyster experiment (from Plato's *Philebus*, 21a-e) may perhaps refute the idea that pleasure is the *only* good, yet this same experiment can also be turned against the Stoic. The Stoic seems to maintain that virtue alone is the good life. But might we not say by the same token that virtue *with* pleasure is better than virtue alone? If pleasure is not the *sole* good, it may yet be *a* good, so why not have as many goods as possible? Put another way, if you are filling up your picnic basket with goodies, why not have them all?

It is easy to see how considerations such as these could have led Aristotle, who studied with Plato for twenty years and who also embraced the composite view, to reach his famous definition of the "happy" man in Book 1 of his *Nicomachean Ethics*. Aristotle was exceedingly learned, having acquired the nickname "the reader" while still a student in Plato's Academy, and he remains one of our major sources for philosophical doctrines from before his own time. He explored a great many such questions, but on the issue of the good life, he thought the oyster experiment decisive. So, according to Aristotle, the "happy" man—meaning the most fortunate man—has not just *one* good thing; he has *all* good things. He leads a life of "complete excellence"—"physical, intellectual and moral"—which he displays in action, but he is also furnished with sufficient "external goods" (including material advantages), and that not for an interval only, but over a complete life. Even the conception of what counts as a "complete" life varies, depending on whether you are a Stoic or an Aristotelian.

For the Stoic, the goodness or badness of a life depends entirely on the mind of the person who lives it. If that person means well and thinks well, then his life is good, complete, fulfilled, and no change in external circumstances can alter this result. The Roman emperor Marcus Aurelius defends this Stoic idea in his *Meditations*:

> a rational soul . . . can contemplate herself, analyze herself, make of herself what she will. . . . [U]nlike dances or plays or such like, where if they are suddenly cut short the performance as a whole is left imperfect, the soul, no matter at what stage arrested, will have her task complete to her own satisfaction, and be able to say, "I am in the fullest possession of mine own."[5]

---

4. *Nicomachean Ethics*, Book 10, chap. 2, 1172b30.
5. Marcus Aurelius, *Meditations*, trans. Maxwell Staniforth (1964; reprint, New York: Penguin USA, Viking, 1987), Book 11, no. 1.

For the Stoic, there is no such thing as being cut off before your time.

For the Aristotelian, on the other hand, external circumstances must cooperate with virtue to make a life worth living. Bad luck can still make even the most virtuous life deplorable, and a life is not good until something external has been accomplished. Thus, the philosophy of the Stoic is thoroughly spiritual; the philosophy of Aristotle is at least partly worldly.

Aristotle and the Stoics are the two great poles of much subsequent ethical discussion, and many other theories will still lead you back to their ideas. Take, for example, the notion that the good life consists of power, a fashionable theory in every century. Still, if you embrace this notion, have you really arrived at an answer to the good life? Actually, you have not made the slightest advance. Why? Because to obtain power is to obtain the *means* to something, but defining the good life is more than a matter of means; it is a question of ends. Put another way, even if you *do* get power, what will you do with it? What will you use your power *for*? Until you have answered this further question, you have not really arrived at a conception of the good life but only a theory of what you would need to grasp it. Of course, power is thought to exist in many forms—economic, political, spiritual, perhaps even magical—and many people seek it avidly. But the notion that power is the good life is still incomplete, and even less clear than I have suggested already, because unless you know what you will do with your power, how do you even know whether you have power of the right sort? If there are several sorts, which is best? The value of power, either as means or as end, seems to depend at least partly on how it is used. (Many writers have celebrated power, but hardly any have said that its use is a matter of complete indifference.) Thus, you are still likely to find yourself posing the ancient question once more: Is the good life entirely in the mind or at least partly in the world?

It is hard to say how either of these views—the Aristotelian or the Stoic—can be definitively proved or refuted, but there is at least one point that still needs to be made in defense of the Stoic, and another that needs to be made as a caution to the Aristotelian. The point in favor of the Stoic is that his philosophy is *not* inconsistent. Stoicism involves no internal contradiction, and the suspicion that it does rests on a confusion.

Let me explain this confusion briefly. Recall the Stoic doctrine that the good life consists in just two things: virtue and a positive attitude. Strictly speaking, then, the Stoic does *not* say that the good life consists in virtue alone. Rather, he says it consists in virtue *and* attitude. Thus, Stoicism also regards the good life as a composite, though a very minimal composite of just two elements.

It is also true that the logical consequence of Stoicism is that a man dying on a cross, after first enduring torture, should regard his life as entirely enviable and fortunate, so long as he acts rightly and thinks positively. A crucified wise man should then have nothing to complain about, even if he has no expectation of an afterlife. (I should add that the ancient Stoics traditionally regarded suicide as honorable, if the torments of life became too great.) Yet however hard and unlikely this result may sound, its unlikeliness does not make the doctrine contradictory. It is still perfectly consistent with this outlook to say that this same man, the man who is ultimately crucified, also has a moral duty to protect others from the very fate that he embraces with indifference. How can this be?

The essential idea of Stoic indifference to the material world is that the mind can determine entirely for itself whether it finds happiness or misery in its worldly destiny. The Stoic thus stresses (though he possibly exaggerates) our capacity to put the best face on events and to embrace them cheerfully. The ancient Stoics expressed this emphasis with the maxim, "Opinion is all." Thus interpreted, Stoicism implies a psychological thesis to the effect that the mind can overcome crushing adversity.

Yet the Stoic can also admit that this reconciling ability of the mind is not equally developed in all persons. Some people make no effort to develop such an ability, and some deny that its development is possible. The Stoic can thus agree with Thomas More that pleasure is a good (if by pleasure we mean content- ment), and he can acknowledge a resulting duty to promote, where possible, the contentment of everyone, including himself. But he can also believe that the means of promoting his own contentment may be fundamentally different from the means of promoting someone else's. Not all people find their contentment in the same way. I have an obligation, where possible, to please little children, but what pleases little children will not necessarily please me. Thus, the Stoic can admit that although physical pleasures may indeed be a means to the good of others, they are not necessarily a means to his own, because of his different psychological temperament. Thus, the Stoic's outlook, though demanding and maybe even condescending, is still consistent.[6]

It may also be noted that a Stoic is not an ascetic (someone who punishes his body); Stoicism and asceticism are different points of view. The Stoic regards the material world as unimportant. An ascetic, on the other hand, regards it as an invitation to evil. In Christianity, the ascetic traditionally seeks to "chastise the flesh" or "mortify the lusts of the body." In Buddhism, the ascetic seeks "joy in renunciation." But the Stoic (and there can be both Christian and Buddhist Stoics) regards the material world as merely inessential. Marcus Aurelius (the Roman emperor) is once again instructive. He expresses the Stoic attitude when he describes his father-in-law, the emperor Aurelius Antoninus Pius:

> He accepted without either complacency or compunction such material com-
> forts as fortune had put at his disposal; when they were to hand he would avail

---

6. Put another way, the criticisms suggested by Thomas More and Bertrand Russell both depend on confusing the *means* of promoting a person's contentment with the end of contentment itself. The Stoic implicitly agrees that contentment is good, but he denies that the means of pro- moting his own contentment are physical.

himself of them frankly, but when they were not, he had no regrets. (Book 1, no. 16)

The warning to the Aristotelian is different. Aristotle's doctrine has the obvious merit of appearing realistic, and it is characteristic of all his teachings that they should conform to the apparent common sense of his day. Aristotle has often been called the first "common sense" philosopher. Yet his doctrine as I have stated it so far still leaves the most important question of morality unanswered. The best life, we are told, consists in having all virtues—physical, intellectual, and moral—and also in having sufficient external goods over a complete life. But to expound this doctrine is not to say which of these various ingredients, which virtues and which "external goods," are most important. The real problem of morality is not to define the ideal life by throwing in every conceivable good. The real problem is to choose which things to give up when we can't have them all. Life involves sacrifice. So which good things should be sacrificed for the sake of which? As it turns out, Aristotle reaches this further issue also, and he answers much like a Stoic: He puts morality ahead of all other goods.[7] So on this further point, the two philosophies seem to agree. Still, from a literary point of view, it is the Stoic writers who seem most adept at conveying the idea of moral courage in the face of adversity.

The Stoic Seneca, who was tutor and later advisor to the Roman emperor Nero, writes, "Men do not care how nobly they live, but only how long, yet it is within the reach of every man to live nobly, and within no man's power to live long."[8] Stoic writers have always appealed to men and women of character whose honor and integrity have been tested by disappointment. Their real purpose has been to teach humanity how to endure blasted hopes.

The Stoic teacher Epictetus, who was himself a slave, advises,

> Remember to behave in life as you would at a banquet. As something is being passed around it comes to you; stretch out your hand, take a portion of it politely. It passes on; do not detain it. Or it has not come to you yet; do not project your desire to meet it, but wait until it comes in front of you. So act toward children, so toward a [spouse], so toward office, so toward wealth.[9]

A similar attitude runs through many of the aphorisms traditionally attributed to the ancient Chinese sage Lao-tzu, and so it is possible to argue that Lao-tzu's outlook is also essentially Stoic. Here is one such passage as rendered by Stephen Mitchell:

---

7. *Nicomachean Ethics*, Book 1, chap. 10, 1100b30–32.

8. Seneca, *Letters*, trans. R. M. Gummere (1917; reprint, Loeb Classical Library, 1989), volume 4, no. 22, 17.

9. *Encheiridion* in *Epictetus*, volume 2, trans. W. A. Oldfather (1928; reprint, Loeb Classical Library, 1996), no. 15.

If you look to others for fulfillment, / you will never truly be fulfilled. / If your happiness depends on money, / you will never be happy with yourself. // Be content with what you have; / rejoice in the way things are. / When you realize there is nothing lacking, / the whole world belongs to you.[10]

Even the American abolitionist Frederick Douglass, who endured countless hardships and numerous setbacks, still sounds on many occasions like an ancient Stoic. He campaigns tirelessly for change, yet he also faces life's defeats with a kind of Stoic composure. He remarks, "We live in deeds, not years, in thoughts not breaths, in feeling, not fingers on a dial. We should count time by heart-throbs; he most lives who thinks the most, feels the noblest, acts the best."[11]

I have spoken so far of what I suspect are the two most important conceptions of the good life, the Aristotelian and the Stoic, but this whole question of defining what makes a life worth living is actually much more complicated than I have suggested already; I say this because suffering and disappointment, which all of us seem at pains to avoid, may even be positive *contributions* to the good life. This sounds implausible, perhaps, but it is a view I mean to defend.

Suffering, considered in isolation, seems undeniably bad. Yet it is conceivable that in due measure, when combined with other factors, suffering might still contribute to the greater goodness of a life as a whole. Nostrils (to use a somewhat strange example) are not particularly beautiful if taken in isolation, but the face as a whole cannot be beautiful without them. Lest this point seem entirely fanciful and abstract, notice that in Shakespeare's play *Othello*, the hero woos Desdemona in precisely this way—by telling her the story of his sufferings. He recounts his pains, his enslavement, his endurance. (At least, this is how he explains their marriage to Desdemona's father in act 1.)

The point I mean to make here is easily confused. The point is not that suffering *improved* Othello's character; the point is that suffering gave his character, already developed, an opportunity to display itself. Suffering gave his character

---

10. *Tao Te Ching*, trans. Stephen Mitchell (New York: Harper and Row, 1988; reprint, New York: HarperCollins, HarperPerennial, 1991), no. 44. Alternatively, the *Tao Te Ching* can be interpreted as fundamentally ascetic.

11. Frederick Douglass, lecture, "Life Pictures," at the Parker Fraternity Course, Boston, winter 1861, in the Frederick Douglass Papers (Library of Congress), reel 14, 28. Quoted in David W. Blight, ed., *Narrative of the Life of Frederick Douglass: An American Slave, Written by Himself* (New York: St. Martin's Press, Bedford Books, 1993), 147–48. Stoicism also has strong affinities with the loose collection of ideas now known as existentialism. The terms "existential" and "existentialist" have been so abused in recent decades that it is sometimes said that both words have become meaningless. Both terms are sometimes used merely as buzzwords. Yet there are also certain traits common to the writers typically called existentialist, and among these is an intense emphasis on attitude as opposed to external accomplishment. Existentialists, like the ancient Stoics, stress introspection, and nearly all these writers have a keen interest in what it means to be moral. Thus, it is only a small step, perhaps, to the old Stoic formula, "action and assent." Stoicism and existentialism both suggest that a good life has nothing to do with external fate.

a moral significance it would otherwise have lacked. Without suffering, his highest qualities would have gone unexercised, but the mere *capacity* for virtue is not the same as the actual exercise of it. And what Shakespeare insists on is that Othello *did* exercise it. To be sure, to wish for hardships in life seems absurd, yet the fact that Othello successfully endured them does seem to change the whole color of his story. At least, this is what Shakespeare implies when he has Othello say of Desdemona,

> She loved me for the dangers I had pass'd,
> And I loved her that she did pity them.[12]

A dictum of the Stoics comes to mind: Say not that this is misfortune but that to bear this nobly is good fortune.

The problem of defining the ideal life is in fact quite difficult, and I am inclined to think that it is actually insoluble. Why? Because the good life is a whole, whereas our usual intuitions about these matters are restricted largely to parts. It is often easy to say that one life in particular is better than another, but it is quite another thing to define the ideal life in general. I can easily say that *this* life is good, but it is much harder to say which things make *any* life good. Our ability to arrive at particular judgments, and our profound inability to arrive at general ones, is a point I shall return to later, and, indeed, it illustrates one of the most persistent errors of contemporary academic philosophy—the tendency to assume that particular moral judgments are rationally indefensible unless supported by a general theory, even though the theories themselves are often highly dubious, and sometimes rather loony. For the moment, however, I content myself with this one assertion: the problem of defining the good life still surpasses the simplistic answers that try to characterize it as all one thing or all another.

Even Aristotle's answer, though it has the virtue of including various elements, still leaves the key questions unsettled. We are told that the good life includes "excellence as displayed in action," but we are not told against what odds, through what dangers, or with how much sacrifice. Nor is it obvious that all good lives must fall under a single definition. Perhaps there is a plurality of ideal lives. Thus, the position I defend in this chapter is essentially negative, yet it may also be possible to add something positive. Though some philosophers have simply disclaimed outright any attempt to define the good life in its totality, they have also supplied, on occasion, a more limited sort of answer. And it happens that one of these philosophers, once again, is Kant.

Kant confines his own remarks on this subject to a carefully restricted assertion. He defines not the best life, but only a better life. He says conscientious-

---

12. 1.3.167–68. References are to act, scene, and line.

ness (what he calls the "good will") is the only good without qualification. This, again, requires some explaining.

By the phrase "good without qualification," Kant seems to mean "good in all possible circumstances, regardless of the situation." What he relies on is a subtle distinction.

Kant thinks many things can be good, but their goodness depends on the situation. Change the situation, and the things you call good can become quite bad. The distinction is easier to see if you think for a moment not about goodness but about beauty. Take, for example, beautiful brown eyes. Some eyes really are beautiful, but their beauty depends in part on the setting. Take the same eyes out of their setting and place them on the anatomist's table (if you can contemplate this possibility without too much disquiet), and though their physical appearance may remain, the beauty vanishes. Again, picture one of those eyes in the head of an octopus; its beauty will likely disappear. Kant thinks the same is often true of the things we call good.

Take poise. Poise is indeed a wonderful quality to have, and it is perhaps the best illustration of Aristotle's famous doctrine of the "mean." To hit the "mean" is to do a thing not too much, not too little. And some such ability does seem to constitute what we call poise. The poised person knows how not to overdo a thing and how not to underdo it. He exhibits the ideal once inscribed at the Temple of Delphi, "nothing in excess," or as it is sometimes phrased, "moderation in all things." He displays what the Chinese sage Confucius (pursuing a similar theme) calls *chung hsing*. Poise in speech, poise in action, poise on the battlefield—all these presuppose an ability to hit a delicate mark between deficiency and excess, between too little and too much. Yet there are times when poise actually makes a person seem *worse*. It is an old maxim of the dramatic arts that the most villainous characters are precisely those who have all the outward virtues, all the grace, the charm, the poise, that make life sweet, but shielding a dishonest intention. The true snake in the grass, the truly slick scoundrel, is odious precisely because he has qualities that in another person would seem admirable. Hamlet finds some such phenomenon in his uncle Claudius: "O villain, villain, smiling damned villain. . . . That one may smile, and smile, and be a villain" (Hamlet, 1.5.106–9). Everything else being equal, a poised villain seems more villainous than a merely bumbling one. As Kant puts it, "the coolness of the villain makes him not only far more dangerous but also more directly abominable in our eyes than he would have seemed without it."[13]

In Kant's view, nearly every virtue can become a defect, given the wrong circumstances. Even kindness can be inappropriate, if showered on the unrepentant. But the one exception, according to Kant, is conscientiousness—the "good will." Kant's doctrine is often obscured by his terminology, but I think it is most

---

13. *Groundwork*, Section 1, 394.

plausible if construed in this way, to mean that conscientiousness always commands respect, even in an opponent. So long as a person strives to do right, his character elicits a certain esteem even if he inadvertently does wrong. Still, the doctrine is easily confused.

Kant does *not* say that wrong conduct somehow becomes right merely because the person who performs it believes in it firmly. For Kant, right is still right, and wrong is still wrong. But he insists that the worthiness of a person's character is logically distinct from his conduct's wrongness or rightness. Just as the right act is not always a conscientious one (the point Glaucon made with his story of Gyges' Ring), so a conscientious act is not always the right one. Sometimes it is inadvertently wrong. Yet it is no less conscientious, and conscientiousness still inspires a form of respect. The same point is sometimes made in war: One's enemy may well be in the wrong, but it is still possible that he is an honorable man.

Kant goes a step further. He asserts that conscientiousness is the true foundation of personal dignity. To be happy, says Kant, we must feel worthy of it. But the whole sense of self-worth comes from the belief that we are indeed capable of acting from duty, capable of doing the right thing not merely because it is profitable but because it is right. On the other hand, when we think we can no longer rise to this, we begin to lose faith in ourselves.

The Comte de Guiche, who is the villain through most of Edmond Rostand's play *Cyrano de Bergerac*, expresses a view much like Kant's in the last act.

> Do you know, when a man wins
> Everything in this world, when he succeeds
> Too much—he feels, having done nothing wrong
> Especially, Heaven knows!—he feels somehow
> A thousand small displeasures with himself,
> Whose whole sum is not quite Remorse, but rather,
> A sort of vague disgust . . .

The comte contrasts his own life with that of Cyrano.

> Yes, I know—I have all;
> He has nothing. Nevertheless, today
> I should be proud to shake his hand.[14]

The sense of duty is for Kant not the *whole* of the good life, but it is still an indispensable element.[15]

---

14. I quote from Brian Hooker's translation.

15. Kant's doctrine also has a further, odd consequence. Though he thinks conscientiousness is indeed indispensable to the good life, he still insists that to act from conscience is *not* to act for this reason. Instead, to act conscientiously is to do something *because it is right*. Thus, it makes no sense from Kant's point of view to say, "Be conscientious, because otherwise you won't feel worthy

All the same, if Kant is indeed right on this point that duty is indispensable to the good life, then why is duty ever violated at all? Why aren't people conscientious always? Of course, our duty often differs from our inclinations, and inclinations also vary from person to person, so that some people have more temptations to overcome. Still, some people seem more devoted to the whole idea of morality. What explains this difference in temperament? Kant's answer is by no means easy to puzzle out, but I think it is most plausibly construed as follows.

Kant thinks nobody can be *argued* into conscientiousness. Instead, he thinks there is a natural tendency to it, innate in the soul. But this tendency must be stimulated, and it is best stimulated by example, real or imagined. Thus, we are inspired to morality not by being badgered into it, or by having philosophers deduce its importance from calculations about the good life, but by seeing morality, real or imagined, in others. That is, we need to think of its being illustrated in other people, who serve as models. Yet there is still an obstacle in this path. The obstacle is this: The person contemplating the example must know what it is an example *of*. He must grasp what the example signifies. Above all, he must not confuse morality with a mere grab for power or comfort, either in this world or the next. He must still see the difference between a truly heroic soul and a merely cunning one.

In the following passage (translated by Lewis White Beck), Kant tries to explain this point further:

> If we imagine an act of honesty performed with a steadfast soul and sundered from all view of any advantage in this or another world . . . it elevates the soul and arouses the wish to be able to act in this way. Even moderately young children feel this impression, and one should never represent duties to them in any other way.[16]

Children are especially drawn to heroism. It plays a large role in their games and fantasies, and in Kant's view the greatest disservice we can do to them is to persuade them that true heroism is really just low cunning in disguise. Children need to believe in heroes as a means to believing in themselves. But the same is equally true in later life. To believe in the heroism of others is also to believe in oneself.

---

of your happiness," or "Be conscientious, because otherwise your conduct won't fit the philosophers' definition of what makes a life worth living." To be conscientious is simply to do right because it is right, and so to give any *other* reason for being conscientious is to lose sight, once more, of what morality really is. Put another way, an act of conscience may have certain logical consequences, but to perform such an act is still to set these considerations aside as irrelevant. Kant stresses this point when he discusses what it means to act "from duty."

16. *Groundwork*, Section 2, 410, footnote.

3.

Is Morality Objective?

IN 416 B.C., the military forces of the Athenian Empire illustrated an old and recurring problem of moral philosophy. They did so by besieging the small Mediterranean island of Melos. Melos had been largely neutral in Athens's long war against Sparta, but the Athenians were unsatisfied. They wanted to absorb the island into their military alliance. And their reason for doing so was *not* that Melos offered any advantage either in resources or location. Instead, the whole attraction of the enterprise was as a stark demonstration of power. The Greek historian Thucydides expressed the Athenian thinking this way: "We rule the sea, and you are islanders, and weaker islanders too than the others; it is therefore particularly important that you should not escape."[1]

Melos resisted. Its negotiators pointed out that its people, though of Spartan descent, had remained independent for seven centuries. The Athenians warned of dire consequences, but the Melians dug in their heels. The Athenians then resumed their siege and soon forced the Melians to surrender. Then they executed all men of military age and sold the survivors, mostly women and children, as slaves. And after that, the Athenians gave whatever was left of Melos to five hundred of their own colonists.

The amoralism that emerged in the latter half of the Peloponnesian War both horrified and mesmerized Thucydides, who saw it unfold. And he took special pains to capture the Athenian thinking. He constructed a small dialogue, unlike anything else in his history, between the representatives of Athens and

---

1. Thucydides, *History of the Peloponnesian War*, trans. Rex Warner (1954; reprint, London: Penguin Books, 1986), Book 5, 97. All citations of this work refer to the reference numbers that are commonly used by scholars and that appear in the margins of this edition.

Melos. The Athenian representatives assert, "It is a law of nature to rule wherever one can" (Book 5, 105).

They declare, "The strong do what they have the power to do and the weak accept what they have to accept" (Book 5, 89). And then they advise the Melians not to worry about "dishonor":

> In many cases men have still been able to see the dangers ahead of them, but this thing called dishonor, this word, by its own force of seduction, has drawn them into a state where they have surrendered to an idea. . . . You, if you take the right view, will be careful to avoid this. (Book 5, 111)

In composing this passage, Thucydides gave expression to philosophical ideas that had only recently become popular in Athens, especially in the 420s, through the influence of the Sophists, Greece's first paid teachers. The Sophists took a keen interest in human behavior, favored natural and scientific explanations, and were highly skeptical of traditional morality and religion (though they also acquired a reputation for rhetorical trickery). And because most of the Sophists were itinerant, they were well acquainted with the cultural differences that often give rise to differences over morality. In the end, many of them came to believe that morality was just a word. Others said it was real, but nothing different from power. Still others thought it was entirely in the eye of the beholder. The war and the Sophists combined in Athenian culture to provoke a recurring question in the history of ideas, and one that is no less common today: Is morality objective? And more broadly, does morality even exist at all, and if so, how is it known?

There seem to be powerful reasons, at least on the surface, for supposing like the Sophists that morality does not exist or that it is at best only an arbitrary invention of particular societies. And it is precisely these same reasons that circulate widely at present. If morality is objective and real, for example, then different people ought to have the same moral ideas. Yet history and anthropology show that different ages and cultures have had radically different moral ideas.

Again, if morality is objective, then how is it perceived? To perceive something objective, it seems, we must see it, hear it, smell it, touch it, or taste it; in other words, we need some physical *sensation* of it. The objects studied by physical scientists, admittedly, cannot always be seen or heard directly, but the reactions of a scientist's instruments occur in plain view. Right and wrong, on the other hand, seem entirely invisible. If I see a murder, then I see the blood, the body, the weapon, and the perpetrator, but I see no further physical fact that would constitute the murder's wrongfulness. The wrongfulness of the deed, it appears, is at best only a reaction in the mind of the observer. And to know about the reaction of an observer is only to know about an observing "subject" rather than an external "object." Thus, morality is not objective; instead, it seems at best only subjective, a mere reaction in the observer's brain.

Suppose, nevertheless, that there is some way around these difficulties. Then what kind of thing would objective morality be? If morality is neither physically observable nor a mere reaction in the observer's brain, then how can it exist at all? Is it a vapor, a ghost, a disembodied spirit? It must certainly enjoy a very queer sort of existence if it is neither physical nor strictly personal and subjective. As the Athenians said of "dishonor," it seems to be just a word.

These criticisms are in fact quite old, and they constitute the three classic objections to the whole idea of objective morality: 1) the objection from moral disagreement (why do people disagree about right and wrong?), 2) the objection from the theory of knowledge (how can objective morality be known?), and 3) the objection from the nature of existence (what kind of existence, if any, can objective morality have?). The three objections were well known in Plato's day, and something very like them may also have appeared in China in the third century B.C. in the mouths of the Legalists. The last two objections, by the way, are properly termed "metaphysical," meaning that they come from the two classic branches of metaphysics: the theory of knowledge (epistemology) and the theory of existence (ontology). But before considering these criticisms further, let me suggest a word of caution about the discipline of philosophy itself.

The reader no doubt realizes that philosophy often involves bewildering questions, some of which may be unanswerable, and it is only natural to wonder whether its overall effect will be healthy. "Beware lest any man spoil you through philosophy," says the Apostle Paul. Nor is this worry exclusive to Christians. The Athenians had a similar experience. A student of the discipline naturally encounters many objections to his or her own views, and it is the business of philosophy to consider these objections. Yet we have no guarantee that the objections will not ultimately undermine our good sense. It is always possible that we will be gulled by some clever but specious argument into believing something not only false but damaging, or perhaps even true and damaging. The final effect of philosophizing might conceivably be the complete abandonment of all moral resolve. In Plato's *Phaedo,* Socrates, believing that truth is beneficial, nevertheless warns before his death that his friends must be careful lest they be injured by his arguments: "I would ask you to be thinking of the truth and not of Socrates: agree with me, if I seem to you to be speaking the truth; or if not, withstand me might and main, that I may not deceive you as well as myself in my enthusiasm, and like the bee, leave my sting in you before I die."[2]

There is no absolute protection against specious reasoning in philosophy, but there is still an available precaution when dealing, as now, with the foundations of morality. The precaution is this: Think of a particular moral judgment of which you are tolerably sure. For example, suppose you were a student in a philosophy class at a school or in college, and suppose your teacher said he

---

2. 91c. (The translation is Benjamin Jowett's.)

would fail you for the course merely because you disagreed with him. Suppose he said he would fail you not because of your behavior or because you had neglected any work for the course but merely because you could not honestly agree with his unsupported opinions. Now, would this threatened behavior be wrong? (In more than twenty years of teaching, I have never heard a student deny that such behavior is wrong.) I venture to say that you know *perfectly well* it would be wrong. More important, you are probably so sure it would be wrong that no philosophical theory whatever could shake you out of this conviction—not if you remember the real measure of your assurance. Of course, it is "possible" that you are wrong. *Possibly* I am not even writing these words at this moment but am instead dreaming them. But what I know to be possible is quite different from what I know to be real, and I know I am writing these words as well as I know anything in the world.

The approach I suggest is roughly equivalent to the approach of the English philosopher G. E. Moore to the theory of knowledge and to the radical skepticism of the seventeenth-century thinker René Descartes. Descartes, whom I shall discuss further in a later chapter, has an enduring place in the history of ideas, because he performed a valuable service for the nations of his own time. Descartes asked how we know what we know. Europe, in Descartes's day, had only just come out of the Wars of Religion, during which many ridiculous claims of knowledge had produced much useless bloodshed, and it was thus vitally important to examine the difference between genuine knowledge and reasonable doubt. Descartes had put his finger on the problem of his age, yet he had also reached the paradoxical result that he did not even know that he had hands and feet unless he could first demonstrate the existence of God through a series of complicated and tendentious proofs. And on this last point G. E. Moore protested. *How* we know that we have hands and feet is an interesting question, but *whether* we know it is an absurdity. Obviously, we know it. And any philosophical theory that purports to show that we do not know it, said Moore, is plainly false.

I suggest a similar attitude toward your basic moral duties. Moral philosophy is often quite serious in its examination of our ordinary persuasions, but on other occasions it is not serious at all, and to take it seriously then is simply the mark of a fool. (As Descartes himself once said, in imitation of Cicero, no proposition is so absurd as not to have been defended at some time or other by a philosopher.) More precisely, philosophy invites its students to contemplate opposing arguments, but contemplating an opposing argument is quite different from surrendering your real moral convictions, many of which cannot be surrendered in the first place, at least not without an elaborate ritual of self-hypnosis. So, as long as you keep this point in mind (that you actually retain many of your own moral convictions regardless of what a clever argument seems to show), you are not likely to be undone by the mere musings and convolutions of philosophy. This much being said, I return to the question at hand: Can morality still be objective?

The alternative view, of course, is not hard to imagine. In fact, there are several alternatives.

The bluntest alternative is to suppose that morality is simply nonexistent and that all moral utterances are then just meaningless gushes of emotion—a view sometimes called "emotivism." Thus, to say that murder is wrong is only to say something like, "Boo, murder!" Another alternative, quite similar, is that moral utterances are really just disguised commands (a view known as "imperativism"), so that to call murder wrong is basically to order your listeners around, as in, "Don't be murderers!" As theories of what people actually *intend* when they use moral language, these views are absurd, but both theories have had philosophical defenders, and both embody a very real fear that morality is at bottom nothing more than an illusion.

More sophisticated is the idea that morality is entirely in the eye of the beholder—an old yet popular doctrine, and one that seems to offer escape from the notion that morality is just nothing. Consider for a moment this further alternative.

The simplest version holds that to call a thing right is only to say that the individual approves of it. Thus, what is right as defined by me could be entirely different from what is right as defined by you. This simple version, called private subjectivism, has no necessary connection with a particular line of conduct, and many private subjectivists would condemn the Athenian treatment of Melos as ghastly. But what distinguishes them as a school is the idea that the immorality of the Athenians' conduct depends entirely on the disapproval of the individual observer, not the other way around. I am not obliged to condemn the conduct because it is wrong; rather, it is wrong only because I condemn it. A line from *Hamlet* puts the theory well: "There is nothing either good or bad, but thinking makes it so" (2.2.259).

One consequence of private subjectivism, if you believe it, is that you are morally infallible. If a thing is right merely because you approve of it, then it is impossible for you to approve of "wrong" things, unless you are somehow mistaken about your own feelings of approval. And in that event, you can probably just dispense with moral reasoning and reflection. (A similar consequence seems to follow, by the way, from the doctrine that any proposition is true so long as you believe it, an assertion I have sometimes heard from students at expensive colleges and universities and never without a certain amazement. I always hasten to point out to them that, if anything is true once they believe it, then they can probably save on the enormous tuition that most colleges now charge by simply making up their educations—all of which then become necessarily true.)

But this is not the only way to put morality in the eye of the beholder, and before trying to decide which theory is correct, consider a few of the more refined possibilities.

A slightly more complicated version holds that to call a thing right is only to say that society or "the culture" approves of it—the theory now called cultural relativism. The cultural relativist believes, like the private subjectivist, that the rightness or wrongness of a deed depends entirely on human approval, but the approval in question is the approval of the *group*. Thus, for a cultural relativist, to call a thing right is only to say that a particular society or culture approves, and to call it wrong is only to say that the society or culture disapproves. The cultural relativist says it is a mistake to think that society *ought* to approve of something because it is right; rather, the thing is right only because society approves of it.

With cultural relativism, it is now the group itself that is morally infallible, because it is precisely the group's opinion that defines the morally correct view. And moral reflection becomes once again unnecessary, except to the extent that you merely seek to find out what the group thinks. Moral inquiry has no real content except what you can learn from a public opinion poll.

Despite their differences, these views still have a common thread, that morality is strictly in the eye of the beholder, and it is easy to see that many further changes can be rung on the same theme. The morality of something (or its beauty) can be defined in such a way that it logically depends on the attitude of an observer, but different persons or groups can then stand in the observer's place—sometimes an individual, sometimes an aggregate. The observer can even be a god. Change the terms of the doctrine slightly, and you have the so-called divine command theory, an early statement of which appears in Plato's dialogue, the *Euthyphro*.

In the dialogue, Plato's character Socrates encounters a young man named Euthyphro, who is prosecuting his own father for murder. And Euthyphro insists that his prosecution is "pious." But when Socrates asks, "What is piety?" Euthyphro replies, "What is loved by the gods is pious" (*Euthyphro*, 7a). Yet Socrates then asks, "But is a thing pious because the gods love it, or do the gods love it because it is pious?" (10a). If we play with the terms of the question slightly, we might rephrase it, thus: "Is a thing right merely because God commands it, or does God command it because it is right?" Put another way, the point of Socrates' question is not to discover *which* things are right (or pious), but *why*. What makes them so? Is it the gods' approval that makes an action right? Or is it the other way around—that an action's rightness leads the gods to approve? Medieval philosophers had a useful way of expressing this distinction, and I shall use their terminology here. The point of Socrates' question is to discover not the "accidents" of morality but the "essence"—that is, the characteristic *in virtue of which* an action is right.

According to the divine command theory, God's approval is the *essence* of morality, and it is thus only the approval of God that makes an action right. Or, put another way, an action is right *only because* God approves of it. If God changes his mind, on the other hand, then right becomes wrong and wrong becomes right. (A necessary corollary of this doctrine, if you also extend it to define the essence of good and evil, is that to call God "good" is only to say that God approves of himself.)

The common feature of all these conjectures is the attempt to identify the essence of morality with the attitude of an observer, and so they can all be broadly termed "subjectivist." That is, they all make the rightness or wrongness of a deed depend necessarily on the observer's approval and disapproval. They differ only in who they take the observer to be. Some say the individual, some say society, some say the gods. (The terms "objectivist" and "subjectivist" are actually used by philosophers in a variety of different ways, sometimes inconsistently, but I think the sense I intend here is not hard to see.) And the logical result is then to give morality a certain arbitrariness. Morality becomes arbitrary in the sense that there is simply no further reason why the observer in question happens to approve of some things and disapprove of others. Or more precisely, there is no further *moral* reason. A moral judgment is justified by showing that it follows from the observer's inclinations, but the observer's inclinations are then incapable of any justification whatever. Many people complain that this arbitrariness is ultimately unsatisfying, yet the Scottish philosopher David Hume, writing in the eighteenth century, tried to soften its effect by ringing still another variation on the same theme—and a clever one. Hume proposed that the observer in question should be the whole human race. Consider for a moment Hume's variation.

Hume believed that all cultures, in all times and places, happen to approve of at least one thing: kindness, or what he called "benevolence." The Christian, the Jew, the Moslem, the Buddhist, the Hindu, and the Confucian all speak well of kindness. This is not to say that all people have always been kind; the instinct for kindness can be easily overwhelmed by other passions. Still, Hume thought that there is a universal tendency, or a nearly universal tendency, to applaud an act of kindness when we ourselves have no role in the proceedings beyond that of disinterested spectator. Even a villain, when he is merely an onlooker at the theater, applauds the dramatic depiction of a desperately needed act of kindness. The essence of morality, Hume thought, is then easily discerned.

Instead of "morality," Hume focused on the word "virtue," but he defined it to be "whatever mental action or quality gives to a spectator the pleasing sentiment of approbation."[3] Put another way, virtue is whatever arouses the disinterested spectator's feeling of approval. And the key word in Hume's definition is "whatever." In Hume's view, we feel approbation for an act of kindness not because it is virtuous; rather, it is virtuous merely because we feel approbation for it. Thus, Hume's definition makes vice and virtue logically dependent on

---

3. David Hume, *An Enquiry Concerning the Principles of Morals* (1751; Indianapolis: Hackett Publishing Company, 1983), Appendix 1, 85.

what he called a "matter of fact" (ultimately, a biological fact) about the likes and dislikes of the human race. Kindness is virtuous only because the human race happens to applaud it disinterestedly. On the other hand, if human nature could be so changed that cruelty was disinterestedly applauded and kindness condemned, then vice would become virtue and virtue would become vice. So, as with the other theories, Hume's doctrine makes morality depend ultimately on someone's attitude, not the other way around.

Hume's theory has been for many philosophers the end of the line. Though later thinkers sometimes make small adjustments to his view, many nevertheless believe that morality can ultimately have no foundation except a biological tendency to applaud certain sorts of actions and condemn others. Recent attempts to postulate an "altruism gene" and to account for its existence by Darwinian principles of natural selection are still only a further variation on this same underlying thesis of Hume's—that the ultimate foundation of morality must be biological. And, personally, I see no way to disprove his thesis. On the other hand, his approach may also have some unsettling consequences. Among the shrewdest observers of these consequences is once again Kant (a name that crops up often), so let me try to express Kant's basic criticism but in terms slightly different from the ones Kant uses himself.

Think for a moment, not about good and evil, but about what it takes to *resist* evil, say, in the form of a sinister political movement. To resist evil courageously, you sometimes need to feel a certain outrage at it. You need to feel its wrongfulness, as it were, in your bones. Still, it is increasingly hard to feel this outrage once you realize that you are outraged not because the thing is outrageous but rather that the thing is outrageous merely because you are outraged. Suppose that the outrage of it depends ultimately on your *sense* of outrage and nothing more, and your own outrage starts to dissipate. Put another way, no one fights with zeal for a mere matter of subjective taste. Instead, he simply begins to compromise his tastes.

In Kant's terms, moral resolve comes from a feeling of "respect," the respect for morality as such. But no one feels respect for his mere biological inclinations (or for his "altruism 'gene'"). Instead, he only feels their effects as agitation. He may try to stifle or gratify these inclinations, but he never stands in *awe* of them. Yet real moral resolve requires precisely this sense of awe. You are unlikely to stand firm for a cause if you think yourself to be standing for nothing more than your own biological impulses. Thus, what is missing in Hume's theory is the idea that in acting from duty we subordinate our biological impulses to something higher.

Religion is no help here either, says the Kantian. Making evil depend on the outrage of a god works no better, because the outrage of God never inspires resolve; it merely inspires fear. Resolve in a religious context comes not from the idea of God as a power to be placated but from the idea of God as an ally in a common, objective cause. (As Martin Luther King Jr. sometimes remarked, "If you struggle for justice . . . God struggles with you.")[4] The essential idea is that God and Man strive for the same objective goal.

Many subjectivists will of course discount these complications, and even if real, they do nothing to prove subjectivism false. After all, such concerns are perhaps nothing more than further psychological facts, strange parts of our queer genetic makeup. The Kantian objection never really *invalidates* subjectivism; all it does is show that people *want* to believe in something higher, something objective and everlasting, and so they find subjectivism psychologically disappointing. But the objection really does nothing to show that this wishful belief is correct.

As it turns out, the result of these difficulties is sometimes a rather odd feeling of longing. We sometimes long for an objective moral standard that is eternal and immutable, yet we also feel that it continues to elude us. This feeling of moral longing is often thought to be quite modern, a special effect of the twentieth century, but it is also the oldest thing in the world. It first arose among the ancient Greeks, for example, as the conflict between *nomos* and *phusis*—meaning, How much of what we take to be morality is merely a matter of custom (*nomos*) and how much is "in nature" (*phusis*)? The Greeks, a seafaring people, had come into contact with other cultures through trade, and as cultural differences then became obvious to them, the philosophical conflict between *nomos* and *phusis* became acute. They worried about it constantly. The historian Herodotus, who was probably involved in international trade himself during the fifth century B.C., displays an intense interest in this question, and sometimes a fanciful one, by continually inviting his readers to reflect impartially on foreign customs. (He remarks, for instance, that, whereas the Greeks burn the bodies of their parents at death, the ancient Callatiae prefer instead to eat them. The Persian King Darius then asks both Greeks and Callatiae, which is the best way to conduct a funeral—by burning or eating the deceased? When he asks the Greeks whether any sum of money could induce them to eat the bodies of their dead parents, the Greeks reply, there is no such sum. But when he asks the Callatiae whether any sum could induce them to *burn* the bodies of their parents instead of eating them, the Callatiae cover their ears and shout, "Stop speaking obscenities!")[5] The thing to notice is that the United States and other modern nations are essentially reliving this Greek experience by encountering other cultures through immigration and trade, and it is thus rather natural for the conflict between *nomos* and *phusis* to be acute for us, too.

Still, this feeling of philosophical longing arises in the first place only

---

4. As recorded in the documentary film, *King: A Filmed Record: From Montgomery to Memphis*, produced by Ely Landau (1970), PMI/Films Incorporated.

5. *Histories*, Book 3, 38.

because many of us are already persuaded that there really are good reasons for rejecting the whole idea of objective morality. In other words, we are already persuaded by the three classic objections that I mentioned at the beginning of this chapter; so I shall return to those objections once more, but this time with a further question in mind: Are they really as compelling as they seem?

Recall the first objection—the argument from moral disagreement. If morality is objective (it is said), then different peoples should agree about right and wrong. Yet history and anthropology show that different ages and cultures have had radically different ideas of right and wrong, so objective morality is impossible.

Is it really true that different peoples radically disagree? Hume has already argued for a universal tendency to esteem kindness, but set aside that assertion for a moment and consider an example or two.

For instance, if I ask, "To what extent does the human race now agree on the morality of abortion?" the answer is probably not very much. But if I ask, "How many people now think Hitler's extermination of millions in gas chambers was morally wrong?" the agreement is nearly universal. If I confine my questions to particular cases instead of general moral rules, it is easy to find countless examples of widespread moral agreement. And the remaining disagreements can often be explained as the result of different physical information, having nothing to do with morality.[6]

Again, consider general moral rules. I may well be able to get wide moral agreement even about rules, so long as I specify not only a rule of conduct but a *motive*. If I ask "Is it always wrong to kill people?" I will perhaps get many yeas and many nays. But if I ask "Is it always wrong to kill people merely for amusement?" or "Is it always wrong to cudgel the sick and infirm for sport?" the agreement is probably much broader. Societies sometimes glorify killing and brutality, yet such killings are often highly restricted and ritualized, which suggests that the killings still provoke latent resistance. Do the restrictions and rituals that surround the killing of human beings demonstrate a general human capriciousness about it? Or do they show instead a latent, universal aversion? Brutalized people sometimes kill indiscriminately, but brutalized people are often impaired in many of their faculties. Why should the depravity of brutalized people cast any doubt on the consistency and rationality of compassionate ones?

The institution of slavery is yet another notorious case. In the first book of his *Politics*, Aristotle calls slavery "natural." Yet the modern world almost universally condemns it. Thus, it seems, the human race has disagreed from age to age about whether slavery is right or wrong. Still, Frederick Douglass once

---

6. Moral disagreement can also be explained as the result of different environmental dangers facing different peoples, which then become embedded in their customs. Different societies may evolve different rules of thumb for their behavior, yet all of them might still express the same underlying desire for the general safety and convenience of their peoples.

replied to this argument by pointing out that no one has ever written a book calling for his *own* enslavement. The only kind of slavery that people will defend, it turns out, is slavery for someone else. In his speech, "What to the Slave is the Fourth of July," delivered in 1852, Douglass remarks,

> Must I argue the wrongfulness of slavery?... Is it to be settled by the rules of logic and argumentation, as a matter beset with great difficulty?... To do so would be to make myself ridiculous, and to offer an insult to your understanding. There is not a man beneath the canopy of heaven that does not know that slavery is wrong *for him*.[7]

The basic point here is that, in assessing the moral agreement or disagreement of the human race, much depends on how you frame your questions. Change the terms of your questions slightly, and what looks like disagreement may turn out to be wide agreement. (In any case, the argument from moral disagreement is apt to be considerably weaker than it seems at first.)

But then there is the objection from the theory of knowledge. How is morality known? How is it perceived? To suppose that right and wrong are literally seen, heard, smelled, tasted, or touched (it is said) is ridiculous. All we literally see or hear are physical objects. But if morality is imperceivable, then it must also be unknowable.

The classic reply this time comes from Plato. His answer, though it sounds at first a little odd, is that there are other ways of knowing. His best examples come from mathematics.

Consider, for instance, this example from geometry—that every triangle can be divided into at least *two* right triangles. This proposition is not only true, by the way, but probably verifiable by the reader with just a little patience and perhaps also a pencil and paper. (Here is a suggestion. The equilateral and the isosceles are in fact obvious cases; all other triangles are scalene.[8] But if a triangle is scalene, meaning that none of its sides are equal, then it has a longest side. So turn the triangle in imagination until its longest side faces downward. The triangle now presents the image of a rather lopsided tent. And all this tent still needs is an imaginary tent pole, from its floor to the point in its roof. Construct such a tent pole, and the triangle will then have been divided into two right triangles. Reflection will show that this same procedure must necessarily work in every instance.)

However, though you can know perfectly well that this proposition is indeed true, you do *not* know it by physical sensation alone. In fact, in a certain

---

7. *The Frederick Douglass Papers,* ed. John W. Blassingame, series 1, volume 2 (New Haven: Yale University Press, 1982), 370.

8. An equilateral has three equal sides, an isosceles has two equal sides, and a scalene has no equal sides.

sense, knowing its truth has nothing to do with physical sensation. You become *acquainted* with the proposition by physical sensation, by reading about it in a book or hearing about it from a teacher, and without any physical senses at all, it is unlikely that you would ever learn geometry. But you *verify* or *confirm* the proposition differently.

The proposition is literally true only of perfect triangles, but there are no perfect triangles in the physical world that you can see, hear, smell, touch, or taste. Still less could you have physical sensations of "all" perfect triangles, even though the proposition refers to all of them. It is a commonplace of geometry that its propositions are proved not by measuring crude diagrams on a piece of paper but by reasoning about the abstractions they represent. The subjectivist complains that morality cannot be physically perceived, but neither can the objects of geometry, and the argument against the objectivity of morality, if valid, would also seem to compromise the objectivity of mathematics. This point will perhaps explain why Plato, according to tradition, admitted no students to his Academy who had not first studied geometry.

Then there is the last objection—from the nature of existence. If morality is neither physical nor personal nor subjective, then what kind of thing is it? How can it exist at all? Is it some sort of ghost or vapor or apparition? Once again, the classical reply comes from Plato, and this time a convenient approach is to ask his famous question, What is a number? That is, ask about the idea of a number the *same* questions that the Sophists were asking about morality: Does it exist, and if so, how?

For example, if I say there is exactly one prime number between six and ten, namely, the number seven, then I seem to imply that there is such a number. Does it exist? It would be odd to say, "There is such a number, but it doesn't exist." On the other hand, if it *does* exist, then *where* does it exist? And in what form? Is it a particular physical object like the Washington Monument, which exists in a specific time and place? Perhaps the number seven is merely a symbol or a word, as the Athenians said of "dishonor," but in that case, how many number sevens are there? There seems to be only *one* number seven, because there is only one prime number between six and ten, yet there are many symbols for it: "7," "VII," "seven," *sept, siete, sieben,* and so on. This suggests that a symbol is not the same as the thing symbolized. (Also, mathematicians say there are infinitely many numbers, even between the integers one and two, yet there can never be infinitely many symbols, unless you have an infinite supply of ink.)

Perhaps the number seven is merely an idea in the minds of human beings. But in that event there was no number seven in the age of dinosaurs, because there were no human beings to have the idea—even though scientists tell us there were still, at that time, more than seven planets in the solar system. Were there more than seven planets in the age of dinosaurs, but no number seven? If there was also no number nine, then how does one answer the question, What was the correct number of planets during the age of the dinosaurs? Would it be correct to say, "The number was nine, but there was no number nine"? The question, What is a number? is old and confusing, but still worth thinking about.

Bertrand Russell once suggested that the number seven, though not a single physical object, could be a *collection* of physical objects. He defined seven as the set of all groups of seven physical things in the universe. And in that event, the number seven is indeed something physical, though a rather exotic something. His suggestion is clever, but not without difficulties. For example, how does anyone *know* about this number of Russell's? I am unacquainted with *all* groups of seven physical objects in the universe, but I still know several things about seven. The only thing I know about *all* groups of seven physical objects is that each such group has exactly seven elements. Yet even to know this fact I must first know what seven is. So in that event, it seems, I must first know the real number seven before I can know Bertrand Russell's number seven.

Yet another tack is simply to give up the idea that there are numbers at all and to say instead that statements about numbers are really just veiled statements about counting. Thus, to say "three plus four equals seven" is just a veiled way of saying "counting to three and then counting to four is like counting all the way to seven." But here, too, there are problems. The counting in question must be mathematically *correct* counting; merely human counting is often inaccurate. And in that event, we can always ask, What makes counting "correct"? Counting is not always difficult, but the procedure must be learned. So why prefer correct counting to a faulty method of counting? There is one answer, of course, that we can never give, the answer, "Because correct counting yields true statements about numbers." We can never give this answer, that is, unless we want to bring back into existence the very things we are trying to banish—those exasperating numbers.

As maddening as it all seems, Plato thought the only tenable solution was to admit that the number seven really *does* exist but to concede also that it is not a physical object of any sort. Rather, it is a nonphysical object. And it is not simply an idea in the mind; rather, it is an object that the mind has ideas *about*. Plato held that the number seven is a nonphysical object whose existence is nevertheless logically independent of our ideas about it, a notion he expressed by calling the number a "form." He attributed a similar kind of existence to Justice, Beauty, Goodness, and other abstract entities and thus arose his famous "theory of forms."

Though these last points look complicated, Plato's underlying strategy is really quite simple. His purpose is to vindicate objective morality by likening it to mathematics. This is not to say, of course, that mathematicians have special insight into morality or that moralists are especially adept at algebra. It is only to say that the two domains are in some ways alike. They are similar, in Plato's view, to the extent that neither depends merely on the opinions of the observer, and neither rests for its verification on physical observation. Instead, both disciplines are what philosophers now call *a priori*—meaning logically prior to observation. Plato conveys this idea in Book 6 of his *Republic* by saying that mathematics and morality are both "invisible but intelligible."

But how does all this abstraction apply to our concrete world of danger and distress?

As it turns out, Plato's outlook is directly applicable to the events at Melos. Plato thinks morality, like mathematics, is eternal, though its truths are not always easily discerned. If the Athenians then destroy just men on a small Mediterranean island, they do not therefore destroy justice, nor do they annihilate honor, any more than a person destroys the propositions of geometry by burning a geometry book or annihilates arithmetic by adding and subtracting incorrectly. Though just human beings often perish, the truths of morality live.

Throughout, Plato is fighting a rearguard action. His arguments do not really *prove* the existence of objective morality. Instead, the most they can do is show the possibility of it. And of course, it is always open to Plato's opponents to challenge the objectivity of mathematics, too, which is a perfectly respectable objection in a philosophy class and which may well seem ridiculous only on payday. On payday, if you expect to earn $400 a week, and if you are then told by your employer that the government has taken $100 in taxes, you will still expect to see $300. It will probably not do for your employer then to say that you are getting only $200 on the grounds that arithmetic is merely arbitrary, or nonexistent, or strictly in the eye of the beholder. Whatever your employer's theories about individuals, cultures, subjectivism, or the gods, you are still likely to demand $300. On payday, nearly everyone is objectivist.

Plato's rearguard action, aimed not at proving his case but merely at undermining his opponents' objections, recalls a remark made much later by Kant: "I have found it necessary to deny knowledge in order to make room for faith." The effect of Plato's points is not so much to *establish* objective morality as to make room for a rational faith in it. And it is perhaps worthwhile to say something more about Kant's attitude toward this whole issue, too.

Kant, like Plato, also believed in the *a priori*, though with important philosophical differences. Nevertheless, it turns out that the *a priori* is exactly where he puts the "good will" (which is the sense of duty discussed in my previous chapters). According to Kant, the existence of the good will (the sense of duty) can never be proved by physical observation. The sense of duty is never seen, heard, tasted, touched, or smelled. All we really see are people's physical actions, but these actions might just as easily spring from some sort of subtle vanity or selfishness on their part rather than from true conscientiousness. There is no way to know (says Kant) whether anyone really does right *because* it is right. And this same ambiguity is apt to be present even when we scrutinize our own conduct. ("Did I really help that person yesterday because it was right, or was I just expecting, secretly, a reward?") Thus, in Kant's view, the existence of a good will, like that of objective morality itself, can never be determined by physical observation or experiment. Nor is there any physical procedure that would show that the sense of duty is the only good without qualification. Instead, all we can do is ask whether we value the sense of duty and whether we *believe* it to be good without qualification. And such questions can only be answered, says Kant, *a priori* (meaning by our own contemplation).

As Kant himself puts it (in his *Groundwork*), "We can cite no single sure example of the disposition to act from pure duty." On the contrary, "philosophers have often denied the reality of this disposition in human actions, attributing everything to more or less refined self-love" (Section 2, 406). The theory that all is self-love, or self-interest, is now called "egoism," and it is by no means stupid. It was expounded with great cleverness by Thomas Hobbes, whose views I shall discuss later, in chapter 6, but for Kant the most important question of morality is different. The most important question (he thinks) is not whether egoism is *true* but whether it is morally *satisfying*. This sounds odd, but it is absolutely crucial to Kant's position. Understand his approach to egoism, and you thereby understand his answer to the whole question of whether morality is subjective or objective.

Kant insists that even the most hard-bitten cynic, if he examines his convictions carefully, will discover that he can defend egoism only with regret. That is, the cynic "regrets the frailty and corruption of human nature, which is noble enough to take as its precept an idea so worthy of respect [the idea of acting purely from duty], but which at the same time is too weak to follow it" (ibid.). The theory of egoism is always disappointing, says Kant; it is always disheartening, if only a little, to hear someone say "all human actions are really just selfish." And if this disappointment is still unapparent to us, it is only because we have not yet noticed it.

Kant then takes one more step. He says that this sense of regret, experienced even by the cynic, arises precisely because the cynic does indeed agree, *a priori*, that the good will *would* be a valuable thing. All the cynic really disputes is its existence in the physical world. He agrees that the world would be better if the good will existed and if people really did right *because* it is right, but he thinks that the way people ought to be is very different from the way they are.

This sounds like only a minor concession on the cynic's part (if indeed he will concede it at all), but it is from just this small concession that Kant derives the main force of his answer to the whole question of objective morality. For Kant, morality is not a physical process but an ideal, and the existence of an ideal has nothing to do with whether anyone actually lives up to it. Its existence cannot be proved, but neither is it *dis*proved by pointing out what people may actually do. Thus, the question he asks us to consider is not whether we live up to the ideal (an issue that he regards as insoluble), but whether we *respect* it. Do we at least *wish* this ideal could be real? If, like the cynic, you *regret* this ideal, then at some level you do indeed respect it. Kant writes:

> This being so, nothing can secure us against the complete abandonment of our ideas of duty and preserve in us a well-founded respect for its law except the clear conviction that, even if there never were actions springing from such pure sources, our concern is not whether this or that was done, but that reason . . . commands what ought to be done. (Ibid., 407–8)

Put another way, the most vital question of morality is not how we really are, but how we really *ought* to be. We ought to do right with a steadfast soul, even if no one can prove for sure that we ever really will. What we respect is not our biology (or our genes) but an ideal beyond, and it is precisely this ideal beyond that is the real focus of our hidden aspirations. Kant's doctrine sounds paradoxical, but he was a great lover of paradoxes, and he remarks, "Pure sincerity in friendship can be demanded of every man, and this demand is not in the least diminished if a sincere friend has never existed" (ibid.).

4.

Can Morality
Be Defined?

WHAT DO ALL right actions have in common? To answer this question would
be to answer many others that have long plagued humanity. It is easy to say that
all right actions are moral actions, or again, that no right actions are wrong
actions, but the most valuable definition of morality would be altogether different. Anyone can look up the word "morality" in the dictionary, but the stub-
born fact is that people often dispute about right and wrong in a way that no dictionary can clear up. These disputes would be greatly lessened if we could agree
on some physically observable property that would distinguish all wrong actions
from all right ones. Thus, in asking whether morality can be defined, what many
thinkers have meant to ask is not whether the word "moral" can be defined by
the words "right" or "not wrong" but whether morality can still be invariably
connected with something empirical—that is, with something whose presence
can be detected by physical sensation. If so, then moral disputes might be settled
by the same procedures used to settle scientific ones, and ethics could then
become, so to speak, a branch of physical science.

One thinker who entertained this vision was Jeremy Bentham, the inge-
nious and eccentric philosopher who eventually had himself mummified. Born
in England in 1748, Bentham became the founder of modern utilitarianism and
the popularizer of the theory that morality consists entirely in promoting "the
greatest happiness for the greatest number."

To determine an action's morality, says Bentham, we need merely ask which
of all possible actions is most likely to bring the most happiness to the most
people. Bentham takes happiness to mean pleasure, and pleasure is for Bentham
strictly empirical. That is, though pleasure is mental and by no means external to
the body, it is still felt as a sensation; it impinges on the mind, much as the feeling

47

of external heat or the sound of external noise impinges on the mind. It is not merely conjured and manipulated by the intellect, like the ideas of numbers or perfect triangles or mythical golden mountains. Whether someone is feeling pleased is a question of scientific reality, not mere hypothetical possibility.

The task of the moralist or legislator is then reduced to measuring a single fact of empirical psychology—the total amount of pleasure produced by a given action. Pain must be subtracted, of course, and we must also ask how many people will feel this pleasure. The pleasures of each person are to be counted equally, and "quantity of pleasure being equal, pushpin is as good as poetry." The total pleasure thus produced, minus pain, then becomes an action's "utility," and the action with the greatest utility is the right one—an idea that Bentham advertises as the "Principle of Utility." So, the great mass of confusion and uncertainty that commonly surrounds a moral quandary is reduced to a relatively straightforward problem of observation and arithmetic.[1]

Bentham's theory has appealed both to those who think morality objective and to those who think it subjective. Instead of disputing whether pleasure is good only because it is approved (or approved because it is good), Bentham's theory invites us to ask the simpler question, What empirical feature do all good things happen to share? Thus, although Bentham does indeed have opinions about what *makes* a thing good, he also asks the more direct question of *which* things are good. And we may still agree on which things are good, even if we disagree about what makes them so. And even if we should reject the Benthamite creed, we can still ask, "Does any other empirical property fit the bill of being common to all good things?"[2]

Bentham believed his theory to be no mere hobbyhorse. He saw it, to the contrary, as an instrument of social reform. The laws and customs of England, he thought, clearly favored the pleasure of the few, not the pleasure of the greatest number, and because he said so publicly, he eventually became leader of the "philosophical radicals," a collection of like-minded writers, agitators, and politicians who campaigned for political change. They advocated adult male suffrage, the secret ballot, limitations on hereditary privilege, prison reform, free trade, the humane treatment of animals, and public sanitation, and their efforts culminated just after Bentham's death in the famous Reform Bill of 1832, a landmark of British social legislation.

Bentham carried his reforming zeal so far that he even wished to promote utility in death, so he asked himself as his death approached, "Of what use is a dead man to the living?" And he could think of only two answers. The first was that he might still be useful as a cadaver for the advancement of medical science.

---

1. Bentham also takes account of the intensity of these pleasures or pains, their duration, whether they will produce further pleasures or pains, and whether their arrival will be soon or far in the future.

2. The question of what makes a thing good now falls under the heading of "metaethics." The question of which things are good is called "normative ethics."

He therefore offered in his will to have himself dissected after his decease, and his corpse was subsequently accommodated (though England was only just learning to tolerate such practices) before a group of invited guests, including his close friend James Mill, the father of John Stuart Mill.

His second answer was that he might also be useful as a continuing inspiration to future generations by having his remains, after the dissection, embalmed and exhibited. So, in accordance with Bentham's wishes, his body was embalmed and exhibited intact at University College, London, where, to this day, it still sits in a chair and wears his real clothing, inside a large wooden box. The head on display, it turns out, is made of wax; the embalming of the real head proved unsuccessful. (The body was restored and restuffed in 1939 by the university's Department of Egyptology, and the clothes have been dry-cleaned at least twice. When a reporter for the *New York Times* ventured some years ago to ask the university provost in whose name the clothes went to the cleaners, the provost replied that he did not know.)

But Bentham's eccentricities aside, his philosophical conjecture deserves serious thought. Is it really true that the right action is always the one that promotes the greatest happiness for the greatest number? An important consequence of this doctrine, if you believe it, is that the ends always justify the means.

Lying, for example, usually seems wrong, at least in the absence of overriding considerations, like the need to save a life or the need to spare someone's feelings. But *why* is it wrong? Is lying wrong in itself, or is it wrong only because of its consequences? The logical effect of Bentham's doctrine (if correct) is to make the rightness or wrongness of an action depend entirely on its consequences.

A consequence of most lies, for instance, is that they sow distrust, and distrust makes life more difficult for everyone. Thus, with various exceptions, lying diminishes the greatest happiness of the greatest number. The essence of Bentham's position is that the consequences of the lie constitute the *whole* of its wrongfulness, and nothing else matters. On the other hand, if you could contrive to tell a lie to a dying man on a desert island—say, by promising falsely to scatter his ashes on the sea—and to tell this lie in such a way that no one else would know about it, then nothing in the lie would be wrong, because the man in question would soon die anyway, and no one else could be hurt by it. Once the man was dead, you could leave the body wherever you liked, despite your promise to the deceased, and the sum of happiness in the world would remain entirely undiminished. On Bentham's scheme, such a lie is entirely permissible. There would be no reason to keep your promise.

The appeal of Bentham's doctrine is its simplicity. It makes morality entirely a matter of adding and subtracting an empirical quantity. On the other hand, Bentham's critics complain that this simplicity is essentially artificial. They say that, in his zeal to simplify and enumerate, Bentham loses sight of what true morality is.

For one thing, say the critics, Bentham takes the ultimate aim of morals and politics to be the sum of pleasure ("the greatest happiness"), yet pleasure alone is an exceedingly narrow vision of the good life. (According to an old legend, the Spartan King Agesilaus was once asked by an outsider to identify the greatest blessing conferred on his city by the stern laws of Lycurgus. Agesilaus replied, "Contempt of pleasure.") But so far as Bentham's theory is concerned, it makes no difference whether the people of a nation are honest or dishonest, courageous or cowardly, intelligent or moronic, so long as the sum total of pleasure is the same. The critics are apt to find themselves saying that a nation of honest and courageous citizens, even if discomforted, is better than a nation of knaves and cowards, even if pleased. Even John Stuart Mill, who followed Bentham on many points and always maintained an immense respect for him, could not quite follow him on this. As Mill remarks in his own essay *Utilitarianism*, "It is better to be a human being dissatisfied than a pig satisfied; better to be a Socrates dissatisfied than a fool satisfied."[3]

Then there is the question of ends always justifying means. Is it really true that any sort of action is permissible, provided that the consequences are good enough? For example, is it ever right, for reasons of state, deliberately to kill the innocent? The orthodox view, in contrast to Bentham's, was laid down long ago by the medieval philosopher and theologian Thomas Aquinas and is now known as the "principle of double effect." And the principle of double effect is itself worth looking at.

Aquinas, who did much of his most important work at the University of Paris in the middle of the thirteenth century and who was later canonized as a saint, believed that certain actions were inherently wrong if done deliberately. And he included in this category the killing of the innocent. It is never right, in Aquinas's view, to kill the innocent deliberately. On the other hand, he conceded that necessary self-defense might still cause certain persons to be killed inadvertently. For example, Aquinas believed there could be just wars, yet nearly all wars result in the death of innocents, and their deaths are often predictable in advance. If a modern army chooses to attack a large military target, it is almost certain that some of its ordnance will go astray and kill civilians.

In Bentham's view, all that matters are the consequences, and if innocents will be killed anyway, it makes no difference whether their deaths are intentional or unintentional. Aquinas, on the other hand, assumes a fundamental difference between achieving your aims by the direct means of killing the innocent, and, conversely, achieving your aims by other means, which nevertheless result in the unavoidable death of innocents as a side effect. In modern terms, there is a moral difference between bombing enemy troops in the certain knowl-

---

3. John Stuart Mill, *Utilitarianism* (1863; Indianapolis: Hackett Publishing Company, 1979), chap. 2, 10.

edge that civilians will be killed inadvertently and killing the same number of civilians deliberately so as to terrorize the enemy. Such, at least, is the orthodox position. According to the orthodox view, the first action is sometimes permissible (if the good achieved outweighs the harm), but the second is forbidden. For Aquinas, some means are never permissible, whatever the end, yet the same consequences can sometimes be tolerated, if unavoidable, as a side effect.

This old conflict between ends and means is actually quite difficult and by no means easily resolved. Another instance of it is the problem of swearing a false oath, and a classic illustration of this problem is the final stand of Sir Thomas More.

Thomas More was one of England's early humanists, a lawyer, a minister of state, and the author in 1516 of *Utopia*, a radical little book in which he seems to have anticipated his own fate. The book's chief character, Raphael Hythloday, sees much to criticize in England, but when he is asked why he doesn't serve as a king's counselor, he replies that one of two things would then happen to him. Either he would be corrupted by ambitious men at court, or his good name would be used as a screen for their wickedness. He calls the aristocratic governments of Europe mere conspiracies of the rich to defraud the poor, and he argues instead for a pure and severe communism. Despite Raphael's radicalism, however, his creator Thomas More later became speaker of the House of Commons, then under-treasurer, and ultimately lord chancellor—the king's highest minister. Finally, in 1532, when King Henry VIII resolved to divorce his wife Catherine of Aragon without the Pope's permission and to bring the Catholic Church in England under his personal control, More resigned. Raphael's prediction had apparently come true: More felt that unless he resigned he would either be corrupted or made a screen for the wickedness of others. King Henry then pushed through Parliament the Act of Succession, which required all English subjects to swear an oath that Henry was supreme head of the church in England. More refused to swear and was imprisoned in the Tower of London.

In Bentham's view, there might well be times when it is necessary to give one's solemn word of honor falsely—for example, to save lives. But this is precisely what More refused to do. As a means, a false oath was simply impermissible to More. The playwright Robert Bolt explains More's thinking in his preface to *A Man for All Seasons*:

> More was a very orthodox Catholic and for him an oath was something perfectly specific; it was an invitation to God, an invitation God would not refuse, to act as a witness, and to judge; the consequence of perjury was damnation, for More another perfectly specific concept.[4]

---

4. Robert Bolt, preface to *A Man for All Seasons* (New York: Random House, Vintage Books, 1962), xii.

The issue was religious so far as More was concerned, yet whatever one's religion, it can also be framed as a matter of moral principle. Bolt continues,

> . . . I am not a Catholic nor even in the meaningful sense of the word a Christian. So by what right do I appropriate a Christian saint to my purposes? Or to put it the other way, why do I take as my hero a man who brings about his own death because he can't put his hand on an old black book and tell an ordinary lie?
>
> For this reason: A man takes an oath only when he wants to commit himself quite exceptionally to the statement, when he wants to make an identity between the truth of it and his own virtue; he offers himself as a guarantee. And it works. There is a special kind of shrug for a perjurer; we feel that the man has no self to commit, no guarantee to offer. (Ibid.)

As Bolt tells it, the question is not merely one of expediency, either for oneself or for society at large. Rather, it is a question of personal integrity, of identity, of who one is. When a person says "I promise" or "I swear," he does not normally mean "I swear, except in the event that keeping my word proves inexpedient, either for myself or for others, and in that event my word isn't worth the time of day." An oath means more than that.

Suppose for the sake of argument that you were on a desert island with no one else except that dying man I mentioned a moment ago, and suppose that before he died he asked you to swear that you would burn his corpse and scatter his ashes on the water. But if you then look him in the eye and give him your solemn word, does it matter later that as soon as he is dead no one else will know whether you carry out his wishes? Does your duty to keep the promise, or the wrongfulness of breaking it, depend exclusively on whether or not the rest of the world is affected? Or do you think yourself obligated all the same? The example is suggested to me by a passage in the second chapter of Sir David Ross's classic treatise *The Right and the Good* (Oxford, 1930), and in Ross's view the wrongfulness of a breach of faith consists not merely in the general social disadvantages of lying. Instead, there is something inherently wrong about it. According to Ross, it *may* be necessary, on occasion, to break one's word, but everything else being equal, it is still preferable to avoid a breach of faith, even to a man who will never be heard from again. Yet the fact that we can say this, that we should avoid such a breach "everything else being equal," shows that consequences are not the whole of the matter, since otherwise we would feel no compunction at all. So, Ross argued, morality must be sometimes more complicated than merely reckoning up the consequences. Whatever the correct answer here, Thomas More adamantly refused to offer what Robert Bolt calls that "shrug of the perjurer," and he was beheaded on the charge of high treason in 1535.

The problem of swearing a false oath is by no means uncommon, and before returning to the general question of whether morality can be defined, I want to mention just one more illustration of the difficulty (which I think interesting) in the person of Abraham Lincoln.

Throughout his career, Lincoln opposed the spread of slavery in the United States, and like other Republicans, he was alarmed at its rapid expansion in the Western territories. Like other Republicans, too, he sought the power of the presidency to contain it. Yet the power of the presidency can be acquired in only one way. The only way to occupy the office is to take an oath prescribed by the Constitution, to "preserve, protect and defend the Constitution of the United States"—which at the time protected slavery in the Old South. Thus, to get the power of the presidency to contain slavery, Lincoln had to swear to protect slavery where it was already legal. He explained the dilemma some years later in a letter to Albert G. Hodges, dated April 4, 1864.

> I am naturally anti-slavery. If slavery is not wrong, nothing is wrong. I can not remember when I did not so think, and feel. And yet I have never understood that the Presidency conferred upon me an unrestricted right to act officially upon this judgment and feeling. It was in the oath I took that I would, to the best of my ability, preserve, protect, and defend the Constitution of the United States. I could not take the office without taking the oath. Nor was it my view that I might take an oath to get power, and break the oath in using the power.[5]

Of course, Lincoln freed large numbers of slaves by the Emancipation Proclamation, but he always denied that the proclamation violated his oath. The proclamation was legal, he said, precisely because the war forced it upon him. Unless slaves were freed and enlisted in the Union cause, he argued, he would lose the war and the constitution both. His letter continues,

> I felt that measures, otherwise unconstitutional, might become lawful, by becoming indispensable to the preservation of the constitution, through the preservation of the nation. Right or wrong, I assumed this ground, and now avow it. (Ibid.)

Put another way, Lincoln conceived of the Emancipation Proclamation not as a violation of his oath, but as the only practical way to fulfill it. This is why the proclamation frees only *some* slaves. The proclamation itself refers to the freeing of slaves as an "act of justice," yet it also says their liberation is "warranted by the Constitution upon military necessity." Thus, the proclamation frees slaves only in areas in "armed rebellion against the authority and government of the United States," because only in these areas does liberation give the Union a military advantage— which is essential to the proclamation's legality. Other slaves must simply wait, and slavery was not outlawed in its entirety until Lincoln and others had pushed through the Thirteenth Amendment, which was ratified after his death.

---

5. *The Collected Works of Abraham Lincoln*, ed. Roy P. Basler (New Brunswick, N.J.: Rutgers University Press, 1953), volume 7, 281.

The key point here is that Lincoln's policy, whether or not you agree with it, is morally complicated—and complicated in a way that not all his defenders or detractors have appreciated. It is complicated precisely because he has taken an oath. He makes this point often, even before the first shots of the war, when he tries to dissuade the Southern states from seceding in the first place. Here is how he expresses the point in his First Inaugural Address.

> . . . think calmly and well upon this whole subject. Nothing valuable can be lost by taking time. . . . In your hands, my dissatisfied fellow-countrymen, and not in mine, is the momentous issue of civil war. The government will not assail you. You can have no conflict, without being yourselves the aggressors. You have no oath registered in Heaven to destroy the government, while I have the most solemn one to "preserve, protect and defend" it.[6]

Like More, Lincoln seems to have taken an oath seriously—more seriously, that is, than a mere reckoning of consequences would suggest. His ostensible behavior is not easily reducible to a mathematical calculation of pleasure over pain, though it is always open to the utilitarian simply to reject his behavior as irrational.

These are just some of the difficulties that utilitarianism seems to involve, but before turning to the underlying assumption behind this whole approach to morality, consider one more criticism of particular importance—the claim that Bentham's doctrine gives no adequate conception of fairness.

The logical effect of Bentham's creed is to offer a theory of the good—that is, a theory of which things are really worth having. And for Bentham, the good is simply the greatest sum total of happiness. The greatest pleasure for the greatest number is all that matters. Yet explaining *which* things are good is quite different from explaining how these things ought to be apportioned. It is one question to ask which items are valuable; it is quite another question to ask who should get how much. For example, it is quite conceivable that the greatest sum total of pleasure would be achieved by making a few individuals suffer abominably, while the vast majority reclines in comfort. (After all, this was essentially the strategy worked out at ancient Rome when gladiators struggled to the death for the amusement of the masses.) Yet will anyone call this fair? A theory of the good is not the same as a theory of fair distribution, and Bentham's great mistake, say his critics, is that he fails to see the difference. (As philosophers sometimes phrase this, Bentham seems to have no conception of "distributive justice.")

In Bentham's defense, it might well be imagined that a proper reckoning of pleasure and pain would reveal that the sum total of happiness is actually reduced by gladiatorial combats and other unfair practices. Utilitarianism will in fact demand fairness. Why? Because the pain suffered by the unfortunate few

---

6. Abraham Lincoln, *Great Speeches* (New York: Dover Publications, 1991), 60–61.

will still outweigh in intensity the momentary pleasure enjoyed by the many. Thus, if the utilitarian arithmetic is properly calibrated, the truly fair approach will always be the one with the greatest utility, and, happily, gladiatorial combats will turn out to be immoral after all.

To the critic, of course, this last reply is particularly lame. It is obviously *conceivable* that the utilitarian calculus will work out in such a way as to pronounce all fair practices as being of highest utility, but no one really knows this in advance, nor does anyone need to know it (says the critic) to determine that certain arrangements are patently unjust. The supposition that fairness always generates the greatest utility is at best only a conjecture, not a certainty; our real sense of fairness, according to Bentham's opponents, springs from another source.

The Harvard professor John Rawls has suggested a different origin of fairness, and his suggestion is highly intuitive. In Rawls's view, the real principle at work is the idea that an arrangement is fair only if those who get *least* under it will still get more than they could expect under any other arrangement. That is, one should always be able to say to the least advantaged, "But someone would get even less than you do now, if we did things otherwise." Or, put another way still, the only fair arrangement is complete equality, unless inequalities somehow lift all boats.

In defense of Rawls's view, observe that the partisans of widely differing policies often invoke a similar idea. For example, in disputing the question of communism versus capitalism, those who favor communism often condemn the treatment of the poor in capitalist countries. The capitalists, they say, treat the poor unjustly. Those who favor capitalism, on the other hand, often argue that the poor in communist countries, especially among the peasantry, are even worse off than under capitalism. Communism merely drags everyone down, say the partisans of capitalism, and it drags the poor down, too. Yet whatever the empirical facts of the case, both sides seem to agree on at least one point, on the relevant moral principle: a just society ought to give even the lowest class their best opportunity. No citizen should be treated as a mere sacrifice to be laid up for the benefit of the rest.[7]

Rawls points out further that a similar conception seems implicit in the classical theory of the Social Contract. Consider for a moment the Social Contract Theory as a philosophical idea.

The Social Contract Theory is the attempt to explain our political obligations by likening society to an implicit agreement, a contract. In other words, in accepting the benefits of society, we implicitly agree to accept certain responsibilities. This contract is not an actual document like the Federal Constitution

---

7. Rawls's idea may also recall in a vague way one of Immanuel Kant's aphorisms: "Act always so that you treat humanity, whether in yourself or another, always as an end and never as a means only."

of the United States, nor is it anything spoken aloud. Instead, it is supposed to be an assumed understanding, unwritten and unspoken—the understanding that, if you receive from society, you also ought to give.

Although the Social Contract Theory aims primarily at explaining why we should obey the law, and when, if ever, we are justified in breaking it, the theory also has implications for the idea of fairness, and this is the key point now. Of course, it is vitally important to see that the question, What is fair? is quite different from the question, Should I obey the law? If society is unfair, it does not follow that you may necessarily break its laws, and no existing society, for that matter, is entirely fair. On the other hand, neither does it follow that you should always *obey* the law, even if your society *is* basically fair. I shall consider the question of obedience to law in a later chapter, but for the moment I want to focus strictly on the idea of fairness.

Historically, the Social Contract Theory has various versions, but three versions have been most influential, those of Thomas Hobbes, John Locke, and Jean-Jacques Rousseau. And all three versions agree on a key point: The contract in question is not merely a contract among *most* citizens; it is a contract among *all* citizens.[8] All citizens are assumed to have consented implicitly to the arrangement, and no citizen is assumed to have consented to his own disadvantage—just as no one signing a contract knowingly agrees to have himself robbed. Thus, the Social Contract Theory implicitly assumes that a just society somehow works to the advantage of everyone, even the least advantaged. Otherwise, the poor would have no reason to enter into the contract in the first place. Here again, says Rawls, we see the implicit principle that a just society should lift all boats. No one is treated as a mere sacrifice.[9]

But where does this leave Bentham's ethical system?

For one thing, Bentham's theory and the Social Contract Theory seem incompatible. You can be a utilitarian or a contractarian, but it is difficult without contradiction to be both at the same time. Why? Because the thrust of utilitarianism is to reduce all moral difficulties to a single question: Which action or policy yields the highest total of good? But the point of the contract is to ensure that each party gets a certain share of this total good, even if the effect is to make the total itself somewhat smaller. Thus, the two theories are at cross-purposes. Utilitarianism aims at simplification, but a contract theory implies that a complete simplification is impossible. If utilitarianism answers all moral

---

8. In Hobbes's version, the contract holds among all "subjects."

9. Rawls's views are laid out in his *Theory of Justice* (Cambridge: Harvard University Press/ Belknap Press, 1971), chap. 2, 60–90. The underlying idea, that fairness should lift all boats, actually goes back to the ancients—at least as far as Book 3 of Aristotle's *Politics*, and perhaps farther than that. Aristotle expresses a recurring theme in Greek political thought, that a just society aims at promoting the interest of *all*, not merely the interest of *most*.

questions, then the contract is unnecessary, but if the contract is indeed necessary, then utilitarianism must be incomplete.

Still, this is not the only point of interest in Bentham's system. What is perhaps *most* curious is the philosophical method he assumes. And though this last observation may at first seem obscure, it is really quite simple.

Bentham has erected a high moral theory (actually a subtle and difficult theory) for the purpose of settling the particular moral disputes of his day. And he supposes that this is how such disputes ought to be settled—by appeal to a theory. He supposes that, to reason about something particular and specific, you must first discover something general and systematic. Wherever your particular moral judgments come from, once you start disputing them, you need a large, inclusive principle like his Principle of Utility to settle the dispute. He conceives of no other way of drawing moral inferences about particular cases. Nor is Bentham alone in this assumption. It is the dominant premise of European moral philosophy since the seventeenth century, and it also lies behind the Social Contract theories of Hobbes, Locke, and Rousseau (as well as the theory of the Harvard professor I mentioned a moment ago, John Rawls). Each of these philosophers tries to settle the particular controversies of his day by appeal to something general and grand—a moral system.[10]

Now, not all philosophers aim at so large an object as defining morality. Instead of asking, "What do all right actions have in common?" they may ask, "What do all legitimate governments have in common?" or "What do all fair arrangements have in common?" Still, there is a consistent assumption of method. To settle a dispute about particular cases, they assume, we should first agree on the general rule; we must first agree philosophically on what all right actions have in common (or all legitimate governments, etc.), and only then do we have reliable grounds for deciding the particular point at issue. The philosopher articulates and defends a broad definition, and he then expects his definition to count as a good reason for or against doing something.

What is most striking about this method is its artificiality. In practice, most people reason about right and wrong in an entirely different manner. Take a simple case.

If I say that shooting my neighbor would be wrong because shooting him might kill him, I have certainly given what counts under ordinary circumstances as a good reason. (No one, hearing my reason, would then reply, "Kill him? But that's no reason not to shoot someone. Go ahead. Fire!") Yet I am by no means prepared to state a general rule that covers the particular case, and philosophers

---

10. Contemporary philosophers are sometimes tempted to suppose that all these systems are merely speculative and explanatory, but any close reading will show they are indeed intended to settle real moral controversies. Again, some canonical writers allow for particular moral intuitions, but when it comes to particular moral *inferences*, they assume that we must include among our premises a general principle.

aside, neither is anyone else. I am not prepared to say that shootings are always wrong, or that shootings in otherwise peaceful neighborhoods are always wrong, or that it is always wrong to shoot a man who lives next door and has nothing in his hands but a spatula and raw hamburger. Still less am I prepared to embrace a sweeping moral conjecture like Bentham's Principle of Utility. Nor am I even prepared to say that such shootings are always wrong in the absence of over-riding considerations, which is the theory defended by Sir David Ross. (Ross's hypothesis is largely vacuous unless you specify what counts as an "overriding consideration," but I can hardly list all such considerations beforehand, nor can I say how I will weigh one against another when they conflict.)

I can at least say this: it would certainly be wrong for my neighbor to kill *me*, but his killing me is not much different from my killing him, so by analogy, my killing him is probably wrong, too. In other words, A is like B, and B is clearly wrong, so A is probably wrong also. But many philosophers, finding this method unsatisfying, wish to replace it with general rules and principles, princi-ples like those of Bentham or the Social Contract thinkers, and the odd thing is that these principles are the very matters over which the philosophers them-selves then conduct prolonged disputes. Indeed, to the uninitiated, it sometimes seems as if the only point on which all these moral philosophers agree is that all the other moral philosophers must be wrong. So, the troubling question of method is, If not even the philosophers themselves can agree on which of their principles are correct, or incorrect, why should anyone else rely on them?

It is important that this point not be misunderstood. Certain principles of morality are easily arrived at. As a general rule (I suppose), all homicidal rapes are wrong. (If there is a real exception to this rule, I cannot picture it.) In addi-tion, moral principles are probably quite plentiful so long as we specify a motive. (For example, it is always wrong, or so it seems, to injure a person permanently, merely for amusement. Again, it is always wrong to strangle kittens merely to watch them suffer.) And there are also various broad and somewhat vague prin-ciples that express the moral aspirations of a society but that owe nothing to the subtle dialectic of philosophy, like the principle of the *Declaration of Indepen-dence* that all men are created equal. But the rules now sought by philosophers are typically different.

Philosophers seek the most basic rules, rules that subsume nearly all others, and they want these rules to hold without exception. (If exceptions were allowed, we could simply say that shooting people is *usually* wrong, which is obvious, and be done with the subject.) Why? Because the point of philosoph-ical analysis today is to make morality *systematic*. Put another way, the point is to turn morality into something like modern physics. After Galileo and Newton, physical scientists managed to reduce most questions of mass, movement, and force to a single set of universal principles, the basic physical laws. Just so, moral philosophers have made a special effort since the seventeenth century to reduce most moral questions to a single set of moral principles, the basic laws of right and wrong. And they have pursued this grail even though none of their principles is susceptible to physical experiment, and none enjoys the sort of broad consensus that surrounds a geometry theorem. To say this is not to *deny* the existence of morality, nor is it to insist that our particular moral judgments are infallible, nor is it to doubt that we often act from a "sense of principle." It is only to say that, when it comes to moral *reasoning*, we often reason by likening one case to another, not by conjuring up the principles of a grand ethical system. So, the underlying question of method is, in seeking to construct such a system in the first place, are the philosophers really doing us a favor?

5.

Is It Reasonable to Rely on a Moral System?

ANYONE WHO THINKS seriously about making the world reasonable must sooner or later confront a bloody episode in the history of change, the French Revolution, and the criticism of its chief philosophical antagonist, Edmund Burke: "It has been the misfortune (not as these gentlemen think it, the glory) of this age, that everything is to be discussed. . . ."[1] To see what he means more clearly, try the following experiment.

Try writing out the first four amendments to the Constitution of the United States, and then try to explain to yourself why each of these amendments is or is not a good idea. The amendments are of course part of the Bill of Rights, the nation's basic list of individual freedoms. Yet without reference books or the help of a few friends, it is questionable whether many citizens can even *recall* the first four amendments (at least in the sense of recalling the wording), let alone mount a philosophical defense of each. This is not to say that no such defense exists but only that the defense is apt to be sufficiently subtle as to require considerable time and energy. Now suppose that instead of writing out the first four amendments, you were to write out all the basic rules of society—governing the state, religion, social intercourse, and property—and then to determine their legitimacy or illegitimacy by philosophical principles. Ask all citizens to do this simultaneously, says Burke, and the result will be chaos.

Burke arrived at this idea quite early in his career. In 1756 (when he was still twenty-seven years old), he wrote in a satirical pamphlet that the effect would be anarchy "if the practice of all moral duties, and the foundations of

---

1. Edmund Burke, *Reflections on the Revolution in France,* ed. Conor Cruise O'Brien (1968; reprint, London: Penguin Books, 1986), 188.

society, rested upon having their reasons made clear and demonstrative to every individual."[2] What really gives order to a society is not reason, says Burke, or even discussion, but tradition.

In regulating the bulk of our behavior, we usually follow custom. Only rarely do we have time and energy to inquire after a moral justification, and more rarely still can we work out a practical alternative. Americans typically believe in the Bill of Rights not because they can defend it philosophically but because they know it to be two centuries old, and because they assume something this old is probably reasonably workable, since it has stood the test of time. They believe in the Bill of Rights, because it comes from the "Founders"—a term often pronounced with awe. The founders themselves often make much the same point. In No. 49 of *The Federalist* (1788), James Madison remarks that in a "nation of philosophers" a reverence for the laws might well flow from reason alone. He continues,

> But a nation of philosophers is as little to be expected as the philosophical race of kings wished for by Plato. And in every other nation, the most rational government will not find it a superfluous advantage to have the prejudices of the community on its side.[3]

This concern for tradition does not make Burke an enemy of reason but rather a believer in its limitations. He thinks reason is perfectly suited to the analysis of particular moral problems on particular occasions. But he regards it as wholly *un*suited to the sweeping comprehension of all social relations at once—something that not even the wisest thinkers can achieve. The opposite view is perhaps best suggested by an early demand of Karl Marx, expressed in an open letter to his friend Arnold Ruge in February 1844: "I am speaking of a ruthless critique of everything existing." Far from "critiquing everything existing," Burke thinks the mystique of tradition is the real glue that holds a society together and that we can stretch this glue only in measured increments. Otherwise, we rend the social fabric. Encourage people to question all customs at once, and you invite pandemonium.

Burke elaborated these views during a long and distinguished career as a member of the British Parliament, and he remains the foremost critic of reducing morality to a system. He is perhaps best remembered today, whether accurately or not, as the first person to call the press the "Fourth Estate," as well as for his conception of a political representative. ("Your representative owes you, not his industry only, but his judgment; and he betrays instead of serving you if he sacrifices it to your opinion.")[4] And he is also credited with a famous

---

2. His pamphlet was called *The Vindication of Natural Society.*

3. *The Federalist Papers* (New York: New American Library, Mentor, 1961), 315.

4. Burke, *Speech to the Electors of Bristol*, November 3, 1774.

aphorism on the results of moral lethargy. ("The only thing necessary for the triumph of evil is for good men to do nothing.") Burke was above all the voice of Britain's loyal opposition—an enemy of England's misrule of India, a friend of the American colonies in their dispute with British authority, and an advocate for his native Ireland. Yet he was also in many ways the archconservative. The last great cause of his life was his opposition to the French Revolution and to a whole class of political philosophies that accompanied it.

Burke's attack on the French Revolution, published as *Reflections on the Revolution in France* (1790), was the first book to anticipate the revolution's fundamental radicalism. And that radicalism is itself worth looking at, because it throws Burke's whole point of view into perfect relief.

Unlike earlier upheavals, the French Revolution not only aimed at social improvement; it aimed at righting the wrongs of a nation, and it encompassed a complete transformation of society. The revolution eventually overthrew most existing institutions: the monarchy, the nobility the established church, the feudal system of property, even the calendar. (France's National Convention decreed that 1792 would become the Year I and that the week would have ten days instead of seven, with one day of rest.) More important, the driving impulse behind these changes was a widespread popular feeling that the previous social order, the *ancien regime*, had been fundamentally unreasonable. Thus, in Burke's opinion, the revolution as a whole was founded on a serious intellectual mistake.

The mistake, in Burke's view, is really quite simple. Nothing is wrong with change as such. "A state without the means of some change," he says, "is without the means of its conservation."[5] Nevertheless, change can be rationally controlled only if it is confined to particular departments, because no one can comprehend more than a few departments at once. As Burke sees it, a society undergoing revolution is like a human body undergoing medical treatment. If one of its limbs is defective, then the defective part can be removed and replaced through the intervention and cooperation of the other parts. If our right hand offends us, then let our left hand cut it off and fashion a new one. But while the one part is being cut off and replaced, the other parts must remain unmolested. The one thing we must *not* do is try to cure all the patient's disorders simultaneously.

The American Revolution is a good illustration of this idea. The American Revolution was in many ways fundamentally conservative. It consisted of an attack on the authority of the British king and the British Parliament, but the authority of the colonial legislatures remained unquestioned. There was no assault on the basic system of property. Even the staggering evil of slavery in the South was left in place. And, indeed, it was the colonial governments themselves that ran the revolution and provided its leadership. Thus, while the head of the body politic was being removed—the preeminent authority of the king and Par-

---

5. Burke, *Reflections*, 106.

liament—the other limbs were kept intact. And the other limbs then succeeded in fashioning a new head, which ultimately became the present federal government. (The American Civil War, it might be argued, was almost equally conservative. Though the social order of the South was dramatically revolutionized, the social order of the North was not, and, consequently, it was the North that became the instrument by which the revolution in the South was carried through.) In effect, Burke's revolutionary strategy is inherently circumscribed, rendering wholesale social transformation nearly impossible, because the essence of his strategy is to pit some parts of the old order against the other parts.

In France, by contrast, nearly all organs of the body politic were attacked within the space of a few years. And the task of regenerating the entire body then became intellectually overwhelming. Because the revolution soon challenged the whole of the previous social order, anyone associated with that order soon became suspect, so the revolution quickly had trouble finding experienced leaders. Burke complains of this difficulty when characterizing the members of France's new National Assembly:

> Who could flatter himself that these men, suddenly, and, as it were, by enchantment, snatched from the humblest rank of subordination, would not be intoxicated with their unprepared greatness? (Ibid., 130)

And again, he complains,

> Among them, indeed, I saw some of known rank; some of shining talents; but of any practical experience in the state, not one man was to be found. The best were only men of theory. (Ibid., 128)

There were numerous schemes for government reorganization and numerous philosophical justifications for them, but the trouble was hardly any two of them matched. And the revolution then became uncontrollable. Veering first in one direction, then in another, it eventually devoured its own managers, until Napoleon, originally an obscure artillery officer, imposed military discipline and finally declared himself emperor.

In place of the example of France, Burke offers an alternative model of how he thinks social change should be conducted—England's Stuart Restoration of 1660 and its so-called Glorious Revolution of 1688:

> At both those periods the nation had lost the bond of union in their ancient edifice; they did not, however, dissolve the whole fabric. On the contrary, in both cases they regenerated the deficient part of the old constitution through the parts which were not impaired. They kept these old parts exactly as they were, that the part recovered might be suited to them. (Ibid., 106)

Thus, though Burke allows various adjustments to the social order, he is still essentially a gradualist. ("[We] should approach to the faults of the state as to the wounds of a father, with pious awe and trembling solicitude" [ibid., 194].) And the one thing he will never support is an attempt to remake the whole of society all at once. He accepts the limited revolutions of Britain but not the total revolution in France, because he has only limited confidence in the ability of any human population to understand its moral and political circumstances.

Burke's doctrine also had a strange corollary—one that completely baffled his former political allies. He defends the cause of American colonists in their dispute with Great Britain (and at great personal risk), because he sees the colonists as defending traditional English liberties, and because he fears that their defeat overseas will threaten traditional liberties at home.[6] But since the essence of his position is tradition and since the traditions of Europe are (at the time) eminently aristocratic, he finds himself defending in Europe what he would never recommend for America—hereditary aristocracy.

It is this strange consequence of his devotion to tradition that now makes me wonder how he would view the current metamorphosis in Russia. It is obviously dangerous to speculate on what a dead political thinker might say. Still, I cannot help believing that he would view the recent reforms with profound misgivings. The demise of communism in Moscow has so far proceeded with much less violence than accompanied the French Revolution, partly because Russia's large middle class tends to resist a sweeping redistribution of personal property. And it is certainly not the only other revolution to aim at extensive social change. (The earlier communist revolutions in Russia and China aimed at the same thing.) Nevertheless, the current transformation is similar to the French Revolution in a key respect: The driving impulse behind it is a widespread popular feeling that the previous social order (the *ancien regime*) was fundamentally irrational. Thus, the effect is to dissolve whatever was left of political tradition. And this is just the sort of situation Burke fears. Dissolve tradition, he thinks, and you invite chaos, followed by dictatorship.

Burke is especially wary of the military. Already in 1790, while the French Revolution is still young, he turns an anxious eye toward the French army:

> In the weakness of one kind of authority, and in the fluctuation of all, the officers of an army will remain for some time mutinous and full of faction, until some popular general, who understands the art of conciliating the soldiery, and who possesses the true spirit of command, shall draw the eyes of all men upon himself. Armies will obey him on his personal account. There is no other way of securing military obedience in this state of things. But the moment in which

---

6. His stand is perhaps best explained in his *First Speech on Conciliation with the American Colonies*, March 22, 1775, in Edmund Burke, *On the American Revolution*, ed. Elliott R. Barkan (New York: Harper Torchbooks, 1966), 70–121.

that event shall happen, the person who really commands the army is your
master; the master (that is little) of your king, the master of your assembly, the
master of your whole republic. (Ibid., 342)

Burke writes this six years before Napoleon achieves fame in Italy and twelve years
before he makes himself consul for life. I quote it not to imply that Russia is now
doomed to a similar fate, or to suggest that Russians should try to bring back communism (which seems to me both improbable and undesirable), but only to say
that this is an especially apt time to give Burke's views a careful reading.

Yet there is much more at stake in his outlook. In making these points, Burke
is attacking not only a theory of revolution but a style of moral philosophy.

Specifically, he renounces any attempt to settle a particular moral or political dispute by appeal to a general theory. Unlike Jeremy Bentham, he has no
definition of what all right actions have in common, or all legitimate governments. And he thinks it fundamentally unreasonable to rely on such a definition. He ridicules the political system of a contemporary (the moral philosopher
Richard Price) by complaining, "[he] proclaims usurpers by circles of longitude
and latitude over the whole globe" (ibid., 96).

Indeed, Burke blames this style of philosophy for the troubles in France.
The French became contemptuous of tradition, he thinks, because they became
far too enamored of generalizations about right and wrong. In earlier times,
famine and tyranny had brought disobedience and rebellion, but the French
Revolution brought much more, and this difference in scope indicates an additional influence—the persistent agitation of the intellectuals. Burke calls them
the "literary cabal," the *philosophes* of the European Enlightenment, many of
whom demanded that European institutions be reformed according to general
rules. The French came to believe that all legitimate governments must have a
certain form and that without this form all their political traditions were only so
much fraud. Thus, insistent on a system different from their customs, they
brought down catastrophe on their heads.

Now it is vital to see that a philosophical theory is not proved irrational
merely in virtue of what some people do in its name. A philosopher may well
engage in general speculations about morality without thereby recommending
that the glue of tradition be everywhere dissolved. And though some philosophers are indeed contemptuous of tradition, many others have a keen appreciation for it and insist that any application of their theories be tempered by deference to the past. Still, Burke thinks that general theories of political legitimacy
are worthless anyway, and he takes a similar view of theories of right and wrong.

Why?

Basically, he discounts these theories, because he thinks they lead us into the
fallacy that logicians now call "begging the question." That is, they invite us to give
for a reason something just as contentious as the point we want to prove. (Logicians

define "begging the question" in several different ways, but the definition I give here is well established and the broadest, and it subsumes all others, including the case of arguing in a circle.) Let me try to illustrate this idea differently, with an example from our own time. Consider for a moment the current debate over abortion.

Many people now oppose abortion because "the fetus is a person," and they suppose that fetuses should therefore have the rights of persons. Others defend abortion on the grounds that "a woman has a right to control her own body." Yet in most cases neither of these arguments is really likely to change anyone's mind. Why? Because the reasons given—that fetuses are persons or that women have rights to control their own bodies—are usually just as controversial as abortion itself. I do not say that either of these reasons is necessarily untrue; what I say is that their truth is no *more* conspicuous than abortion's morality or immorality. Put another way, anyone who disputes your opinion of abortion will probably also dispute your opinion of the status of the fetus or the anatomical rights of women. You are merely preaching to the converted.

Long before Burke, Aristotle expressed this same point by saying that the premises of a rationally persuasive argument must be "better known" than the conclusion (*Posterior Analytics*, Book 1, chaps. 2 and 3, 72a25–73a5). What Aristotle means, in part, is that the person to be persuaded must already be less inclined to dispute your reasons than the idea you want to prove. Otherwise, he will simply dispute your reasons, too—and no one is rationally persuaded by a reason he disputes. (It is absurd to say, "I am persuaded by the reason you give, but personally I dispute it.")[7]

In Burke's view, this is just the trouble with generalizations about morality and government. They are all highly disputable. To invoke such a generalization to settle a practical moral controversy must therefore beg the question. Far from settling the dispute, you merely invite further controversy over the generalization itself. During a debate in Parliament about the general principles of government, he once remarked,

> These are deep questions, where great names militate against each other, where reason is perplexed, and an appeal to authorities only thickens the confusion. For high and reverend authorities lift up their heads on both sides, and there is no sure footing in the middle. This point is the great Serbonian bog betwixt Damiata and Mount Casius old, where armies whole have sunk. I do not intend to be overwhelmed in that bog, though in such respectable company.[8]

---

7. Aristotle adds that this same consideration rules out arguing in a circle. Historically, many authors have tried to show that circular reasoning is sometimes rationally persuasive, but the trouble with all such attempts is perhaps best expressed by a dilemma. If each element of the circle depends for its acceptance on all the other elements, each being justified by appeal to the rest, then all elements are accepted or none are accepted. If none are accepted, the circle is unpersuasive, since there are no accepted premises. If all are accepted, the circle is unnecessary. It can never rationally change your mind.

8. I quote from his *First Speech on Conciliation*, 95–96.

Nevertheless, as it turns out, Burke's view is by no means popular today. Among academics, for example, it is decidedly *un*popular; in academia, systems, generalizations, and abstruse theories are still very much in fashion. And many writers now say that these systems are inescapable. Some say, for instance, that our everyday view of the world is colored by tacit assumptions that systematically distort our thinking. All our particular judgments (they say) depend on systematic biases. And, of course, some of this talk is easily debunked. (Except in statistics, for example, the word "bias" connotes unreasonableness or unfairness, but if everything is "bias," then what does the word "bias" mean?) Still, there is a more important disagreement here with Burke, in fact, a crucial one. Were Burke alive today, he might well agree that our perceptions and judgments often involve tacit assumptions. But it is quite another thing to say that these assumptions must be *systematic*. If my perception of some object A involves assumptions, perhaps this is only because A resembles another object, B, that I am acquainted with already. In that event, I do indeed make assumptions, but they derive not from a system of rules; instead, they derive from a limited analogy between two cases. What Burke resists is the tendency to squeeze everything into a system.

This current zeal for system is a fascinating subject in its own right and deeply embedded, at present, in several academic disciplines. But for the moment I want to focus on Burke's idea of an alternative. How *else* should we reason about right and wrong, if not by constructing a system? Burke answers, by analogy. "By following wise examples, you would have given new examples of wisdom to the world."[9] A good way to see what he means is to consider the approach of a very different but equally well-known figure, Martin Luther King Jr., in his *Letter from Birmingham Jail*.

King was arrested in Birmingham, Alabama, in April 1963, for "parading without a permit," and he was attacked by his critics as an outside agitator, a fomenter of tension, and an extremist. When his nonviolent supporters were assaulted by thugs, it was said that King's civil-rights activities in the South, though peaceful, precipitated violence. Yet, in reply, King's letter asks, What was the Apostle Paul, if not an outside agitator? Who were Jesus, Martin Luther, John Bunyan, and Lincoln, if not "extremists" of a sort? And what did Socrates do, if not create tension? Again, if King is a precipitator of violence merely because his nonviolent supporters are themselves attacked by violent thugs from the opposition, should we not say by the same method of reasoning that a robbery victim is a precipitator of violence, merely because his having money precipitates the evil act of robbing him? King's strategy, in part, is to argue from similar cases. A is like B, and B is legitimate. Therefore, A is probably legitimate, too.[10]

9. Burke, *Reflections*, 123.

10. *Letter from Birmingham Jail* in Martin Luther King Jr., *Why We Can't Wait* (1964; New York: New American Library, 1991), chap. 5. Consider how the abortion controversy might now look if

Broadly, Burke feels that the need for systematic moral theory has been greatly exaggerated. And he doubts nearly all of it, because he sees no obvious way to prove it. How, after all, *is* such a theory proved? Theories in physical science can be supported by empirical observation and experiment, and they often yield striking consequences that can be tested. But there is no obvious physical experiment to test Jeremy Bentham's Principle of Utility, or John Locke's theory of government legitimacy, or Thomas Hobbes's definition of justice. Philosophy, regrettably, is mostly just talk, and the only way to confirm or refute it is with more talk. To be sure, mathematics is also insusceptible to empirical proof, but given enough time, mathematicians tend to agree. The architects of general moral systems, on the other hand, usually disagree. (In chapter 3, I pointed out some alleged similarities between morality and mathematics, but here I mean to point out a difference.) Even when the question concerns alternative geometries, mathematicians do not normally range themselves into competing camps, the "Euclideans" versus the "non-Euclideans." The situation in moral philosophy is quite otherwise. Take, for example, the famous (or notorious) Social Contract Theory.

Burke *does* agree (in his *Reflections*) that society is a contract. Still, it is one thing to admit the existence of such a contract; it is quite another thing to invoke the details of such a contract to settle a real moral issue. The Social Contract Theory is not a hypothesis about anything written down. Instead, it is only an assertion about an implicit agreement, unwritten and unspoken, to which a citizen presumably consents whenever he accepts society's benefits. Thus, consulting the contract is not like looking up the relevant clauses in the Federal Constitution. It is a matter of consulting the invisible and intangible. How, then, does anyone know what the contract really says?

As it turns out, there are various historical versions of the Social Contract, but few of them match. The version in Rousseau's *Social Contract*, for example, is different from the version in Locke's *Second Treatise of Government*, which is different from the version in Hobbes's *Leviathan*, which is different from the version in Plato's *Crito*. Harvard professor John Rawls also has a version in his treatise, *A Theory of Justice*, and it, too, is different. And the trouble is, different versions jus-

---

conducted with an eye to analogy. A late-term abortion bears at least a superficial likeness to infanticide, whereas an early-term abortion bears at least a superficial likeness to the ordinary removal of one's own tissue. Thus, the analogy in defense of abortion is stronger the earlier the abortion is performed; the analogy against it grows stronger as the fetus develops. I do not say that either analogy is necessarily compelling but only that both analogies might be developed, depending on whatever empirical similarities or dissimilarities were discovered. The need to preserve the mother's life or health would then be a further complication. But much current debate on the subject takes an entirely different approach. Many of the debate's participants seek instead a clear and convincing definition of what all human life has in common—a definition of personhood, so to speak—and being unable to agree on such a definition, they then plunge headlong into metaphysics. In truth, probably no one knows how to define human life in general.

tify different conduct. So which version is the right one? Far from settling controversies, we seem only to be starting new ones.[11] To borrow Burke's phrasing, "High and reverend authorities lift up their heads on both sides." The complaint here is not that general moral systems like the Social Contract are false but rather that their details are never so conspicuously true that they could be good reasons for settling a real moral dispute. The better way, in Burke's view, is to reason by analogy.

The defender of high moral theory still has an obvious reply. He can always say that he has studied his own philosophical system with so much caution that he is reasonably sure for all practical purposes that it is correct. And if other philosophers refuse to agree, this is only because they have failed to study the system with sufficient care.

I must confess that I see no way for Burke to argue a philosopher out of this kind of confidence in a grand moral hypothesis, except by asking him to think again. Burke often remarks on the intoxicating effect of abstract philosophizing. We often suppose that we have more confidence in a theory than we really do, because we get carried away with it. On the other hand, I think it is indeed possible to design a test for precisely this kind of "intoxication"—that is, a psychological test to determine whether the architect of such a theory really has as much confidence as he imagines. We can test his confidence by asking him to trust his theory in a hypothetical case, but a case sufficiently serious to give him pause. And we can thereby determine, perhaps, whether his cherished philosophical system is really the basis of his actions or is just a showy facade. So I suggest a test for those who take high moral theory seriously, but I should also warn that the test is difficult. I intend it, as it were, only for the aspiring professional in the field—for someone genuinely prepared to carry an abstract idea to its logical conclusion. But if you never take such theories seriously anyway, then you can just as easily pick up the main thread of my discussion by skipping now to the beginning of the next chapter. Do that, and you will have missed nothing vital.

To the adherent of a general moral theory, I propose this experiment: Pick a theory of what all right actions have in common. That is, pick a theory that completes the sentence "An action is right if and only if. . . ." But I also ask that the theory you pick do what Jeremy Bentham wished for: Your theory must lay out empirical conditions for thinking an action right. Thus, it will not do to offer a merely subjective theory like "An action is right if and only if I personally approve of it" or "An action is right if and only if my culture approves of it." What I ask is that you go a step further and say what everything achieving the relevant approval has in common. I ask you to define morality in the way that philosophy has long sought to define it—by connecting it with something physically verifiable. And I

---

11. Professor Rawls's system is primarily intended to justify claims of fairness rather than claims of government legitimacy. Still, his system is frequently at odds with those of Hobbes, Locke, and Rousseau—a point he makes often.

then ask one thing more. I ask you to use your theory to decide a man's fate. I ask you to suppose that you must decide whether to imprison a man, a man you must imagine, but without knowing anything of his conduct. He is a faceless man, so to speak, and I give you nothing about his background or how you got him in your power, except for one point, but I do indeed give you this one point as a dead certainty. I give you as a premise of the experiment that by imprisoning this man you will satisfy your general moral theory. Given only this one broad piece of information, and nothing more, would you think it reasonable to send the man to prison?

The question is hypothetical and abstract, and just the kind that practical people dismiss, but which philosophy sometimes relishes, so to avoid confusion I want to explain in just a bit more detail exactly what I am asking and what I am not asking.

I ask you to decide whether to send a man to prison without knowing what he has done. You are not told whether he has had a fair trial, though it is quite possible that he has. You are not told whether you have the legal authority to imprison him, though perhaps you do, and in any event you have the real power to do it. But you *are* given the crucial piece of information that the duty to imprison him follows from your general moral theory. If you are a utilitarian after the manner of Bentham, I give you as a certainty that by imprisoning this man you will produce the greatest happiness for the greatest number. If you are a follower of another philosopher, like, say, John Rawls, I give you as a certainty that by imprisoning this man you will (in Rawls's words) "conform to principles that would be acknowledged by rational persons in the original position."[12] Again, if you are a strict Kantian, I give you as a certainty that by imprisoning this man you will (in Kant's words) "act on that maxim that you can at the same time will to be a universal law." Pick whatever philosophical theory you like; whatever conditions the theory requires to send a man to prison, those conditions are met. You are assured that everything in the theory after the words "if and only if" has been satisfied, but what you are not told is how.[13]

No doubt it is hard to imagine how you would ever get such information, and, indeed, you might well object: "If another person understood my general moral theory very well, and knew also how to determine whether the conditions it names had been fulfilled, then perhaps he could verify for me that these conditions had been met, and pass this fact along to me. I would then have to decide the case. But in that event [you say], I am being asked to send a man to prison solely on another man's word."

But this is not what I am asking.

---

12. More precisely, I give you the following stipulation: If Rawls's theory of choice in the original position is indeed correct, then imprisoning the man is morally obligatory. (For Rawls on the original position, see *A Theory of Justice*, 17–21, 46–53, and 118–92.)

13. In chapter 1, I construed Kant's categorical imperative as a criterion of moral motivation, but I now consider its possible use as a criterion of right actions.

I ask you to take it as a certainty, for purposes of argument, that the right-ness of sending the man to prison follows from your theory. The conditions your theory imposes have been fulfilled, but there is no intermediary from whom the information comes. Rather, the information is a supposition, like the supposition in the Pythagorean Theorem that the triangle ABC has a right angle. I ask you simply to suppose it. (On the other hand, if you *cannot* suppose it, then I suspect that your theory is already useless for justifying the vital practice of imprisoning people, even in ordinary cases. Consider: to justify imprisonment, you would first have to *know* that your theory's conditions were satisfied. But to know they were satisfied, you would first need the ability to *suppose* they were satisfied—and this is all I ask.)

There is another confusion I want to avoid. I ask you to decide a man's fate only by appeal to your *general* moral theory, not by appeal to the lesser convic-tions that you believe it to imply. I assume that your theory is distinct from its consequences, and though you no doubt believe it to imply many good things, I give no guarantee that your belief is correct. All you are given in deciding the man's fate is that your general theory is satisfied. Any further inference is your own responsibility. I give you an initial supposition, but I do not therefore guar-antee the further conclusions you want to draw from it, any more than a geom-etry teacher, giving the students axioms, guarantees whatever theorems the stu-dents might try to derive.

Thus, what you are given is *not* that sending the man to prison follows from sentiments you learned at your mother's knee, or from an idea avowed on the editorial pages of the best newspapers, or from the hodgepodge of legal princi-ples that find expression in the criminal code. You are given only that sending the man to prison follows from a principle with the words "if and only if" in it, a principle you have gleaned from *philosophy*—a grand theoretical principle that purports to sweep across the whole of morality or a large stretch of it. Your deci-sion must rest on precisely the kind of principle that has traditionally divided moral philosophy into competing schools, and that, by point and counterpoint, has provided for their mutual vexation. I ask whether your confidence in any such principle is so great that you would stake a man's freedom on it.

In consequence, the fate of the man I ask you to imagine hinges entirely on the question of just how sure you are that your grand moral theory is correct, while anything that might influence you *independently* of the theory has been removed. And your situation is thus unlike anything you would face in the real world. Unlike the typical judge, you have no law to go by. Unlike the typical jury, you have no particular facts to go by. Unlike the typical prison warden, you have no legal document commanding the man's imprisonment and no informa-tion about how such documents are issued. And unlike the typical citizen, you have no information about the political and social system. (Unlike the typical physical scientist, moreover, you have no physical experiments to support your claim that your grand moral hypothesis is really reliable, since no moral theory can be verified in this way.) Your situation is perhaps a plain man's nightmare, but like the old story of Gyges' Ring (or perhaps like the possibility once suggested by Descartes, that everything we see is really only the work of an "evil, deceiving spirit"), your situation is still, I think, within the bounds of human fancy. And in one respect it is exactly what moral philosophers have always wanted. You are given as a dead certainty, beyond all possible dispute, that your preferred philosophical theory applies to the case.

A final point: In asking whether, on the ground of your general theory alone, you would send a man to prison, I am not asking whether you would do it if you were in the mood for it. Nor am I asking whether you would have the grit for it. I am asking whether you would think it *reasonable* to do it. Would any reasonable person, whose philosophy had not become his fanaticism, send another person to prison on so speculative and disputable a basis?

For those who answer yes, I have no further argument. But for those who answer no, I draw this inference. Your theory is useless for justifying the morality of your conduct. If the theory can't establish the reasonableness of something it actually entails, then it is no help in establishing the reasonableness of anything else.

I can draw the inference several ways. Try this way first: If your theory *could* help, as a premise, to establish the reasonableness of anything else, then it would have to be reasonably established itself. But if it were, then anything it was known to entail would also be reasonably established—including the imprisonment of the man. Since you reject imprisoning the man, it follows that your theory helps to establish the reasonableness of nothing else.

But here is a second way to draw the inference, in somewhat different terms. You are given as a certainty that imprisoning the man satisfies your preferred philosophical theory. If you understand the supposition correctly, you can then have no more confidence in the theory than you have in the morality of sending him to prison, since the theory entails it. But unless you are morally indifferent (or paralyzed), you also have more confidence in the morality of your *real* conduct than in the morality of any conduct you would conscientiously refuse. If you would conscientiously refuse to imprison the man, you must then have more confidence in your real conduct than in the theory. And this is exactly the situation Aristotle warns against. You are no longer reasoning from the "better known." You are more likely to dispute your theory (which is your premise) than your conduct (which is your conclusion). And the logical result must then be a dilemma: If you dispute your conduct, you will also dispute the theory; if you accept the theory, you already accept your conduct—since you find it less disputable. To justify your conduct by appeal to the theory must, therefore, be unpersuasive or unnecessary. It can never rationally change your mind. Your theory is not a real reason for doing anything in particular; quite the contrary, it is at best just a showy facade.

I am at pains not to be misunderstood. The little experiment I suggest is highly abstracted, and I want to avoid claiming too much for it. Most important, I want to say that, personally, I have always enjoyed the discussion of general moral systems, and I have spent a number of years professionally, arguing, back-tracking, and modifying, in an attempt to determine which of the many systems was best. Such disputes are fine exercises for the mind, and in old age a grand moral hypothesis can be a wonderful hobbyhorse. But it only seems fair to add, heaven help the sage who actually relies on one.

6.

Why Obey the Law?

I RETURN ONCE more to ancient Athens, which plays an exceptional role in the history of ideas.[1] In 406 B.C., the Athenian Assembly wrestled with a fundamental problem of law and fair play. The Assembly sought to try eight generals for their lives on the charge of murder. The generals had won a desperate sea battle during the Peloponnesian War, but they had also allowed more than a thousand of their own sailors and soldiers, who were clinging to the wrecks of Athenian ships, to drown. The relatives of the dead then accused the generals of deliberately killing them, but the generals said they had abandoned the men only out of military necessity. They had left the men behind, they said, because of dangerous weather and because enemy ships were still within range. What made the case especially peculiar was that the generals were to be tried not in a court of law but by a simple popular vote in the Assembly. And they were to be tried *en bloc*, meaning that only one verdict could be given for all eight. Thus, either all eight men would be guilty by popular vote and so executed, or all eight would be innocent.

By chance, the philosopher Socrates was chosen to put this item on the Assembly's agenda, but when it came time for Socrates to act, he refused. A clear majority wanted the item included, but Socrates, selected by lottery for the presiding committee, defied the will of the majority and insisted that the procedure was "contrary to the *nomoi*"—meaning contrary to the fundamental laws. He apparently wanted the men tried in a court of law or not at all. And he then tried to block the Assembly's vote. The rest of his committee was intimidated,

---

1. I shall try to explain the cause of this unusual prominence in the next chapter.

75

however, and the Assembly's majority soon bypassed the philosopher and executed each general who dared to attend the proceedings.[2]

This is one instance in which Socrates defied the apparent will of the state,
but not the last. He did so again in 404/3 B.C., when a new oligarchic government called the Thirty (and led by Plato's cousin) demanded that he help arrest
a man for execution without trial, a man named Leon of Salamis. Socrates
refused once more, and he remarks in Plato's Apology that he would have been
executed himself for disobedience had the Thirty not been overthrown shortly
afterward in a revolution.

Socrates' stubbornness in these episodes is in many ways remarkable, but
more remarkable still is the fact that he nevertheless submitted to the state quite
readily when his own life was at stake. In 399 B.C., Socrates was himself indicted
on charges of corrupting the young and of believing in gods not recognized by
the city but of his own invention. As the Apology recounts his own trial,
Socrates steadfastly maintained his innocence. Little real evidence was offered
to the jury, and the jury seems to have been deeply prejudiced. Still, Socrates
also insisted that he was morally obligated to abide by the jury's verdict whether
or not he agreed with it (or so Plato tells us), and with that verdict came a sentence of death. So, about a month after the trial and in accordance with the law,
Socrates obediently drank the poison that ended his life.

There is much reason to think he could have escaped had he wished. Escape
from Athenian jails was fairly common for the intellectually prominent. About
a generation earlier, the philosopher Anaxagoras escaped from Athens with the
help of the outstanding politician of the day, Pericles. In another dialogue, the
Crito, Plato indicates that an elaborate plan for Socrates' escape was already in
motion but that it was finally abandoned only because Socrates insisted that
escape would be wrong. Thus, Socrates seems to have believed, at least implicitly, that the state had a right to execute an innocent man, provided he had had
his day in court; Socrates thought it wrong to interfere with his own execution,
yet he never ceased to maintain his innocence.

The upshot is that Socrates, like Mohandas Gandhi and Martin Luther King
Jr. after him, seems to have cooperated with the state on some occasions, but not
on others, and he seems to have regarded some of its actions as lawful, yet others
as unlawful. How, then, did he decide when to go along? When did he think it
right to obey the state, and when did he think himself obligated to resist? The
question of when to submit to the state's authority is called the problem of legitimacy, and it is equally the problem of when to obey the laws of man.

Many thinkers have, of course, wrestled with this issue, and I shall return to
Socrates' views later, but the most surprising, elaborate, and daring answer ever

---

2. The story of the affair is told in both Plato's Apology, 32b-c, and Xenophon's Hellenica, Book
1, chap. 7.

suggested comes neither from an ancient Greek nor from a philosopher of our own time, but from the seventeenth-century, during the English Civil War, in the person of Thomas Hobbes, who expounds and defends this answer in his fearless treatise *Leviathan*.

According to Hobbes, Socrates was wrong on all counts. Yet this is no reason for the student of Socrates not to be also a careful student of Hobbes. To the contrary, the great advantage of the lives of these two philosophers is that they represent intellectual opposites, so that by studying one we learn more about the other. Likewise, Hobbes's outlook is probably the clearest antithesis to the rarified metaphysics of Socrates' friend Plato, so that an easy way to understand Plato is to contrast him with Hobbes, and vice versa.

Consider, for example, Hobbes's stark materialism—which is nothing if not plucky. Hobbes defends the risky proposition that the only things that exist are physical bodies, an assertion that thoroughly incensed England's religious authorities and later got him investigated. Thoughts, appetites, and aversions are but physical motions in the brain, says Hobbes, and so good and evil are nothing more than the things picked out by human beings as the objects of their likes or dislikes. He remarks,

> . . . whatsoever is the object of any man's appetite or desire; that is it, which he for his part calleth Good: And the object of his hate, and aversion, Evil. . . . For these words Good, Evil, and Contemptible, are ever used with relation to the person that useth them: There being nothing simply and absolutely so; nor any common rule of Good and Evil, to be taken from the nature of the objects themselves.[3]

Hobbes is thus a moral subjectivist, and this subjectivism indicates the whole strategy of *Leviathan*.

Beginning with the assumption that the only things that exist are physical, Hobbes sets out to redefine the entire vocabulary of the human sciences—psychology, sociology, politics, and even morality, mathematics, and religion—so that all terms signify physical bodies.[4] If a term does *not* signify a physical body (or at least some feature of one), then Hobbes calls the term meaningless. *Leviathan* is consequently an elaborate system of materialist definitions, which, when combined with certain generalizations about human behavior that he thinks to be observable, yield a great variety of political inferences, just as the definitions of Euclid, when combined with Euclid's postulates and axioms, yield a variety of theorems. In fact, there is an old story that the fundamental inspiration behind Hobbes's philosophy was his discovery of Euclid's geometry.

---

3. *Leviathan*, ed. C. B. Macpherson (1968; reprint, New York: Penguin USA, Viking, 1982), chap. 6, 120.

4. Though the term "sociology" was not yet invented, Hobbes is indeed concerned with many of the same issues.

Being in a gentleman's library, Euclid's *Elements* lay open, and 'twas the 47 El.
libri I [the 47th Proposition of Book I]. He read the proposition. By G[od], said
he, this is impossible! So he reads the demonstration of it, which referred him
back to such a proposition; which proposition he read. That referred him back
to another, which he also read. *Et sic deinceps* [and so on] that at last he was
demonstratively convinced of that truth. This made him in love with geometry.[5]

Just so, at least half the charm of *Leviathan* is its systematic quality. Quite
apart from whether or not you are a materialist, you can always ask, What would
a materialist's conception of the world look like? Could all human knowledge be
redefined, at least in theory, so that all of it was ultimately reducible to physics?
And if so, then what would terms like "justice," "right," "obligation," and "duty"
mean—if anything? Is morality simply some sort of complicated physical law? Of
course, I have already argued (in the previous chapter) that relying on a philosophical system of this sort would actually be quite unreasonable, even if the
system *could* be devised, but I now ask you to suspend this judgment for the time
being, because Hobbes's sweeping ideology still has much to teach, whether or
not you agree with him.

Hobbes is above all the towering adversary of Platonism. Plato, you recall,
liked to think that justice was similar to a number—timeless, placeless, eternal.
Hobbes, on the other hand, says numbers are merely names, invented for the
convenience of human beings. And justice? Things like "justice," "right," "obligation," and "duty" are only the various parts of political agreements made by
people, and these agreements are themselves only complicated physical
processes in the brains of the participants. Thus, everything that Plato wanted
to call "invisible but intelligible" (the Platonic "forms"), Hobbes wishes to make
material and tangible. According to Hobbes, without human beings to think of
the names, there can be no numbers, and without human beings to make the
agreements, there can be no justice.

As for the proof of Hobbes's materialist hypothesis, which is both the foundation and rationale of his whole system, Hobbes relies on a theory of language,
a theory of great influence today, though by no means obviously true. And at the
bottom of this theory is an idea of how we think.

Hobbes says all our thoughts are but "decaying sensations." For example, if
I think of eating an ice-cream cone, and if I imagine the experience in enough
detail, then I can almost taste it. But not quite. Thus, my imagining of the ice-
cream cone is not an actual sensation of ice cream; rather, it is a decaying sensation, meaning that it is drawn from previous memories. I can also manipulate
my memories of various sensations so as to imagine new entities, like ice-cream
cones made of plastic, or ice-cream cones made of putty, but my imaginings

---

5. The story is told by Hobbes's friend John Aubrey in his *Brief Lives*, ed. O. L. Dick (London:
Secker and Warburg, 1950), 150.

always derive from my original stock of remembered stimuli, so that my imagination is forever limited, in certain ways, by my personal experience. Had I never seen plastic or putty before, I would have to make my imaginary ice-cream cone out of something else—like plaster.

Hobbes's next move is simple. Because sensations are always of something physical, it follows, he says, that only physical objects, or possible physical objects, can be thought about. Thus, any assertion about the existence of *non*-physical objects, such as nonphysical numbers or nonphysical morality, is meaningless, because it expresses no thought. The effect is to dismiss all competing philosophies as verbally absurd.

The usual rejoinder, it should be added, is to attack Hobbes's underlying notion of thinking. The whole thrust of the philosophies of Plato and Descartes, for example, is to argue that much intelligible thought, especially in fields such as mathematics, is about the *in*tangible and even the unimaginable. Descartes was probably the greatest of Hobbes's opponents in his own lifetime, and his outlook is typical.

Descartes implicitly denies that you can ever have a sensation of the number five. You can have the sensation of seeing the symbol for it, or hearing the word for it, but the number five is not the symbol. Rather, it is the *thing symbolized*. There are many symbols for the number five, but only *one* such integer between four and six. Thus, Descartes thinks that you do indeed reason about numbers, and much of your reasoning may be correct, but you have never experienced physical sensations of them or even imagined them. Instead, all you really imagine are the symbols. Thus, abstract thought consists precisely in the ability to reason about things that are strictly *un*imaginable. (To test this hypothesis for yourself, try imagining something like the idea of causation or the idea of infinity. Can you picture it? Hobbes's opponents will deny that such things can be imagined in the same way a plaster ice-cream cone can, yet scientists and mathematicians reason about causation and infinity all the time. Thus, they argue, Hobbes's attempt to derive all human knowledge from sensation must be mistaken, and with it his contention that all opposing philosophies are necessarily meaningless.)

Hobbes was well aware of this contrary view, and while living in Paris as a refugee, he got a chance to read Descartes's acclaimed *Meditations on First Philosophy* when it was still in manuscript. His resulting criticisms led to an acrimonious exchange of letters between the two philosophers, and each man finally concluded that the other must be a fool. Hobbes told the biographer John Aubrey, "had [Descartes] kept himself to geometry, he had been the best geometer in the world, but his head [does] not lie for philosophy."[6]

Hobbes's radical materialism got him into considerable trouble personally.

---

6. Ibid., 158.

Asked by the Anglican Bishop John Bramhall what he took God to be, Hobbes replied, "I leave him to be a most pure, simple, invisible spirit corporeal."[7] The key word is of course "corporeal," and Hobbes therefore denies that there can be angels, a Holy Ghost, miracles, or any of the other traditional adjuncts of Christianity, except to the extent that these things are physical processes. The whole second half of Leviathan is then devoted to showing how such a religion is still possible, though many readers (myself included) find it hard to construe these chapters as anything other than a staggering piece of irony.

Readers in his own time apparently had the same problem. After the Great Plague swept through London in 1665 and the Great Fire swept through it in 1666, Parliament passed a bill for the suppression of atheists, believing that God was displeased, and it assigned to a committee the special task of investigating Hobbes's book. But the investigation was abandoned after the intervention of Hobbes's former student and good friend, King Charles II.

Hobbes was nevertheless suspected of atheism for the rest of his life and was thoroughly distrusted by England's various political factions. Yet he remained vigorous and witty, playing tennis to the age of seventy-five and at eighty-six publishing translations of both the Iliad and Odyssey. He never lost an opportunity to mock the remote learning of the universities (which was easy for him, because he made his living as a private tutor), and he quipped that if he had had the patience to read as much as other men of his time, he would have remained just as ignorant as they. When his death finally came at the age of ninety-one, his last words, according to one version, were, "I am about to take my last voyage, a great leap in the dark."[8]

But what advice would Hobbes have given Socrates in facing the Athenians? In a word, Hobbes would have said to run—just as he himself did in 1640 with the approach of the English Civil War. ("I was the first of all that fled.")

The whole purpose of government, says Hobbes, is to "preserve men in numbers" and offer them "commodious living." But the person whose preservation and convenience matter most is always oneself. Thus, Leviathan is an intricate calculation of self-interest, where self-interest is construed in material rather than spiritual terms. And Hobbes believes that self-interest always permits you to save your own life. His defense of self-interest is, of course, highly controversial, but more important, he is also a political absolutist—meaning that, except to save yourself, you must always obey the ruler. And the issue of absolutism is crucial whether or not you believe in self-interest.

Absolutism is a theory of legitimacy. That is, it tries to answer once more

---

7. Hobbes's remark is quoted by R. S. Peters in The Encyclopedia of Philosophy (1967; reprint, New York: Macmillan, 1972), volume 4, 32.

8. John Watkins, Anecdotes of Men of Learning (n.p., 1808), 276, quoted in The Oxford Dictionary of Quotations, 4th ed. (New York: Oxford University Press, 1992), 340.

the old question, When, if ever, is it morally permissible to defy the state? And Hobbes's answer illustrates most of the classic features of political philosophy.

For one thing, Hobbes conceives of the state as an instrument of coercion. Put another way, the very *idea* of a state assumes that someone, somewhere, must be compelled. And the kind of compulsion he has in mind is not the mild and metaphorical one of a harsh word or angry glance but the solemn and severe one of threatening lives, liberties, or possessions. Here, perhaps, is a way to see this first point more easily. Many organizations exercise authority; they lay down rules, regulations, and punishments, yet not all of them amount to a "state." A modern church, for example, may proclaim "laws" of a sort; it can claim divine legitimacy and punish its miscreants by condemning them. But rarely does it constitute a sovereign "government." Why not? For Hobbes, the answer is simple. Unless the church tries to kill its enemies (or imprison them, or confiscate their possessions), it fails to exercise the requisite force. Instead, it is merely a private association, because its punishments have not yet reached the level of deadly intimidation. Thus, although the question of political legitimacy is usually phrased as a problem of when to obey the state's authority, it can also be construed as a problem of coercion (though only the most severe *type* of coercion). The problem can be posed like this: If such coercion is used at all—the taking of lives, liberties, or possessions—then how should it be rationally managed? Answer this, and you have already propounded a theory of the state.

This is not the only way in which Hobbes's outlook is typical. He also thinks that the power to kill, imprison, or confiscate (or beat, wound, and maim) can reasonably arise among human beings only because they are already prone to violence. As Hobbes says, "The way of one competitor to the attaining of his desire, is to kill, subdue, supplant or repel the other."[9] In other words, if all men were invariably good and peaceful, why would anyone inflict such awful penalties in the first place? And why, then, would there be "government" at all?

This assumption is by no means unique to Hobbes, and, in fact, it receives one of its clearest expressions from one of Hobbes's staunchest opponents, the bold revolutionary Thomas Paine, in his pithy little pamphlet *Common Sense* (1776). Here is how Paine explains the idea:

> Society in every state is a blessing, but government even in its best state is but a necessary evil. . . . Government, like dress, is the badge of lost innocence; the palaces of kings are built on the ruins of the bowers of paradise. For were the impulses of conscience clear, uniform, and irresistibly obeyed, man would need no other lawgiver; but that not being the case, he finds it necessary to surrender up part of his property to furnish means for the protection of the rest. . . .[10]

---

9. *Leviathan*, chap. 11, 161.
10. *Common Sense*, ed. Isaac Kramnick (1976; reprint, London: Penguin Books, 1986), 65.

The whole origin of government, says Paine, is the "inability of moral virtue to govern the world."

The idea that moral virtue might "govern the world" is the essence of several species of philosophical anarchism, but as it turns out, Hobbes is famously pessimistic about it. He writes, "I put for a general inclination of all mankind, a perpetual and restless desire of power after power, that ceaseth only in Death."[11] And he not only is pessimistic about moral virtue but also about the rule of law, which is precisely what makes him an absolutist.

The very idea of the rule of law implies that no man's power is absolute. In a state under the rule of law, each person's authority must have limits. Thus, even if one person has the power of life and death over another, the rule of law still requires that he exercise this power only according to known regulations, and if he exceeds these regulations, his legitimate power disappears. So, though one person may well be above another, it must still be the case that "no man is above the law." On the other hand, unlimited authority implies not a "government of laws," but a "government of men," an idea that was perhaps best expressed in the famous remark attributed to the French king Louis XIV, "L'etat, c'est moi" (I am the state).

Hobbes's theory expresses this distinction well. The absolute sovereign that Hobbes favors in *Leviathan* is bound by no human rules whatever. Instead, unlimited freedom and authority are precisely what define him. Everyone else in the Hobbesian state binds himself by contract to obey the commands of this absolute sovereign (whom Hobbes calls "that mortal God"), but the sovereign is in turn the one person who remains outside the contract and, being outside it, becomes its enforcer. According to Hobbes, if the sovereign wishes to execute his subjects arbitrarily, then none of them is rationally entitled to interfere, except to protect his individual safety. Also, Hobbes's sovereign shares his authority with no other branch of government; there is no separation of powers in Hobbes's scheme, since if there were, the separation would require a basic law or agreement to regulate it, and in that event, the ruler would be once again *under* the law instead of above it. And on the whole, Hobbes thinks that the very idea of the rule of law is a recipe for disaster.

Hobbes's great fear is civil war. He knew its effects during the disturbances in England, "a war of every man against every man," and he also saw its consequences in the uprising of the Fronde in France in 1648. And he fears civil war so much that he thinks any attempt to limit the sovereign's authority will itself be a matter of dispute, which will then steep the nation in blood. Let this happen, says Hobbes, and all commerce disintegrates, all industry ceases, all joys vanish, and all life becomes "solitary, poor, nasty, brutish and short." Something of the sort did indeed happen in Hobbes's own day, when England's king,

---

11. *Leviathan*, chap. 11, 161.

Charles I, fell into a dispute with Parliament over the proper limits of his power, and both sides then raised armies. But what is peculiar is Hobbes's diagnosis of the cause. The cause of the English Civil War, according to Hobbes, was not the king's attempt to *assert* absolute power but Parliament's attempt to *deny* it. And as a general rule, Hobbes thinks that the odds of causing a civil war by denying a ruler absolute power are always greater than the odds of provoking an equally destructive conflict by seizing absolute power.[12]

Hobbes's theory is of course sweeping and extreme, but let me try for a moment to put the case for absolutism in its most plausible form. Even constitutional governments sometimes see the necessity, at least temporarily, of martial law; but if martial law can be temporarily necessary, why can't it be permanently necessary? Again, isn't it conceivable that in certain times and places the inhabitants of a particular society might be so violent as to be ungovernable except by a Draconian hand? The ruler might then be just as wicked as the rest, but his own devastations, aimed only at satisfying his own will and that of his army, might still be less than the many smaller devastations of a thousand warring wills. Even that apostle of nineteenth-century liberalism, John Stuart Mill, remarks,

---

12. The only circumstances in which Hobbes permits defiance is to save one's own life, an exception that is warranted, he says, by the "law of nature." The law of nature is a thoroughly ancient idea and one that deserves special consideration in its own right, but Hobbes's version happens to be particularly unorthodox. One of the best expressions of the *traditional* view comes from Cicero, who says the law of nature is moral law, an eternal emanation from God, and "neither the Senate nor the people can absolve us from our obligation to obey this law." Human laws are then morally binding only to the extent that they conform to this law of nature. If the two conflict, the law of nature comes first. Thus, if we ask, "When is it permissible to defy the state?" Cicero answers, whenever its own laws violate the law of nature.

Cicero's idea (expressed, for example, in Book 3, Section 22, of his *De Re Publica*) has descended largely intact into modern times. It is adjusted only slightly by the medieval philosopher Thomas Aquinas to adapt it to Christian theology. John Locke assumes the tradition quite easily in his *Second Treatise of Government* (1690), and so does Thomas Jefferson in the *Declaration of Independence* (where he invokes "the Laws of Nature and of Nature's God"). Martin Luther King Jr. also assumes it in his *Letter from Birmingham Jail*. In fact, the seeds of the doctrine go back at least as far as Sophocles' play *Antigone*, where Antigone invokes a higher law in asserting her right to bury her dead brother—and to defy all Thebes if necessary.

The very idea that morality is objective and independent of human whims may indeed suggest something like this natural-law doctrine, but what distinguishes Hobbes is his egoism and his materialism. Hobbes recognizes nineteen different "laws of nature," all interrelated, but he says they are only "qualities that dispose men to peace, and to obedience." What he means is that these laws of nature are only psychological tendencies—tendencies that actually prevail among human beings and that derive from the desire for self-preservation and for "commodious living." Thus, the laws of nature are for Hobbes merely the dictates of rational self-interest, which is itself only a physical process in the brain.

Because the laws of nature always permit us to save our own lives, says Hobbes, they also permit us to refuse dangerous military service, to decline to testify against ourselves, and to seek the protection of a more powerful sovereign whenever we can find one.

> Despotism is a legitimate mode of government in dealing with barbarians. . . .
> Liberty, as a principle, has no application to any state of things anterior to the
> time when mankind have become capable of being improved by free and equal
> discussion. Until then, there is nothing for them but implicit obedience to an
> Akbar or a Charlemagne, if they are so fortunate as to find one.[13]

Much would depend, of course, on the character of the particular ruler in question and on the nature of the little bandits who would constitute the alternative.

On the other hand, the opposite situation is equally conceivable. In truth, many societies with established limits on government authority are far safer places in which to live than the regime of an absolute despot, whose army plunders the people with impunity. And in a constitutional regime, even martial law includes limits on the use of force. John Locke offers one of the best criticisms of Hobbes's basic idea—the recommendation that we escape the many little tyrannies of anarchy by erecting the one big tyranny of absolutism. Locke remarks, "This is to think that men are so foolish that they take care to avoid what mischiefs may be done them by polecats or foxes, but are content, nay, think it safety, to be devoured by lions."[14]

Still, what is most striking about Hobbes's theory, and even Locke's for that matter, is that both authors try to generalize for all cases. Neither confines his argument to particular historical periods or social circumstances. Instead, each proposes a theory of what all legitimate governments must have in common. Thus, their approach is quite different from that of Edmund Burke, who stresses the particular and circumstantial.[15]

---

13. John Stuart Mill, *On Liberty,* ed. Gertrude Himmelfarb (1974; reprint, London: Penguin Books, 1985), 69.

14. John Locke, *The Second Treatise of Government,* ed. Thomas P. Peardon (1690; Indianapolis: Bobbs-Merrill Company, 1952), chap. 7, Section 93. All subsequent citations refer to section numbers.

15. One might also ask, Why do philosophers feel the need for such general theories in the first place? Why don't they rest content with deciding moral and political questions by analogy—as Burke does? The answer, I suspect, lies in the staggering pace of social change in the recent history of Europe.

Europe experienced some of its deepest social upheavals from the beginning of the sixteenth century to the close of the nineteenth. Under the immense pressure of these disruptions, many of Europe's traditional moral and political rules had to be rethought, and many philosophers naturally hoped to ease this process by finding some single set of principles that would define a well-ordered society. Thus, it is no accident, perhaps, that many of the most famous theories coincide with specific revolutions or dislocations. Hobbes's *Leviathan,* for example, appeared just after the English Civil War. Locke wrote the *Second Treatise* in the years surrounding the Glorious Revolution of 1688. Rousseau published *The Social Contract* in 1762 in the years leading up to in the French Revolution. And Bentham and Mill defended utilitarianism in the midst of the Industrial Revolution.

Philosophy's reaction to these events is probably understandable, but Burke's basic point is that the reaction is exaggerated.

I shall have more to say about the particular circumstances of the modern era in chapter 8, but there is still one further important point that needs to be made about both these theories of legitimacy. To say that a state has behaved *ill*egitimately is to say that the state has done something *wrong*. But it is quite another thing to determine the appropriate *remedy*. Even if a state *is* illegitimate, it does not follow automatically that the correct remedy is revolution. This distinction between a wrong and a remedy is fundamental in law and politics, and a classic illustration is the story of the old woman of Syracuse.

According to the story (told by Thomas Aquinas), Syracuse was ruled in the fourth century B.C. by the hated tyrant Dionysius, but one day he learned that an old woman always prayed for his welfare. Surprised to hear that any of his subjects thought so well of him as to pray for him, Dionysius then sought her out, and when he found her, he asked what he had done to earn her affection. She replied, "When I was a young girl, we had an evil tyrant for a ruler, and I prayed for his death. But then he died, and we got a worse tyrant, and I prayed for his death, too. But when he died also, we got a worse tyrant still, and that was you." The result of overthrowing a tyrant may simply be a worse tyrant. To say this, of course, is not to deny that revolution is sometimes appropriate, but only to say that the whole question is apt to depend on a great many factors, some local and impermanent.[16]

Still, it is important to see that the problem of legitimacy is not just a question of when to make revolutions or set up "mortal gods" or overthrow tyrants. It is equally a problem of ordinary life, whenever the state asks you to cooperate—a difficulty that I discovered for myself some years ago in a rather unusual way, when I was first called to serve on a criminal jury. Perhaps the story of my experience will help to explain this point further.

I was called to serve in a murder case in which two brothers were accused of killing a third brother. And the judge was quite specific about my duty. He said we jurors were to determine the facts of the case and then to apply to the facts whatever law he laid down. As the judge himself expressed it, "The jury is the judge of the facts, but the judge is the judge of the law." Yet the judge then added something more: He said the jury was to apply the law as he gave it "without exception, no matter what."

Now part of his remarks were simply a restatement of ordinary American law. Since the nineteenth century, most American courtrooms have followed the dictum that the jury must take its law from the judge. And the reason is simple. In a complicated society, law is so technical a business that it needs to be construed by professionals; ordinary citizens often lack the training necessary to determine precisely what the law means, yet the defendant is entitled to be tried by the law as it is, not as I merely fancy it.

---

16. Aquinas tells this story in the sixth chapter of his treatise on kingship, *De Regimine Principum*.

The judge in front of me, however, took this settled legal doctrine one step further. He not only said that his instructions were legally binding on the jury; he also said they were binding on the jury "without exception, no matter what." (Notice that it is one thing for a judge to assert binding legal authority over a jury; it is quite another thing to say that this authority therefore extends without limit. By analogy, a king may well have binding legal authority over his subjects, yet only Hobbes would say that the authority is therefore unlimited.) And the judge then did what, from my point of view, was the worst thing imaginable. He called a five-minute recess.

Nothing is so unsettling to someone who teaches philosophy for a living as to be presented with such a conundrum and then to be given five minutes in a corridor to worry about it. People in my line of work tend to make mountains out of molehills, and already my brain was off and running. Various ideas began vexing me. The first was John Locke's "law of nature" (which is Locke's way of expressing the limits of government authority over the individual), and I asked myself what would happen if the judge's construction of the law somehow violated the law of nature as construed by Locke. Wouldn't I then be guilty of helping to violate the law of nature myself? This was not my only worry. I thought next of Socrates' behavior at the trial of the generals in 406 B.C., and I recalled that even Socrates had set limits to what any legal system might require him to do. I also reflected that from a practical standpoint it was entirely ridiculous to worry about such questions. After all, whatever legal errors a judge might commit during a trial, they were unlikely to be so gross as to exceed the bounds of legitimate government, and even if they *were* that gross, they could still be corrected on appeal. (Even Locke remarks, *Second Treatise*, 207, that resistance is unjustified while an appeal to the law is still possible.) And even if I were then to have doubts about the reliability of the courts of appeal, and thus have doubts about whether the required corrections would ever take place, I could still simply forswear the juror's oath once I was in deliberation and construe the law however I liked, and no one could ever punish me for it. I could simply ignore the judge's instructions outright.

On the other hand, an opposing set of practical considerations also came to mind. For one thing, I knew from having worked briefly for a public defender many years earlier that the murder case in question would almost certainly fall under the felony-murder rule, an old piece of common law that now varies from state to state and that sometimes has unforeseen legal effects. Could I be sure that one of the brothers would not be technically guilty of murder in a way that was morally absurd?

But this was not the only problem. I also knew that criminal convictions that ought to be overturned on appeal sometimes never are, because no one hears the appeal and because no lawyer or judge takes an interest. As a newspaper reporter some years earlier, I had once come across a man who had been convicted and sentenced to prison for three months, without legal counsel, for the sole crime of having insulted the secretary of a local district justice. (The man, who was poor, ill educated, and apparently shiftless, had told the secretary as she walked past that her figure was attractive—only he said it more graphically.) The secretary's father turned out to be a police lieutenant, and he arrested the man in his home that same evening. The magistrate who heard the case then failed to arrange for a lawyer to be present, and so the man was hustled off to prison for three months for disorderly conduct. My own knowledge of the law was quite paltry at the time (and still is), but I knew enough to realize that the handling of the case violated the U.S. Supreme Court's rules on legal representation. Yet the man remained in prison, and no lawyer or judge took the slightest interest in his situation until I began to write articles about it.

And I had in mind one further consideration, too. My scruples up to this point were of course entirely hypothetical, though they could hardly impede the court's business anyway, because many other jurors were available for service. But more important, there was also a question of moral principle at the bottom of it all. The judge was looking me in the eye and asking for my word of honor, under oath and in the most solemn way that a modern society can devise, that I would participate in the application of a law that I couldn't know in advance, and that I would also swear not to carve out exceptions to it if I later discovered it to be something monstrous or barbaric. So I decided what I would do.

When the court reconvened, the judge asked whether every juror had understood what his or her duty would be. I then asked the judge, "Do you mean your instructions are binding on the jury even if absurd or tyrannical?" The judge replied instantly, "I want to make this perfectly clear: My instructions are binding on the jury even if absurd or tyrannical," and with that I refused to take the oath.

To avoid further difficulties, I had myself transferred from criminal to civil cases, but the first case I was then called for turned out to be the eviction of a defendant who could neither hear nor speak. The courtroom was in Manhattan, which was just beginning to witness a dramatic increase in the number of homeless people during the 1980s. As it turned out, some of these homeless people later perished from exposure and at least a few were murdered by thieves. The city's shelters, meanwhile, were notoriously unsafe. And again I was asked by the court whether I would follow the law as the judge gave it. I replied that I would almost certainly do so, but that I would reserve the right to consider the overall legitimacy of the proceedings in just one circumstance: if the defendant could show that eviction would threaten him with death or serious injury. (At the time, I recalled Locke's dictum, *First Treatise*, 42, that even the right of property must give way if necessary to save a man's life.) And again I was dismissed from the case.

What I finally discovered from these incidents was something quite strange about jury service, in fact, wholly unique. Many courts now ask their jurors something officially asked of no other U.S. citizen in any other context. They ask their jurors, once sworn, to put entirely out of mind the question, Is this, after all, morally defensible? A soldier, though strictly obligated to obey orders, is still expected to determine whether his orders are lawful and legitimate; no soldier, for example, may obey an order to commit murder, and if he receives such an order, he is expected to defy it. Yet the jury is seemingly forbidden to ask whether it has perhaps been roped into some sort of judicial murder or some equally monstrous project, since to ask this question would be to ask whether the judge's instructions are really binding after all. Put another way, if the judge's legal authority over a jury has no limits whatever, then how does his relation to the jury differ from that of a Hobbesian sovereign?[17]

But my personal experience aside, how did Socrates handle this sort of problem? How did Socrates decide when to obey the state and when to defy it?

As frustrating as it sounds, no general answer is likely, because Socrates left no general theory. We know his particular deeds but not his general principles (if indeed he had such principles). Still, it *may* be possible to lessen this frustration slightly, by looking once more at the three incidents I related earlier: 1) the trial of the generals, 2) the arrest of Leon of Salamis, and 3) Socrates' own trial and execution. The three incidents may still suggest a common idea.

The common idea is this: Socrates refuses to participate in executions without first giving the prisoner a chance to defend himself in a court of law. Or so it seems. Put another way, Socrates takes no part in executing people summarily, or, put another way still, what all three cases seem to have in common is a special concern for the right of trial.

In his own case, Socrates is summoned by a lawful court, tried, and sentenced, and at each stage of the process he obeys. The rationale is not hard to see. If men no longer obey lawful courts, then there will no longer *be* lawful courts, and men and women will then have to settle their affairs in the alley, with very little justice.[18] On the other hand, Leon and the generals are all executed without a judicial trial, and in each of these cases, Socrates refuses to participate.

That Socrates had special concern for the right of trial is, of course, only a conjecture, but in defense of this view I would add that there is indeed a close connection between the right of trial and the Socratic life. That is, there is a

---

17. The most authoritative discussion of this question is the United States Supreme Court's majority opinion in *Sparf and Hansen v United States*, 156 US 51 (1895), where the Court insists that the judge is indeed the judge of the law and that the jury's practical power to defy the judge does not logically entail a legal or moral right to do so. Yet nowhere in the opinion does the Court say that the judge's authority over a jury in matters of law extends "without exception" or "without limit." In recent years, various American courts have considered the problem under the heading of "jury nullification." But they have used this term so broadly that it now covers defiance of a judge even out of mere pique, or out of a belief that the law or the judge's interpretation of it is merely imperfect. By contrast, a juror's refusal to participate in an act of tyranny has been discussed only rarely.

18. For what it's worth, Socrates makes a similar point in Plato's *Crito*, at 50b.

close connection between the right to be tried in a law court and the ability to engage in moral discussion. The connection is actually rather obvious. No one calls attention to a question of justice without at the same time calling attention to himself. But without a secure right of trial, the conspicuous people are easily cut down. They can be assassinated or simply arrested and killed, and because there is no public hearing, with known rules of evidence and established procedures, there is no way for anyone else in the community to verify that the victims were really guilty. Thus, where criminals are executed summarily, there is also an easy opportunity for those in power to stifle moral criticism by simply murdering the critics—on the pretext that the critics were criminals, too. So, quite apart from the death of the victims, the effect of assassinations and summary executions is also to make moral discussion more dangerous for the whole community. About the only way to prevent this effect, on the other hand, is to give trials to everybody, even those you believe to be guilty from the start. (Summary executions in combat, it should be noted, are a different case.)

The danger inherent in summary executions is quite distinct from other questions of politics. When people now discuss what they regard as basic political issues, what do they ask? They typically ask 1) whether their country should be democratic, 2) whether it should have free speech, 3) whether it should be capitalist or socialist, and 4) whether it should enjoy national independence. But these questions are still different from asking whether their country should execute its alleged enemies without trial. And the logical independence of this last issue may also explain a further peculiarity of Socrates' behavior: his conspicuous silence on the burning question of his own time—the problem of democracy versus oligarchy.

Nearly everyone in fifth-century Greece had an opinion about the best form of government, rule by the many or rule by the few, and nowhere does Socrates give the simple democracy of Athens a ringing endorsement. Yet neither does he condemn it at his trial. Scholars in later ages have often suggested that the real reason he was executed was that he opposed democracy as such, yet if this is really so, why doesn't he simply condemn democracy plainly? Plato depicts him in the *Apology* as rebuking the jurors for neglecting their duty, and also boasting of his courage, yet he apparently forgoes this chance to lecture the jury on the virtues of oligarchy and the evils of popular rule. (Socrates does indeed condemn democracy in the *Republic* and also criticizes it obliquely in the *Crito*, but these dialogues are much less reliable historically than the *Apology*; the *Apology* records an event to which there were many witnesses. The *Republic* and the *Crito* may simply reflect the views of Plato.)

The more likely explanation, I think, is that Socrates regards questions of the proper form of government as far less important than the basic problem of legal process. Allow citizens to be executed summarily, and perhaps it makes no difference who is in charge; you simply exchange one form of tyranny for another. But whether or not this was Socrates' real view, we can still ask the same question today. If you execute wicked men summarily, do you really make the world better? As Robert Bolt's Thomas More remarks in *A Man for All Seasons* (38), "I'd give the Devil benefit of law, for my own safety's sake."

7.

Are Some Races Intellectually Superior?

WHY DO PEOPLE of European descent exercise disproportionate power over the earth? Why, in literature, philosophy, mathematics, and science, have Europeans also exercised unusual influence? More than blame or commendation, the question cries out for straightforward explanation. How did Europeans get such power in the first place?

This old conundrum still puzzles observers on all sides of the political arena, and the want of a solution gives extra impetus to racism. After all, to solve it in terms of culture only raises the further difficulty of explaining why the same cultural tendencies haven't been equally present everywhere. Why Europe rather than Nigeria? The belief that Europeans are somehow biologically superior often persists, secretly, even among those most likely to deny it, and this secret conviction gains strength from the fact that many classics in the history of ideas do indeed come from Europeans. Recent attempts to tease an answer out of I.Q. scores are another effect of this old and persistent riddle, yet the riddle was actually solved more than two centuries ago by a professor of moral philosophy, a shrewd and engaging writer, still widely touted but not nearly so often read, Adam Smith. According to Smith, the dominion of Europeans has nothing to do with race; it derives instead from a simple accident of geography.

Smith's ideas on this head look at first glance like the exclusive domain of the social scientist, yet they should also engage the philosopher. Why? Because they can also affect how we interpret philosophical classics. Ignore Smith's ideas, and you are more likely to fall into a common misconception: that the traditional classics of philosophy are essentially conservative endorsements of an intellectual status quo. Keep his ideas in mind, on the other hand, and you are more likely to see their radicalism and daring. The most celebrated works of phi-

91

losophy are typically bold departures, and Smith's observations help to show how this is possible. Such, at least, is what I hope to demonstrate in the remarks that follow.

The trouble is, Smith remains one of the most misunderstood authors of modern times. His name now suggests immoderate riches, though his real sympathies were always with the poor. His ideas are said to justify monopoly, though the "wretched spirit of monopoly" was always his principal target. And he is usually conceived as the businessman's advocate, though his warning about the businessmen of his own day could hardly be plainer:

> The proposal of any new law or regulation of commerce which comes from this order ought always to be listened to with great precaution, and ought never to be adopted till after having been long and carefully examined, not only with the most scrupulous, but with the most suspicious attention. It comes from an order of men whose interest is never exactly the same with that of the public, who have generally an interest to deceive and even to oppress the public, and who, accordingly, have, upon many occasions, both deceived and oppressed it.[1]

How did this misunderstanding of Smith come about?

Actually, very simply—and before I relate his explanation of Europe's preeminence, I want to say something to clear up this misimpression.

Smith held the Chair of Moral Philosophy at the University of Glasgow in the 1750s, and he was thus (in his own words) "a man of speculation—whose trade is not to do anything but to observe everything" (1.1.10). Smith was notorious for his absentmindedness, so much so that on one occasion he apparently fell, while talking with a friend, into a tanning pit. On another occasion, he is supposed to have brewed himself a mixture of bread, butter, and water and then to have pronounced it the worst cup of tea he had ever tasted. His eccentricities aside, however, he was an astute observer of his times; so why does Smith embrace the doctrine now called laissez-faire—a doctrine that condemns nearly all government regulation of the economy and that no modern nation has put into practice since the Great Depression? Actually, for a perfectly sensible reason. Smith embraces laissez-faire not because he wants businesses to be free to set up monopolies. Instead, he embraces it because he views government as the chief means by which monopolies are set up. In the last decades of the eighteenth century, before the Industrial Revolution and while capital investment is still relatively small, Smith thinks the main barriers to competition are those erected by government itself—usually in league with a few businessmen. Votes in Parliament can be openly bought, and monopolies legally established for the

---

1. Adam Smith, *An Inquiry into the Nature and Causes of the Wealth of Nations*, ed. Edwin Cannan (1776; New York: Modern Library, 1937), Book 1, chap. 11, 250. Subsequent references are to book, chapter, and page number.

benefit of the few. Thus, the most likely outcome of government interference is not that the government will regulate business for the public good. Instead, the most likely outcome (he thinks) is that government and business will conspire together to restrain competition and so "levy, for their own benefit, an absurd tax upon the rest of their fellow citizens" (1.11.250). On the other hand, had he lived to see an expansion of the right to vote, or the rise of industrial robber barons and predatory corporate tactics, it is quite possible that his analysis of government intervention would have been different. (His classic argument for the "invisible hand," though highly schematic, is intended for a land of cottage manufacturers, not for a nation of heavy industries and business cycles, neither of which existed in his own day.)

This is not the only way in which Smith's real views are now frequently misconceived. Another example is his attitude toward the laboring poor, and here again I want to add a word of explanation.

Smith thinks that to improve the condition of the poor now is only to undermine their status in the future; if you raise wages today, you will only get more laborers tomorrow. But this will simply drive wages back down. Thus, the whole idea of helping the laboring poor is self-defeating. Should we conclude that Smith writes the poor off?

As it turns out, Smith keeps up a regular campaign in *The Wealth of Nations* for *higher* wages.

> That a little more plenty than ordinary may render some workmen idle cannot well be doubted; but that it should have this effect upon the greater part, or that men in general should work better when they are ill fed than when they are well fed, when they are disheartened than when they are in good spirits, when they are frequently sick than when they are generally in good health, seems not very probable. (1.9.82–83)

On the other hand, Smith thinks that higher wages will allow the working poor to bring up more children, thereby increasing the pool of laborers in competition with each other and thus driving wages back down again. Look at how he arrives at this peculiar conclusion, and you see him wrestling with the great evils of his age.

> It is not uncommon, I have frequently been told, in the Highlands of Scotland for a mother who has borne twenty children not to have two alive. . . . In some places one half the children born die before they are four years of age, in many places before they are seven, and in almost all places before they are nine or ten. This great mortality, however, will everywhere be found chiefly among the children of the common people, who cannot afford to tend them with the same care as those of better station.

Having described this reality, Smith then explains the resulting mechanism.

> Every species of animals naturally multiplies in proportion to the means of their subsistence, and no species can ever multiply beyond it. But in civilized society it is only among the inferior ranks of people that the scantiness of subsistence can set limits to the further multiplication of the human species; and it can do so in no other way than by destroying a great part of the children which their fruitful marriages produce.

Thus, the effect of reduced wages is more dead children. He continues,

> The liberal reward of labor, by enabling them to provide better for their children, and consequently to bring up a greater number, naturally tends to widen and extend those limits. It deserves to be remarked, too, that it necessarily does this as nearly as possible in the proportion which the demand for labor requires.

Smith concludes, "It is in this manner that the demand for men, like that of any other commodity, necessarily regulates the production of men."

What is especially remarkable about these passages (all taken from *The Wealth of Nations*, Book 1, chap. 8, 79–80) is the combination of moral indignation and dispassionate analysis. Smith grieves for the plight of the poor; his anger is only thinly disguised when he remarks, "A half-starved Highland woman frequently bears more than twenty children, while a pampered fine lady is often incapable of bearing any, and is generally exhausted by two or three" (79). He tells his reader that he has made inquiries with military officers from the Highlands, at foundling hospitals, and at parish charities, all to determine the rates at which children die. Still, in the midst of tragedy, while discussing the death of babes and the anguish of their parents, he simply cannot resist making the further observation ("It deserves to be remarked, too") that the whole thing is really just supply and demand. Is it not odd, he seems to say, that the production and destruction of human beings should be like that of any other commodity—shoes, corsets, carriages, or spectacles? It is basic economics. He wishes the truth were otherwise, but he is simply too honest to deny it.

This same observation—that the demand for men necessarily regulates the production of men—led the English preacher Thomas Malthus to argue at the very end of the eighteenth century against all forms of public charity. Feed the poor, says Malthus, and you only generate more of them. Many nineteenth-century figures adopted a similar doctrine, and its prevalence led to the eloquent protests of Charles Dickens. But the curious fact is that Smith himself never embraces such a policy. Quite the reverse; he is entirely against it. He continues to argue for *higher* wages. Why? Oddly, for no reason, except that his compassion requires it, even if renouncing the poor *is* the logical consequence of his reasoning. Put another way, Smith will sooner embrace an implicit contradiction than advocate something that he believes downright barbarous, or deny what he thinks is downright obvious. Smith is no Malthus, and though sometimes mistaken, he is never cruel.

(Smith's analysis of the "production of men," it should be pointed out, also happens to be fallacious, but for reasons that Smith himself could not foresee. The demand for men regulates the production of men only because of two additional factors: a high birthrate and high child mortality. But the mortality of children not only depends on poor food; it depends also on poor sanitation, and what Smith fails to anticipate is that improvements in sanitation during the nineteenth century will cut the deaths of children dramatically. Today, it is simply false to say that the demand for men regulates the production of men. Birth and death rates may still have causes, but neither simply fluctuates with wages.)

I mention these points for one reason only: to show that Smith was a man of liberal and humanitarian instincts, whose views are often misconceived because of our tendency to read current economic conditions back into the past. But I now return to the principal question: How does he explain Europe's preeminence?

Smith's explanation is really quite simple. It appears in the first three chapters of *The Wealth of Nations*, first published in 1776, and can be summed up in a single sentence: "The division of labor is limited by the extent of the market."

Let me summarize his explanation briefly. Smith points out that all peoples trade. Anyone who uses money trades, as does anyone who barters chickens for a coat. This not only holds good for modern capitalist or socialist societies but also for virtually every known society of the past. (*The Wealth of Nations* is, in fact, the first book to make trade its specific focus of study, which is why it constitutes the founding document of modern economics.) And Smith also remarks that specialization is greatest where this trade is most extensive. For example, a businessman in Manhattan must specialize to a far greater degree than one in rural Pennsylvania, because he is in competition with more suppliers. But this increased specialization (which Smith calls the "division of labor") has a further effect. It tends to spur invention. The more you specialize, the more you see ways to cut corners. Thus, inventions will be most common where the markets are largest. If you then wish to know which regions of the earth will probably generate the greatest changes in technology, either in the past or the future, you need merely ask, Where are the markets biggest?

Now a market is not a mere courtyard or building. Rather, it is an exchange of possessions, and most exchanges are a swap of physical objects. Thus, participating in a market is usually a matter of transporting goods from one person to another. But in that case, the whole problem is really quite simple. The essence of Europe's preeminence boils down to a question of transportation. Find the places where transportation has been easiest, and you thereby trace the real economic history of the human race.

Smith sees at once that in his own period (and in every earlier historical period) the easiest way to transport goods is by water—by raft, boat, or ship, not by a horse-drawn wagon. Today we would include railroads, auto routes, air traffic, and electronic transmissions, but none of these techniques was available when Smith wrote. Thus, Smith gives special attention to the geography of rivers and seas. And he is then within easy reach of a general explanation. He sees the cardinal principle that early civilizations, whether defined by opulence, technology, architecture, or literature, almost always planted themselves along waterways. But more important, he is the first person to understand why. What civilization required was not just water to drink or water to irrigate, but water to navigate.

Consider first the example of Egypt. Smith writes,

> Of all the countries on the coast of the Mediterranean Sea, Egypt seems to have been the first in which either agriculture or manufactures were cultivated and improved to any considerable degree. Upper Egypt extends itself nowhere above a few miles from the Nile, and in Lower Egypt that great river breaks itself into many different canals, which, with the assistance of a little art, seem to have afforded a communication by water carriage. . . . The extent and easiness of this inland navigation was probably one of the principal causes of the early improvement of Egypt. (1.3.20)

With navigation came a larger market, and with that market came an increase in specialization and, consequently, discovery.

Smith also points out the fundamental importance of river traffic in the early rise of civilizations in India and China. On the other hand, he contrasts the geography of those regions with that of sub-Saharan Africa. He remarks,

> There are in Africa none of those great inlets, such as the Baltic and Adriatic Seas in Europe, the Mediterranean and Black Seas in both Europe and Asia, and the Gulfs of Arabia, Persia, India, Bengal and Siam, in Asia, to carry maritime commerce into the interior parts of that great continent; and the great rivers of Africa are at too great a distance from one another to give occasion to any considerable inland navigation. (1.3.21)

If Smith is right, of course, the explanation of Europe's preeminence should lie not in the races of its peoples but in the nature of its waterways, and the most stupendous waterway of all, anywhere on earth, is the Mediterranean Sea. Here is how he describes it:

> That sea, by far the greatest inlet that is known in the world, having no tides, nor consequently any waves, except such as are caused by the wind only, was by the smoothness of its surface, as well as by the multitude of its islands and

the proximity of its neighboring shores, extremely favorable to the infant navigation of the world. . . . (1.3.19)

The Mediterranean is quite unique. Its shores are close, its islands plentiful, and it is the largest body of placid water in the habitable world; you might almost say, the world's largest "lake." Thus, taking Smith's basic principles as a guide, the real story of the world's economic growth may be briefly told.

Mankind has always been a trading species, as far back as any record could possibly indicate, and trade has always required people to transport goods. But during the earliest stages of navigation, men were able to travel on rivers only; seas and oceans were still too formidable. Thus, the earliest civilizations tended to cluster along rivers: the Nile, the rivers of India, the rivers of China, and the Tigris and Euphrates. Then, when seafaring had improved, traders ventured out across the Mediterranean—less perilous than an ocean but still quite dangerous. The chief difficulty of the Mediterranean is its violent and unpredictable winds. The sailor is often becalmed, but when the winds do come, they change rapidly and are often too strong for sail. (Odysseus, by the way, faces just these difficulties in the middle books of Homer's *Odyssey*.) So, early navigation on the Mediterranean was largely an affair of rowing, with sail used only for running downwind. The result is that Mediterranean commerce developed more rapidly among the Greek islands of the Aegean, where the distances for rowing are short, than in the Western Mediterranean.

The civilizations of China and India, on the other hand, rested like Egypt's on inland navigation. China lacks natural harbors in the north and it was thus prevented from developing an extensive maritime trade; most of India's ancient cities were inland, in the plain of the Indus and Ganges. So, civilizations founded on river traffic mostly got off to an earlier start than the settlements of the Mediterranean, but once the Mediterranean market was established, it ultimately dwarfed all others. And with each of these expansions in trade, founded on an expansion in the system of transportation, there was a corresponding increase in specialization, in opulence, and in the accidents of discovery.

As for the Americas and sub-Saharan Africa, they are surrounded by treacherous oceans, and their sea traffic was thus quite confined until modern times. (The east coast of Africa conducted a small but ancient oceanic trade with Arabia.) Still, the most important point is that all these developments rested not on differences between peoples but on differences between waterways. Europe's dominance came from the sea. And in terms of structure, Smith's theory is logically explanatory in the same way that Newton's mechanics is logically explanatory or that Darwin's theory of evolution is logically explanatory. That is, Smith accounts for a wide variety of different phenomena by appeal to a few basic principles: all peoples trade, competition forces them to specialize, specialization tends to hasten discovery, and specialization is most extensive where transportation supports the largest market. (His theory can also explain the longstanding emphasis on European authors in intellectual history, but this is a point I shall come to in a moment.) To explain different rates of economic development among different peoples, we need merely ask, How has geography created differences in their methods of transporting goods? In effect, Smith has propounded one of the most sweeping historical explanations of all time.

Consider for a moment the opposing view—that some races are biologically superior. How can a racial theory account for these different rates of development?

If the ancient Greeks and Romans were genetically superior, for example, why did Egypt, India, and Mesopotamia develop first? On the other hand, if the Egyptians, Indians, or Mesopotamians were genetically superior, then why did the markets of Greece and Rome subsequently dwarf their own? Similar difficulties arise for any theory that uses racial differences to explain the later preeminence of Northern Europe. Northern Europe, through most of human history, was simply a backwater, but if a racial theory is correct, we should expect the Northern Europeans to have been technologically and culturally advanced (or perhaps culturally and morally degenerate) in all periods. In fact, Northern Europe's dominion is quite recent, and it is merely the effect of another change in the system of transportation—the Age of Exploration.

The Age of Exploration, during the fifteenth and sixteenth centuries, gave Northern Europe unparalleled power over the earth by turning it into a collection of competing maritime states, much like the ancient city-states of Greece. And therein lies the secret of Europe's extraordinary power for good or ill. Europe dominated the world because it dominated the oceans. Europe's many natural harbors directed its energies outward: through most of the last four centuries, it was simply easier for a European state to win an overseas empire than to consolidate one on the continent. What first pushed the Europeans to expand across the seas? The lucrative trade in spices.

Europe had long imported spices from Asia for reasons that are quite puzzling, unless you recall that without refrigeration and quick transportation the European diet was decidedly bleak. The traditional route for this trade was through the Middle East, across the Mediterranean, and into Italy, where it was then carried by land or sea to the rest of Europe (and in consequence, Italy and the Middle East grew rich). But in 1453, Constantinople fell to the Ottoman Turks, and much of this trade was cut off. Portugal and Spain then found a new way to Asia that bypassed the Mediterranean altogether—they sailed around the coast of Africa—and once the spice trade shifted to Europe's Atlantic coast, the maritime states of Northern Europe grew in power, while Southern Europe and the Middle East went into gradual decline.

The determining cause once more was a change in the system of transportation, which is the essence of Smith's theory. The new sea routes, opened by the effort to restore the spice trade, now gave the Europeans vast, new opportunities for profit. The demand for spices stimulated seafaring, but the advance of seafaring then gave Europeans a gigantic new intercontinental market, with all the innovation that a larger market entails. In effect, the Europeans merely repeated what the Egyptians, Chinese, and Greeks had done before them, but on a larger scale.

The colonization of America and the European enslavement of Africans then began as afterthoughts. Europe had almost no interest in colonizing America until the accidental discovery of gold, but then the European powers introduced African slaves to mine it. A cascade of further effects suffused the earth; Asian societies such as that of the Japanese were soon forced or drawn into international trade, with the consequence that many of their respective countries have now become major seafaring states. But the overriding historical point is that all these events had their origin in a change in trade, wrought by a change in the method of transporting goods. The determining cause in each case was transport by water. No racial theory is likely to explain so much of the world's history.[2]

But what does Smith's theory say, if anything, about the history of ideas? What explains the large number of European authors still studied in the universities, especially ancient Greeks, ancient Romans, Renaissance Italians, and Northern Europeans? Why does so much literature come from Europe?

It is easy to imagine that this so-called Eurocentrism comes from power. Smith has already explained why the European states became powerful, but the power to control trade, by controlling the sea, *might* seem to carry with it the power to control ideas, so that Europeans could prescribe their literature to all corners of the globe. Thus (it seems), we read European books today mainly because they defend and perpetuate a European system.

This conjecture is now quite popular, and there is a good deal more to be said for it, but there is also a fatal objection. The objection is that it assumes the classics of European literature to be justifications of Europe—either of Europe's institutions or ideas. Justification is the supposed motive for disseminating these classics in the first place. Yet the great majority of such books are actually quite different; they are radical attacks. In fact, it is safe to say that almost every great book of philosophy or political theory is in some sense a radical but intelligent attack on the intellectual status quo. Some books, such as Locke's *Second Treatise*, were radical when written and only later became orthodox. (Locke, it may be recalled, wrote much of the *Second Treatise* as a refugee in Holland; the king of England had already declared him a traitor.) Likewise, any book, no matter how

---

2. Whether I.Q. scores really do demonstrate a genetic difference in the intelligence of different races is a question beyond my competence. But even if there are such differences (and personally I doubt it), they will do little to explain major historical trends. Smith's theory, by contrast, explains much more, and it is essentially environmental.

radical, must share at least some points with conventional opinion, if only to serve as common premises for the argument. Still, many traditional classics are just as extreme now as the day they were conceived. Plato's *Republic*, for example, recommends pure communism for the "guardian" class and periodic mating festivals. How could disseminating such ideas possibly strengthen European hegemony? It is certainly true that European colonization carried with it European literature, but it is absurd to suppose that this literature makes a convincing justification of European colonization—not unless it is thoroughly bowdlerized.

One way to see this point better is simply to add up the large number of European authors who have nasty things to say about their own social order. I have already mentioned the opinion of Raphael Hythloday (the chief character of Thomas More's *Utopia*) that the governments of Europe are but conspiracies of the rich to rob the poor. Jean-Jacques Rousseau argues that Europe's "advanced" civilization is degenerate. Erasmus's attacks are equally scathing, whereas the works of Martin Luther are filled with charges that Europe is being overwhelmed by the Antichrist. Rabelais, to cite another instance, is interested not in defending European notions but in laughing at them, and he is joined by a large and distinguished company: Molière, Voltaire, Jonathan Swift, Laurence Sterne, Edward Gibbon, Mark Twain, and many others. Marx is, of course, no friend of the Chamber of Commerce, and many nineteenth-century novelists fill their books with bleak portraits of the Industrial Revolution. Many of these writers may *assume* the legitimacy of various institutions, even the legitimacy of overseas colonial empires, but it is quite another thing to say that they try to *justify* these institutions.

There are exceptions to this basic radicalism of European literature, such as Aristotle or Edmund Burke, but even these authors are locked in battle with the intellectual authorities of their age—Aristotle with the inheritors of the Academy, Burke with the Enlightenment. More generally, few celebrated authors in any culture, east or west, have ever spent much time exalting their own civilizations and for a simple reason. Nothing could be more tedious. You write a lasting book not by congratulating your contemporaries, but by challenging them.[3]

The real explanation of Eurocentrism in literature is different, and the easiest way for me to express it is to put it rather strangely. Odd as it sounds, many of the world's famous dead authors (too many to be mere accident) took to the sea.

Those taking the typical sea voyage include Herodotus, Thucydides, the Sophists, Plato, Aristotle, Demosthenes, Julius Caesar, Cicero, St. Paul, Averroës, Maimonides, Erasmus, Thomas More, Descartes, Thomas Hobbes, John Locke, Montesquieu, Voltaire, Rousseau, David Hume, Adam Smith, Thomas Paine, Mary Wollstonecraft, Heinrich Heine, Tocqueville, Frederick Douglass, Charles Dickens, Emile Zola, Marx, Engels, Darwin, Mark Twain, Herman Melville, John Stuart Mill, and Freud. Some will construe this as an argument

---

3. The principal exceptions to this rule are probably Livy and Virgil.

for the bracing effect of salt air, but the real mechanism is different. The destination of each voyage I cite was the territory of a foreign power or (in the case of the Romans) a region beyond the reach of the author's local government. Thus, what all these authors had in common was the ability, if they wished, to escape from their own rulers.

Escape from political authority today depends largely on wheeled machines (on "trains, planes, and automobiles"), but your best bet in a seafaring age was to live among competing maritime states. Then, in the event of a collision with the government, you simply floated away. The place you were leaving needed no prior commitment to the freedom of thought. The political geography encouraged it anyway. This is why the most intellectually fertile societies of the past were maritime: ancient Greece, ancient Rome, Renaissance Italy, and Northern Europe after the fifteenth century.[4]

Writers and talkers in other parts of the world could also escape from their rulers but only by surmounting formidable geographical barriers. Many nevertheless succeeded. Among those reputedly traveling to foreign states by land or on rivers were Confucius, the Buddha, Mencius, Sun Tzu, the Legalists, Mohammed, al-Farabi, and Avicenna, and among those who undoubtedly undertook such journeys were Luther, Calvin, Nietzsche, and Lenin. But the political control of ideas in land-locked communities still tended to be more intense, and it was nearly absolute once these societies were unified into large territorial empires. It is surely no accident that the most fertile epoch in Chinese intellectual history is precisely the age when China was still divided into contending states—the waning years of the Chou Dynasty and the so-called Warring States Period. Once China was unified, its intellectual originality diminished sharply, just as Greece's originality diminished sharply after the conquests of Philip of Macedon and Alexander the Great.

Thus, the real reason certain periods of European history have been exceptionally fertile in the realm of ideas is again an accident of geography. Europe's maritime contours, combined in later times with an increase in oceangoing commerce, made it especially easy for controversial authors to escape violence or arrest. This is not to say that all such authors found escape necessary. Many never left home, and many never even contemplated a foreign retreat. But the option of escape, even if unexercised, still tended to widen the limits of what was politically permissible. Many of the world's great writers and talkers have spent at least part of their lives as exiles or refugees.

(I have omitted Dante and Machiavelli from my list of itinerants only because both men seem to have traveled to foreign states by land, even though Italy as a whole might fairly be called maritime. Still, their personal histories

---

4. Athens was the wealthiest of the Greek states in classical times, which is why it attracted more than its share of professional philosophizers.

illustrate the general rule: A society is intellectually fertile to the extent that its inhabitants can escape from it. Only an exile could have written the words of the *Inferno* [Canto 26, 1–3] "Rejoice, Florence . . . through Hell thy name is spread abroad.")

Europe's geography was certainly not without its drawbacks. The same conditions that gave Europe its controversial literature also gave it terrible wars, and ancient China had a similar experience. But the key point is that both these effects, warfare and literary output, share a common cause—the existence of an easy mode of transportation that connects independent states. And it is also worth noting, perhaps, that the same conditions now prevail among modern nation-states. Today's nations are stitched together by traffic, transport, and trade, and it is, therefore, no surprise that they should form complex alliances like those of ancient Greece, or that many of today's writers and talkers, like the ancient world's writers and talkers, should carry on the venerable tradition of running for their lives. (The preponderance of men over women in classical literature, though a complicated matter, also involves a similar effect: Men tend to be heavier than women and to have more weight in the shoulders; thus, women in the ancient world, where combat was usually hand-to-hand, could escape political control only at greater physical risk—a disparity that modern technology has partly erased.)

The truly puzzling question is why this mechanism has for so long escaped notice. Smith's explanation of Europe's ascendancy has been on the table for more than two centuries, and it is only a slight extension of his theory to say that geography also accounts for most of the continuing emphasis in intellectual history on the authors we now call European. (Some of this emphasis may still be attributable to prejudice, but my point is that most of it is not.) Yet Smith's insight is still largely ignored, and many able commentators, despite readily available evidence, still imagine the usual European classics to be mainly endorsements and justifications of European institutions instead of radical attacks. And, strangest of all, this fancy is shared both by the defenders and opponents of traditional learning. What accounts for this odd attachment to an implausible idea?

The answer is that most of us still labor mentally under the influence of the Age of Exploration and especially the domination of other peoples by European seafarers. Because of Europe's overseas empires, our key words have become "European" and "non-European" instead of "maritime" and "nonmaritime." This takes some explaining.

Before the sixteenth century, almost no one called himself European or non-European, nor did earlier peoples call themselves white, black, or Asian. Earlier societies had their prejudices, many as absurd as our own, but their bigotry ran along lines of tribe, clan, and religion—not race. Even the idea of "the West" is comparatively recent. The Greeks of the classical period, for example, did indeed refer to Europe and the West but only to distinguish themselves from the opulent Persian Empire immediately to the east. In thought and sensibility, Greek affinities went eastward, not westward, and they would be profoundly shocked to learn that modern readers now link them with the descendants of the illiterate "barbarian" tribes of the north. Rome, likewise, was fundamentally Mediterranean, and the last place a literate Roman would want to find himself would be among Germans or Britons.

Thus, until the rise of Europe's modern empires, most people divided up the world in a different way. Their favored terms were not European, Asian, and African, but Greek, Roman, Barbarian (originally meaning only "non-Greek speaker," from the sound "Bar-bar-bar"), Christian, Infidel, Florentine, Frenchman, and so forth. Herodotus remarks in the fifth century B.C. that Ethiopians have black skin, but it simply never occurs to him to call other tribes "whites" or to distinguish what we now call races. Once these empires were established, however, their architects, under attack for the enslavement of overseas populations, justified this practice by saying that the white races of Europe were intellectually superior. In consequence, modern readers now see literature differently. They look automatically for the *race* of an author instead of the author's method of traveling from place to place. Thus, the maritime literature of ancient Greece becomes a "white, European literature," though the very idea of a white, European literature would have struck the Greeks themselves as unintelligible. It is then only a small step to suppose that this same literature must somehow aim at justifying a great many other white, European enterprises, such as the British Empire.

Of course, from a strategic point of view, the maritime cities of modern Tokyo and modern London have far more in common with ancient Athens and ancient Corinth than any of these cities has with medieval Paris. But the steady habit of dividing the world into European and non-European now leads us to lump Athens, Corinth, London, and medieval Paris into one incongruous lot and to regard Tokyo as disparate. As a result, intellectual history seems to center on Europe, whereas its real center is the sea. Thus rendered especially sensitive to race by imperialism across the waters, we lose sight of the real mechanisms of history—so pervasive are the lingering effects of some of the modern world's great evils.

8.

Is Democracy a Blessing?

MODERN TIMES ARE the age of democracy, but strangely, not all thoughtful observers have seen this as a good thing. Edmund Burke warns,

> Of this I am certain, that in a democracy, the majority of citizens is capable of exercising the most cruel oppressions upon the minority. . . . In such a popular persecution, individual sufferers are in a much more deplorable condition than in any other. Under a cruel prince they have the balmy compassion of mankind to assuage the smart of their wounds . . . but those who are subjected to wrong under multitudes, are deprived of all external consolation. They seem deserted by mankind; overpowered by a conspiracy of their whole species.[1]

To understand his fear a little better, consider for a moment the nature of fascism.

Fascism looks at first sight like the *opposite* of democracy, but in fact both democracy and fascism spring from a common source. Each expresses the overwhelming force of majority opinion in modern politics—an effect that is historically quite recent. The medieval serf never dreamed of being consulted in political matters. Kings and aristocrats ruled not in deference to public opinion but in contempt of it. Modern rulers, on the other hand, usually exercise real political power only by appearing as champions of the many. Hitler and Franklin Delano Roosevelt were radically different in aims and methods, but both came to power by popular demand. Of course, the term "democracy" can be defined in such a way as to exclude fascist regimes, but the example of fascism still demonstrates the danger inherent in majority rule. The majority may simply *choose* to crush dissent and oppress various minorities. Fascism is a contemporary form of

---

1. *Reflections on the Revolution in France*, 229.

what some thinkers now call the "tyranny of the majority," and if recent history demonstrates anything, it is that the effects of this tyranny can be just as bad as anything from the Middle Ages.

In a word, though the nature of tyranny has changed, it has not therefore gone away. The danger of the past was the despotism of the few, but the danger of the future may be the despotism of the many. And one of the best accounts of why the danger has shifted comes from a writer much influenced by Burke, but working more than a generation later, that is, the French social philosopher Alexis de Tocqueville, in his classic treatise *Democracy in America*, first published in two parts in 1835 and 1840. According to Tocqueville, the cause of this shift is the coming of "social equality," by which he means the rise of a dominant middle class.

During the Middle Ages in Europe, the tiny class of kings and nobility enjoyed more real wealth than all the peasants put together. The ruling elite stood at one extreme of the social order, the vast majority at the other. In the future, however, Tocqueville thinks most people will see themselves as falling somewhere in the middle. The rich may still live unequally and splendidly, but their consumption will never seem to represent the bulk of society's resources. The poor may still be desperate, but their desperation will play itself out largely in the shadows.

In customs and manners, too, all classes seem to be merging into a nebulous mass in the middle. In eighteenth-century France, peasants and aristocrats were immediately distinguishable by dress, accent, manners, and amusements. Peasants watched cockfights; an aristocrat might enjoy chamber music. The rich and poor today, however, have roughly similar aspirations. They have different opportunities to indulge their tastes, and different individuals have different idiosyncrasies, but large numbers of people in all social classes now have the same idea of a night on the town: dinner in a restaurant, followed by a movie. In many modern societies, culture is rapidly becoming mass culture.

As for the origin of this merging of classes and melding of manners, Tocqueville thinks every innovation since the Crusades has encouraged it, but behind it all is probably the dissolving power of commerce. Commercial wealth, unlike landed wealth, is fluid and therefore less stable. Take, for example, America's patrician families, its upper crust. A Kennedy or Rockefeller can often go where a Smith or Jones cannot, but trace the lineage of the patrician back to his great-grandparents, and you often find forebears living in complete obscurity. Riches now reside in a single family only for a few generations, not for centuries, as in the past. Tocqueville thinks this effect to be most advanced in his own day in the United States (which is why his book centers on America), but a similar trend has since emerged in many countries. Many modern societies are becoming demographically volatile; the status of one generation often differs from the next because of commerce. And, in the long run, the psychological effect of this tendency is to make most people think of themselves as middle class, even if they are prosperous and even if they are poor.

What effect, then, should we expect in politics?

As this middle class seems to consume the bulk of society's proceeds, so it comes to assume that society as a whole exists primarily for its benefit. And if society exists for the benefit of this middle class, then it seems to follow with equal necessity that this same middle class ought to be obeyed. So, once social equality is established, the middle class expects, and indeed demands, that its will be decisive. Thus arises (according to Tocqueville) the "sovereignty of the people."[2]

By no means does Tocqueville oppose this trend; quite the opposite, he regards it as historically inevitable. But he thinks an enlightened democracy must take conscious steps to avoid putting too much power in the hands of its leaders. The authority of a feudal regime was often checked by class antagonisms; now that the middle class has depressed these antagonisms, something else must take their place, or the leaders of the future will be virtually unstoppable. And thus Tocqueville sounds one of the great themes of modern politics.

What he seeks above all are ways to check the majority's power. For one thing, he stresses "voluntary associations," by which he means newspapers, political parties, business organizations, and what we now call "interest groups." The function of these associations is mainly to inform, but they also represent a division of power in society as a whole. Any politician who fails to take account of these associations will probably be stymied. Tocqueville concedes that the interference of these groups is often harmful; after all, the leaders of the majority might be preeminently good. Still, in the words of James Madison (one of the nation's founders), "Enlightened statesmen will not be always at the helm."[3] The greater evil, in Tocqueville's opinion, would be to have no such associations at all.[4]

---

2. The doctrine of the sovereignty of the people first appears in literature in Rousseau's *Social Contract*, published in 1762, and the speed with which the idea has spread is perhaps a partial confirmation of Tocqueville's thesis that some sort of mass psychological change is under way. Before Rousseau, political writers spoke of the *consent* of the people, but consent is not sovereignty. To consent is to agree, but the people may still be forced into a variety of compromises with their rulers before this agreement is reached. To be sovereign, on the other hand, is to command. It is this latter idea that most people now have in mind when they speak of popular government.

3. *The Federalist Papers*, no. 10, 80.

4. John Locke's thesis that property is a "natural right" may also be relevant here. Locke is often construed as defending capitalism (an interpretation that involves serious difficulties), but quite apart from this question, his doctrine also has the effect of protecting the government's political opponents from economic reprisal. In industrial nations, opponents of the majority are sometimes destroyed by setting up a blacklist among the nation's employers. In the agrarian society of Locke's time, however, the opposition consisted mainly of landed gentry, and they could therefore be destroyed by confiscating their landed estates. Thus, Locke is at pains in his *Second Treatise* to deny that the "supreme or legislative power of any commonwealth can do what it will and dispose of the estates of the subject arbitrarily, or take any part of them at pleasure" (chap. 11, 138). The key point is that Locke and Tocqueville both have their eyes fixed on the economic and social means by which power is consolidated.

This is not the only way Tocqueville thinks a modern society should divide power. He also stresses a division of power within government, especially the so-called "separation of powers" of the American Constitution, which is usually thought to derive from the French philosopher Montesquieu but which is actually much older, having its origins in the ancient theory of the "mixed constitution." The Federal Constitution of the United States divides power between the executive, the legislative, and the judiciary (and also between the national and state governments), and Montesquieu's ideas are indeed the direct antecedent of this scheme, but it is really the ancient theory of the mixed constitution that shows why this system is now politically stable while other systems sometimes are not. Consider for a moment the ancient theory.

The theory of the mixed constitution derives indirectly from Aristotle, who says there are really just three kinds of "natural" government: 1) monarchy, or rule by one; 2) aristocracy, or rule by the few; and 3) polity, or rule by the many.[5] (Later writers often substitute the word "democracy" for Aristotle's "polity.") Aristotle was a careful observer of his times, and his account describes much of what he saw in Greece, but when later thinkers tried to apply his ideas to ancient Rome, they were frustrated. The greatest of these, the historian Polybius, came to believe that the Roman Republic was neither monarchy, aristocracy, nor democracy but a combination of all three. The Roman consuls, who controlled military forces in Italy, seemed to have the power of kings, so Polybius described them as a kind of monarchy. But their power was limited by the Senate, which represented the wealthy patricians, so Polybius described the Senate as a kind of aristocracy. Yet there were also tribunes, who were elected by an assembly of the common people (the plebeians), and the tribunes had the power to veto various actions of the consuls and the Senate. So Polybius said the tribunes represented a kind of democracy (the structural equivalent of Aristotle's "polity"). Thus, Polybius inferred, the Roman Republic was actually a mix of all three constitutions— monarchy, aristocracy, and democracy—and therein lay the secret of its stability. The effect of the system was to force the different social classes to compromise.[6]

Now the thing to notice is that Polybius's theory, though quite old and still couched in terms of a rigid class structure, nevertheless explains much of what we see in the modern world. If a single social group gains complete control of the state, it often has little incentive to offer concessions, and other groups may then have no recourse but revolution. If a revolution succeeds, the result is then apt to be what ancient writers called the "cycle of states," in which different forms of government succeed one another over a period of generations, because a single class in each case insists on complete power. (The most famous of these

---

5. *Politics*, Book 3, chap. 7, where Aristotle elaborates an idea introduced by his teacher Plato in the *Statesman*.

6. Polybius lays out this theory in Book 6 of his *Histories*.

cycles is the one sketched in Book 8 of Plato's *Republic*, where a military elite evolves into the enfeebled aristocracy of its descendants, which is then over-thrown by the common people. The common people, however, finding them-selves threatened by counterrevolution, rally around a popular leader, who soon becomes a tyrant. It is sometimes remarked that the French Revolution supplied an almost exact analogue to Plato's old progression—from the conquest of ancient Franks to the degeneracy of the *ancien regime* to the despotism of Napoleon.) The idea of the mixed constitution is to break this sort of cycle by forcing compromise among the different social factions.

This idea of the mixed constitution was actually the model for a great many European regimes until the nineteenth century—in Great Britain, it was repre-sented by the king or queen, the House of Lords, and the House of Commons—but its fundamental weakness is its vulnerability to demographic change. The mixed constitution divides power by assigning different parts of the government to *hereditary* classes, but when the classes shift, either in numbers or influence, the mixed constitution is fatally rigid. And it is precisely this rigidity that shows why the Federal Constitution of the United States, by contrast, is both histori-cally novel and better adapted to the modern world.

One of the best examples of this fatal rigidity appears in the subsequent his-tory of Rome, and it serves as a sort of cautionary tale for most modern states. The conquests of Rome's armies brought new slaves into Italy and cheap grain from the provinces, but the side effect was to drive small Italian farmers into bankruptcy. As their own farms became unprofitable because of foreign imports, the small farmers then found their labor worthless, because they were in com-petition with slaves. So, many soon drifted to Rome to become a sullen, listless mob. As the number of landowners steadily declined, Rome finally was forced to recruit its armies from the landless poor, who had no stake in preserving the status quo and who became totally dependent on their generals. The soldiers wanted substantial land grants, but when the Senate refused to agree, the easiest path for the generals was to march their armies against Rome itself. (In indus-trialized nations, demobilized soldiers want jobs, but the economy of Rome was agrarian.) Thus, Rome's constitutional structure began to fall apart.

So far as political stability is concerned, the underlying problem was that the distribution and power of social classes in Italy had changed, yet the Roman constitution never responded to this change. As the Senate came to represent a smaller and smaller portion of society, and the tribunes a larger and more des-perate one, their respective privileges within the government remained largely the same, so the poor soon began to look elsewhere for leadership. And, ulti-mately, many supported dictatorship.

The United States sometimes faces similar difficulties, but consider how its Federal Constitution regulates them. The Federal Constitution achieves a sim-ilar stability but in a different way.

Set aside for a moment all matters of justice; leave aside the question of whether you think the Federal Constitution is moral. The Federal Constitution is nevertheless uncommonly *stable*, because it distributes power among different groups, but in a way that still responds to underlying changes in the population and its economy. The Constitution is flexible because the distribution of its offices depends not on hereditary groupings but on the staggered timing of elections and appointments. At any one moment, for example, some parts of the federal government are more congenial to the rich, others more congenial to the poor; some we call more "conservative," others more "liberal"; some more favorable to reform, others more favorable to preservation. Thus, the Federal Constitution, like the old Roman one, tends to represent different social factions and presses them to compromise. Yet such differences arise not from assigning different parts of the government to hereditary groups but from the inability of any majority to capture the entire structure in a single election. To change the political complexion of the House of Representatives can take as little as two years, since the entire House stands for election biannually, but to change the presidency takes four years. To change the Senate typically takes longer, because senators serve for six years, and only a third are up for reelection at any one moment. And it often takes a generation to change the political direction of the Supreme Court. As a result, different officials have usually entered government service in different decades, and they therefore tend to represent different constituencies, which were ascendant at different times. The staggering of these elections and appointments, combined with the swing of the political pendulum, thus produces a division of power, but a division that can still evolve to reflect further changes in society itself. If some *new* group enters the country's electorate in large numbers, it, too, can capture part of the structure, given enough time.

The ultimate effect is to slow down needed reforms and to force unwelcome concessions, but the corollary is stability, the stunning singularity of which sometimes escapes notice. The Federal Constitution is quite young in comparison with, say, the constitution of the ancient Spartans, which lasted more than four centuries. But it is really quite old when considered against the vast expansion of America's territory and population. The Civil War amendments notwithstanding, its basic organization is unaltered, whereas all other national democracies have a more recent set of laws. In a word, no constitution in the history of the world has ever changed so little while the people it governs have changed so much.[7]

Tocqueville focuses on one further aspect of American government that is especially important—that is, the unusual power of the judiciary—because it serves as a further check on a potential tyranny of the majority. And Tocqueville says this extraordinary judicial power comes precisely from the fact that the power is limited.

---

7. Tocqueville makes much of these divisions of power, yet he also tends to regard the ancient theory of the "mixed" constitution as somehow illusory. On this last point, which is perhaps merely verbal, I can only say that I disagree with him.

The authority of the courts to strike down popular legislation as "unconstitutional" is nowhere expressly stated in the Constitution itself. Instead, the authority was inferred in 1803 by John Marshall, chief justice of the United States Supreme Court, in his remarkable decision *Marbury v Madison*, 1 Cranch 137 (1803)—perhaps the most influential judicial opinion ever written. But this potent authority is politically palatable in the first place, says Tocqueville, only because the decisions of even the highest tribunal can still be circumvented by constitutional amendment. And so the courts' authority is acceptable to the people precisely because they think they have a way around it. Jury trial has a similar effect: It relieves judges of responsibility for an unpopular verdict by giving it to the people, while also communicating the thinking of the judges to the jurors themselves.

Still, there is one further limitation on judicial power in America that is probably most decisive—that judges are powerless to decide any matter of law until they are first called to decide a particular case. Tocqueville writes,

> If the judge had been empowered to contest the law on the ground of theoretical generalities, if he were able to take the initiative, and to censure the legislator, he would play a prominent political part. . . . But the American judge is brought into the political arena independently of his own will. He judges the law only because he is obliged to judge a case. The political question which he is called upon to resolve is connected with the interests of the parties, and he cannot refuse to decide it without a denial of justice.[8]

Because the judge is apparently "obliged" to decide such cases (so as to do justice to the parties), he is relieved of at least part of the blame that attaches to an unpopular ruling. The people will more likely forgive what a judge can't avoid.

Tocqueville also remarks that in America the lawyers are the "natural aristocracy," and here he means that political power falls disproportionately into their hands. Most politicians in America today are lawyers—and always have been. Tocqueville writes,

> Men who have made a special study of the law derive from this occupation certain habits of order, a taste for formalities, and a kind of instinctive regard for the regular connection of ideas. . . . Some of the tastes and habits of the aristocracy may consequently be discovered in the character of lawyers. They participate in the same instinctive love of order and formalities; and they entertain the same repugnance to the actions of the multitude, and the same secret contempt of the government of the people. . . . In a community in which lawyers are allowed to occupy without opposition that high station which naturally belongs to them, their general spirit will be eminently conservative and

---

8. *Democracy in America*, ed. Phillips Bradley (1945; reprint, New York: Alfred A. Knopf, 1993), Part 1, chap. 6, 102–3.

anti-democratic. When an aristocracy excludes the leaders of that profession from its ranks, it excites enemies who are more formidable as they are independent of the nobility by their labors, and feel themselves to be their equals in intelligence, though inferior in opulence and power.[9]

Readers today sometimes find Tocqueville's remarks on lawyers shocking, and most lawyers in America would probably reject the label "antidemocratic." Still, there is a sense in which his comments are perhaps true. Most lawyers believe in democracy, but as a profession they are indeed uncommonly contemptuous of public opinion. Lawyers on both the left and right can often be heard in private speaking disparagingly of public attitudes. And the reason is simple: They have been trained from the start to regard the unpopular and the unlawful as different things. And Tocqueville's point is that on the whole such habits are good. More than any other group, lawyers preserve the memory of a vital distinction without which popular government descends into chaos—the distinction between majority rule and the rule of law. (As for lawyers excluded from power by a jealous regime, it is perhaps well to remember that Danton, Robespierre, Lenin, and Fidel Castro were all trained as lawyers.)

On the whole, Tocqueville's book expresses a general fear of public opinion, because he thinks it easily manipulated, and his whole strategy is thus to water down its force. The one vital point he does *not* discuss, however, is *how* public opinion is manipulated, and to better understand this further aspect of modern democracy, it is sometimes useful to consult two other students of popular sentiment, the ancient historian Thucydides and the Renaissance diplomat Machiavelli.

Thucydides and Machiavelli remain important authors for the modern age, because both were products of city-states—which, because of their small size, were especially sensitive to popular feeling. Thus, both authors pay careful attention to how public opinion is exploited. Thucydides observed such tactics while serving the Athenian Assembly as general, and then, after being banished for losing a battle, as a historian wandering from state to state. Machiavelli witnessed the manipulation of public sentiment as envoy of Florence, and then studied it in books after being exiled on suspicion of treason. And Machiavelli's most famous analysis is, of course, *The Prince*.

The Prince, written in 1513, is notorious for its ruthlessness. (Though some commentators now try to sanitize the book, its third chapter is really quite frank about exterminating the families of deposed rivals.) Yet it is also keenly attentive to how public opinion is influenced, and if only for this reason, though there are others, it remains a political classic.

For example, Machiavelli recommends that any cruelties a ruler needs to commit be accomplished all at once, in a flurry, not prolonged. The great mis-

9. Ibid., chap. 16, 273–75.

take is to extend such deeds over a longer period in the belief that they will be better absorbed in increments. What the public remembers, says Machiavelli, is not the intensity of your deeds but their duration. Machiavelli is of course talking about executions and assassinations, but a similar rule can be applied even to the politics of a society at peace. If you have unpopular news to announce, you usually do best to disseminate all of it immediately, not ration it out in small doses in the mistaken hope that it will be better absorbed gradually. Bad news should come briskly, "so that being less tasted, it will give less offense; benefits should be granted little by little, so that they may be better enjoyed."[10]

Another of Machiavelli's recommendations: give the privilege of arms even to those whose loyalty you suspect, "for by arming them these arms become your own, those whom you suspected become faithful . . . and from being merely subjects become your partisans" (20.77). During a civil war, private armies are often recruited in just this way, not by appeals to ideology but by the gratitude that results from giving frightened men and women the means to defend themselves. Again, however, Machiavelli's advice also applies to the politics of a genteel age. Gratitude is often stronger than ideology. A political campaign often recruits its operatives not by dwelling on the complexities of the issues but by giving the newcomer a chance to represent the campaign at the local level. The sheer privilege of an appointment will overcome many people's scruples.

On the whole, the thing to notice about Machiavelli is that, although the bloody tactics he recommends have no place under the rule of law, his advice still depends on certain generalizations of psychology that may well hold true everywhere, and it is for this reason that *The Prince* can prove useful in contemporary politics and business. Of course, not all his advice is universally approved. He takes a dim view of the power of forgiveness. ("Men must be either caressed or annihilated; they will revenge themselves for small injuries but cannot do so for great ones; the injury therefore that we do to a man must be such that we need not fear his vengeance" [3,9].) And he is equally pessimistic about the power of love to achieve political aims. ("Better to be feared more than loved. . . . Men love at their own free will, but fear at the will of the prince" [17.61–63].) He also gives a remarkable and entertaining portrait of fraud in the person of Pope Alexander VI. ("No man was ever more able to give assurances, or affirmed things with stronger oaths, and no man observed them less; however, he always succeeded in his deceptions, as he well knew this aspect of things" [18.65].) And his contempt for the people's judgment is undisguised. ("Everybody sees what you appear to be, few feel what you are. . . . The vulgar is always

---

10. *The Prince and the Discourses*, trans. Luigi Ricci (New York: Modern Library, 1950), chap. 8, 35. (All subsequent references are to chapter and page number.) Acting in disdain of this advice is sometimes said to have cost Richard Nixon the presidency. Had he revealed the full extent of the Watergate scandal immediately, he might well have been forgiven by the electorate.

taken by appearances and the issue of the event; and the world consists only of the vulgar, and the few who are not vulgar are isolated when the many have a rallying point in the prince" [18.66].) Nevertheless, Machiavelli is a shrewd observer, and one can easily appreciate his shrewdness without thereby recommending his cynicism, which is at once both poignant and pathetic: "How we live is so far removed from how we ought to live, that he who abandons what is done for what ought to be done, will rather learn to bring about his own ruin . . ." (15.56).

Also, in Machiavelli's defense, it is worth noting, I think, that Thomas More's character Raphael Hythloday has an equally grim view of Renaissance politics in Book I of Utopia; the only difference is that Raphael thinks the whole business of politics to be unworthy of a good citizen's time. Machiavelli and More both urge us to give up naive assumptions when dealing with ruthless men. But then, the odd thing about Machiavelli's heroes is that, after achieving momentary "glory," most of them end up murdered. Cesare Borgia is killed in Spain. Hannibal poisons himself to avoid execution by the Romans. Remirro de Orco, "a cruel and able man" (7.27), is found cut in half in a public square. Oliverotto da Fermo is strangled, "together with Vitellozzo, who had been his teacher in ability and atrocity" (8.34). The Prince is a sad book, but there is also a certain dark comedy about it.

Thucydides (the other great author in this field) is equally concerned with public opinion, but he analyzes it differently. As a historian, he offers long public addresses from the key politicians of his day, but he admits frankly that he has made the speeches up, being unable to recall or discover their exact words. Readers sometimes complain that his history is therefore inaccurate, but in many ways this is a mistake. The great advantage of Thucydides' history is that it consequently bypasses the usual bombast of political oratory and reveals instead the underlying strategy. Put another way, what it lacks in fidelity, it gains in candor. For example, when the Corcyraeans try to induce Athens to intervene in their colonial dispute with Corinth, Thucydides has them say this:

> The whole thing can be put very shortly. . . . There are three considerable naval powers in Hellas—Athens, Corcyra and Corinth. If Corinth gets control of us first and you allow our navy to be united with hers, you will have to fight against the combined fleets of Corcyra and the Peloponnese [which includes Corinth]. But if you receive us into your alliance, you will enter upon the war with our ships as well as your own. (Book 1, 36)

Thus, where ideology might have induced the Athenians to oppose Corcyra—on the grounds that it was thwarting democracy in a small town (Epidamnus)—the temptation of strategic advantage leads them to befriend Corcyra instead, in the hope of gaining leverage over Corinth. Thus, they sacrifice their principles to their security. By showing how great powers act in his own time, Thucydides opens a window on later times.

Thucydides is especially alert to the danger of demagogues, and here his archetypal figure is the Athenian politician Cleon. In the course of trying to persuade the Assembly to execute the entire adult male population of Mytilene, Cleon goes out of his way to accuse his opponents of taking bribes. But Diodotus, speaking for the opposition, replies that Cleon's attack is essentially personal. Diodotus warns,

> This sort of thing does the city no good; her counselors will be afraid to speak and she will be deprived of their services. . . . The good citizen, instead of trying to terrify the opposition, ought to prove his case in fair argument. . . . [W]hen a man's advice is not taken, he should not be disgraced, far less penalized. (Book 3, 42)

Diodotus puts his finger on the great danger to democracies inherent in personal abuse. In politics, if you win your case merely by wounding your opponent personally, you also inflict a subtle wound on your country. Good men and women will then be less willing to enter politics in the first place, and the nation will be deprived of their services. There are, of course, exceptions to this rule, as when an opponent unquestionably deserves rebuke, but on the whole, democracies are in better shape if their politicians can respect each other's honor.

Thucydides blames demagogues for Athens' defeat in the Peloponnesian War, but against them he sets up the image of Pericles, a leader he idolized.

> [Pericles] could respect the liberty of the people and at the same time hold them in check. It was he who led them, rather than they who led him, and since he never sought power from any wrong motive, he was under no necessity of flattering them: in fact, he was so highly respected that he was able to speak angrily to them and to contradict them. (Book 2, 65)

Thucydides is sometimes accused of exaggerating Pericles' abilities, since he hardly ever criticizes this interesting politician, but even if the charge of exaggeration is true (and I don't say that it is), Thucydides still shows us what a democratic leader *might* be.

There is still one other important effect of democracy that I have not yet mentioned, but equally vital in the mind of the French observer Alexis de Tocqueville—to whom I must return once more. It is the tendency of social equality (as Tocqueville construes the term) to obliterate diversity.

As people become more alike, says Tocqueville, they become less and less tolerant of people who are different—either in thought or behavior. ("I know of no country in which there is so little independence of mind and real freedom of discussion as in America.")[11] The pressure to conform is a natural consequence

---

11. *Democracy in America*, Part 1, chap. 15, 263.

of social equality, he says, and it turns out that his remarks on this subject resounded with special force in the thinking of another celebrated writer, John Stuart Mill. Mill was Tocqueville's contemporary and later served as his host during a tour of England, but it also happens that the details of Mill's personal life, strange and fascinating, became one of the best illustrations of Tocqueville's main point. Let me say a word about those details.

John Stuart Mill was above all a nonconformist, from a long line of nonconformists. And his education was highly peculiar. His father James, the intimate friend of Jeremy Bentham, resolved at John Stuart's birth to educate his son in a new manner, so John Stuart was never sent to school. Instead, he was set to learning ancient Greek at home at the age of three and Latin at the age of eight. By the time he was twelve, John Stuart had composed his own history of Roman law. By the age of fifteen, he had read widely in literature, mathematics, philosophy, and economics and was already responsible for producing analytical abstracts of one of his father's forthcoming books. As a teenager, Mill associated with many distinguished thinkers of the day, including Bentham, the economist David Ricardo, and the legal philosopher John Austin, but at the age of twenty, he suddenly had a mental breakdown (an episode that would now be diagnosed as depression). He complained later that his father, though eminently rational, failed to express tenderness and had consequently neglected to cultivate in his son a life of passion and emotion. Mill remarks of him, "He seems to have expected effects without causes."[12] Also, the whole of Mill's education had left him with no chance to mix with other children of his own age. Mill's mental crisis lasted nearly a year, but when it finally abated, he met a woman who would then become the love of his life, Harriet Taylor. The trouble was, she was already married.

Mrs. Taylor was estranged from her husband, and before long she began to see a great deal of Mill. They spent weekends together, then went on trips abroad. Soon, Victorian society was scandalized, and Mill received considerable interference from his own family. Yet his friendship with Harriet continued on this same intimate basis for twenty years, until her husband died, and then after another two years (considered the proper period of mourning), she and Mill were married.

Finally, when Mill considered the elements of his own life against Tocqueville's warnings about the pressure to conform, he saw in himself a perfect example of the modern predicament. He knew that he had been strangely educated and that his relationship with Harriet had provoked the "tyranny of opinion." But he also had the rhetorical and analytical abilities to combat this "despotism of society." So, out of this mix of personal experience and careful reflection, he set about to write, with Harriet's extensive help, a profound meditation on individual freedom in a democratic age, the book *On Liberty*.

---

12. Mill, *Autobiography*, 26.

Published in 1859, *On Liberty* considers both freedom of thought and the freedom to manage one's personal life. Mill makes many of the classic points for free speech. False and offensive speech, he reminds us, often has the wholesome effect of training the mind to distinguish the false from the true. In many subjects, "three-fourths of the arguments for every disputed opinion consist in dispelling the appearances which favor some opinion different from it. . . . He who knows only his own side of the controversy knows little of that."[13] Mill repeats the advice of Cicero that the secret to success at law lies not in studying your *own* arguments, but in studying the opposition's—which is impossible unless you let them speak freely.

The study of opposing views, not all of which can be true, has other effects, too. Not only is it essential to understanding the logic of your own position, says Mill, it is also essential to acquiring the emotional equanimity required of a skilled reasoner. People are not born liking to hear themselves contradicted. Rather, they learn to tolerate it only by debating. Otherwise, they remain permanently disabled in their efforts to analyze a difficult issue, because they will brook no opposition. They lack the ability to reconstruct their opponents' arguments "in their most plausible and persuasive form" (2.99). What an exact thinker needs most of all, says Mill, is the ability to see the opposing view clearly—in Mill's own phrase, to "feel the whole force of the difficulty" (2.99).

Aside from this equanimity, he also speaks of intellectual courage, which depends likewise on a climate of mental freedom:

> Who can compute what the world loses in the multitude of promising intellects combined with timid characters, who dare not follow out any bold, vigorous, independent train of thought, lest it should land them in something which would admit of being considered irreligious or immoral? (2.95)

Mill describes such people as "cowed by the fear of heresy."

The logic of Mill's position is that false and offensive speech is often beneficial and that, consequently, though much speech is indeed harmful, there is no way to define what is harmful by a general rule. But unless there is indeed a rule defining which speech is permissible and which is not, the beneficial will be suppressed indiscriminately. Thus, the only rule available is to make all speech legally permissible, so long as the circumstances of its utterance allow for reasoned debate.[14]

As for the freedom to manage one's personal life, which Mill calls "individ-

---

13. *On Liberty*, chap. 2, 98. Subsequent references are to chapter and page number.

14. Mill remarks, "An opinion that corn dealers are starvers of the poor, or that private property is robbery, ought to be unmolested when simply circulated through the press, but may justly incur punishment when delivered orally to an excited mob assembled before the house of a corn dealer, or when handed about among the same mob in the form of a placard" (3, 119).

uality," his arguments amount to an extended defense of privacy. Individuals vary enormously, he says, and what is harmful to one may be beneficial to another. Individuals usually know their own circumstances better than outsiders anyway, and there also needs to be room in any society for "experiments in living." Further, individuals need experience in the art of making their own choices, even if they often choose badly, as a means to their own development. "The mental and moral, like the muscular, powers are improved only by being used" (3.122). The same point is often made in defense of democracy as a whole: Even if the people sometimes choose their political destinies badly, the chance to choose still contributes to their mental cultivation. Even if inefficient, democracy exercises the citizens' sense of justice. Mill plainly echoes Tocqueville's fear that too much social control will only generate a "pusillanimous and enfeebled" citizenry, and his doctrine of individuality is also strongly reminiscent of Aristotle's dictum that the mean is "relative to the person" and that it can be attained only by practice in making one's own choices.[15]

Mill's book involves some obvious strains. For one thing, though he defends free speech, he also says the tyranny of opinion can be an even greater threat to privacy than the officers of the state. Thus, there is obvious tension in his analysis between the defense of free speech, on the one hand, and his concern for privacy on the other. Free speech is often the very thing that destroys privacy. Mill is, of course, keenly aware of this tension, and much has been written on the subject since, but despite these difficulties, I think it is important to note (as Mill does) that there is indeed a genuine difference, in most cases, between speaking of a person's private affairs for the purpose of reasoning with that person, and, conversely, doing so merely to badger or intimidate him. Again, there usually is a difference between discussing a person's private affairs with an outsider so as to give the outsider reason for caution and, on the other hand, as a device for injuring the offending person through gossip and reproach. On the whole, Mill allows the first kind of conduct but opposes the second. Most of his key distinctions depend on his confidence in the power of reason to improve our behavior and on his view that other forms of influence should never be used merely to protect the individual from himself.

Mill and Tocqueville are both deeply dissatisfied with what they see around them, and both writers may be justly accused of a certain "elitism." Each rises above the crowd, and at times looks down on it. But in another sense, they are both eminently democratic. Their aim is not to flatter the mass of their contemporaries but to encourage the mass to lead the life of the mind. Similarly, to study the weaknesses of democracy is not to be against democracy as such; quite the contrary, an enlightened democracy needs to study its shortcomings with

---

15. Aristotle affirms these points in Book 2, chaps. 6 and 1, of the *Nicomachean Ethics*, 1106a30–b8 and 1103a32–b25.

exquisite care, as a means to resisting them. To do so is only to follow the guidance of Delphi, quoted by Socrates, "Know thyself." And on our success or failure in this effort really depends the whole future. As Tocqueville remarks at the close of his book,

> Around every man a fatal circle is traced, beyond which he cannot pass, but within the wide verge of that circle he is powerful and free: as it is with man, so with communities. The nations of our time cannot prevent the conditions of men from becoming equal, but it depends upon themselves whether the principle of equality is to lead them to servitude or freedom, to knowledge or barbarism, to prosperity or wretchedness.[16]

---

16. *Democracy in America*, Part 2, Book 4, chap. 8, 334.

9.

Is Marxism Still Tenable?

WHEN THE INDUSTRIAL Revolution first gripped Europe in the nineteenth century, a celebrated writer dreaded its effect on laborers and industrialists alike. His fears have been echoed ever since.

> When a workman is unceasingly and exclusively engaged in the fabrication of one thing, he ultimately does his work with singular dexterity; but, at the same time, he loses the general faculty of applying his mind to the direction of the work. He every day becomes more adroit and less industrious; so that it may be said of him that, in proportion as the workman improves, the man is degraded. What can be expected of a man who has spent twenty years of his life in making heads for pins?

Such a man, said this celebrated writer, is no longer really himself.

> His thoughts are forever set upon the object of his daily toil; his body has contracted certain fixed habits, which it can never shake off: in a word, he no longer belongs to himself, but to the calling which he has chosen.

As for the industrialist, the typical result is just the opposite:

> The mind of the latter is enlarged in proportion as that of the former is narrowed. In a short time, the one will require nothing but physical strength without intelligence; the other stands in need of science, and almost of genius, to insure success. This man resembles more and more the administrator of a vast empire; that man, a brute.

And the two men grow ever farther apart.

> The one contracts no obligation to protect, nor the other to defend, and they
> are not permanently connected by habit or duty . . . the manufacturing aristoc-
> racy of our age first impoverishes and debases the men who serve it, and then
> abandons them to be supported by the charity of the public.

There, in a nutshell, is a description of what many commentators now call
"industrial alienation," the theme of Karl Marx's Paris Manuscripts of 1844. But
the writer in question is not Marx. Rather, it is once more that champion of classical liberalism, Alexis de Tocqueville, in the second part of his instant best-
seller, *Democracy in America*, published in 1840.[1] What is most peculiar about
Marx is that many of his claims are not new. Four years after Tocqueville
expressed the problem of degraded labor in specific and graphic detail, the young
Marx was still wrestling with it in the abstract jargon of the German universities, having yet to arrive at the concrete and punchy style of his *Communist
Manifesto*. When Marx became a socialist, he merely followed in the footsteps of
many earlier writers (Saint-Simon, Charles Fourier, Robert Owen, and François-
Noël Babeuf, among others). And the notion of pure communism is, of course,
quite old, having appeared in Plato's *Republic*, in Thomas More's *Utopia*, in the
monastery movements of Stoicism and Christianity, and in the Acts of the
Apostles. Yet it is always Marx we now remember, at least in passing, when we
discuss these ideas. Why?

Marx's fame actually owes little to the Russian Revolution of 1917 or to the
Soviet empire that followed; his was already a distinguished name before the
Russian Revolution occurred. Instead, Marx had already won for himself a per-
manent place in the history of ideas, and for the same reason, he is unlikely
simply to disappear from the scene now. His place rests on having been the first
widely circulated author to pose a question that remains vitally important to the
modern world: Will capitalism survive?

The *Communist Manifesto*, which struck like a thunderbolt in the revolutionary year of 1848, asserted that capitalism contained within it the seeds of its
own destruction. The system of making money from money would ultimately
destroy itself in a cataclysmic upheaval, in which a vast army of impoverished
workers would overwhelm a small elite of successful industrialists. The workers
would then seize for themselves the basic means of production—factories,
finances, and natural resources—and operate them as collective property.

Since the collapse of Soviet Communism in 1991, many people have come
to regard this hypothesis as nearly impossible, but, of course, one swallow does not
make a summer. Take, for example, the idea that economic development may

---

1. I have quoted from Book 2, chap. 20, 158–61.

ultimately generate vast inequalities—and perhaps destabilizing ones. Jean-Jacques Rousseau suggested this possibility even *before* the Industrial Revolution. To develop technology, said Rousseau, is rather like asking a dwarf and a giant to walk down the same road; with each step, the giant moves farther ahead. Just so, the effect of technological development (Rousseau argued) is to magnify whatever physical or mental differences exist between individuals, so that some men eventually become paupers, and others live in glass towers. (Rousseau defends these claims in his *Discourse on the Origin of Inequality* [1755].) And, at the moment, at least, the difference between rich and poor in the United States does happen to be greater than at any time since World War II, a difference that seems to grow daily and a difference that is vastly larger if you look across national boundaries to the condition of foreign laborers. Even if it would require an extraordinary series of blunders on the part of industrialists and governments alike to make a marxist revolution occur, human beings have blundered into a lot worse. In fact, there is a sort of historical inevitability to the whole idea of Marx's outlook. After all, market forces are still apt to bring unpredictable changes to the world economy, and as long as this is so, there may still be reason to ask how much of our current economic system will change and how much will endure. Could these changes actually destabilize society? Thus, we may still find ourselves asking whether Marx's predictions, or something like them, could ultimately be right. If you think Marx is wrong, how can you be sure?

When it comes to Marx himself, most people now picture an old man with a gray beard, just as he appeared in his sad, later years in London. But most of his key ideas were really worked out while still in his twenties, so his later output is essentially an elaboration of that young man's philosophy. And Marx was the very model of a young revolutionary.

Drawn while still a university student to the "Young Hegelians" in Prussia, he completed a doctoral dissertation in ancient philosophy, then found work as a writer for a liberal newspaper, where he soon became editor. There he met another young contributor, the son of a wealthy industrialist, who was later to be his chief collaborator for the rest of his life—Friedrich Engels.

In 1843, when Marx was just twenty-four, censors of the Prussian government cracked down on his newspaper, and he moved with his wife to Paris to escape government control. In Paris, he soon brought out a new radical journal (the *Deutsch-Französische Jahrbücher*) to which Engels contributed, but he was expelled by the French government within fourteen months and moved to Brussels. He immersed himself in economic studies, collaborated with Engels on a variety of manuscripts, and then attended the Second Congress of the Communist League in London in 1847, where he was asked with Engels to compose a declaration of the League's principles. The result, written mostly by Marx himself, was the famous *Manifesto*, perhaps the most succinct overview of his thought.

All previous history is but a history of class struggles, says the *Manifesto*, and

Marx thus announces in its opening paragraphs not only a specific prediction about the fate of capitalism but a general thesis: that class struggle is somehow the chief engine of all previous social change. (And the collapse of the Soviet Union notwithstanding, this general thesis remains particularly influential among academics.) From a logical standpoint, class struggle is still compatible with the class compromise of Polybius, since the very idea of compromise seems to assume an underlying struggle, but Marx is at pains to show that the struggle within capitalism will never be papered over. The question of capitalism's fate is naturally crucial, and I mean to consider it in a moment, but his claim about history in general is also important, because Marx draws from it a startling consequence: Any means, even ruthless ones, are appropriate if they achieve a progressive economic order. Put another way, it makes no difference whether your tactics are legal or illegal, so long as they work. And it is just this consequence, I suspect, that makes marxism persistently appealing to many revolutionaries in the developing world. Thus, quite apart from the collapse of Soviet Communism or other recent events, it still makes sense to ask: How much of this political view remains tenable?

Consider the general thesis first.

Marx not only says that class hostility is always present; he says it is somehow fundamental to almost everything we do. By "classes" he means economic groups (his examples are slaves and masters, serfs and lords, workers and capitalists), and so his apparent meaning is that economic conflicts are the principal cause of all historical change.

Actually, he expresses this thesis, now known as "historical materialism," as a metaphor: society is an edifice in which the economy is the "foundation" and its other aspects are the "superstructure." Also, the foundation "conditions" or "determines" the superstructure, and the whole doctrine is then apt to have profound consequences, depending on how you construe it.[2] The consequences are especially important, for example, when you think about political revolution.

---

2. The main historical source of this doctrine is the preface to Marx's *Contribution to the Critique of Political Economy* (1859). See Robert Tucker, ed., *The Marx-Engels Reader*, 2nd ed. (New York: W.W. Norton and Company, 1978), 3–6. Marx says: "In the social production of their life, men enter into definite relations that are indispensable and independent of their will, relations of production which correspond to a definite stage of development of their material productive forces. The sum total of these relations of production constitutes the economic structure of society, the real foundation on which rises a legal and political superstructure and to which correspond definite forms of social consciousness. The mode of production of material life conditions the social, political and intellectual life process in general" (4). Thus, expressed in one sentence, the "economic structure of society," also known as the "mode of production," is the foundation of the "legal and political superstructure," as well as the ideology of the age. Broadly, the economy is the basis for everything else. Marx has also noted that the economic structure derives from the technology of the period, which he calls the "material productive forces," and from the various kinds of economic classes that such a technology requires—what he calls the "relations of production." So, the two elements, forces and relations, make up the mode of production, which, in turn, gives rise to everything else.

Consider for a moment the predicament of a revolutionary. In a revolution, your classic problem is always to defeat the enemy without setting the wrong precedents at the same time. The great temptation is to expand from regular warfare into summary executions and assassinations, but the chief danger is that the new regime will then perpetuate these tactics indefinitely—and thereby crush legitimate dissent. Put another way, governments tend to imitate their founders, and a lawless revolution often produces a lawless state. But historical materialism seems to make this problem go away. How? Very simply. Questions of law are merely questions of the "superstructure," not the economic foundation, and since the foundation *determines* the superstructure, it follows (or so it seems) that the only real problem is to insure the triumph of a new foundation. In other words, the legal process of the future will depend solely on the *economy* of the future, not on your present tactics, so a lawless revolution can do no lasting harm. If you prefer to execute your enemies summarily, all well and good. As Marx suggests in the *Manifesto*, "your jurisprudence is but the will of your class made into a law for all, a will whose essential character and direction are determined by the economic conditions of existence of your class."[3] Does historical materialism really entail this? Much depends on just what the doctrine means—and this requires a closer look at it.

Marx's emphasis on economic conflict happens to recall a similar (and famous) remark by James Madison, in No. 10 of *The Federalist*:

> A landed interest, a manufacturing interest, a mercantile interest, a moneyed interest, with many lesser interests, grow up of necessity in civilized nations, and divide them into different classes, actuated by different sentiments and views. The regulation of these various and interfering interests forms the principal task of modern legislation and involves the spirit of party and faction in the necessary and ordinary operations of government.[4]

Sometimes, Madison sounds just like a marxist. Notice, however, that there is a crucial difference between these two writers. It is one thing to say that most government operations consist in regulating economic interests (which is Madison's view); it is quite another thing to say that the economic foundation of society *determines* its legal and political superstructure (which is Marx's view). Madison's remark says nothing about how to preserve legal process.

Part of the problem is that Marx's doctrine is actually much less clear than it seems. Consider for a moment the terms "condition" and "determine." In saying that the foundation "determines" the superstructure, what exactly do we mean? Do we mean only that the foundation *affects* the superstructure? In that case, the doctrine turns out to be trivial: No one would deny that economic phe-

---

3. *The Marx-Engels Reader*, 487.
4. *The Federalist Papers*, 79.

nomena have effects, since nearly everything does, yet nothing of importance follows. In other words, if Marx could speak to us now, he would surely want to avoid the reduction of his thesis to something plainly insignificant or rigidly fatalistic. The thesis becomes insignificant if it means only "the economic structure sometimes has important effects," or "economics sometimes affects politics." (Being told that economics *sometimes* matters is like being told that presidents are sometimes assassinated; unless you know which president or when, the information is largely useless.)

On the other hand, the doctrine becomes rigidly fatalistic if it means that economics is *all* that matters. If every political event has economic causes, but no economic event has political causes, then why write the *Communist Manifesto* in the first place? The *Manifesto* is itself a political phenomenon (unless the term "economic" is inflated to include everything), and in that event the *Manifesto* would have no effect on society. Put another way, Marx's doctrine must still leave room for political initiative of some sort, if only a marxist one. Again, the doctrine would reduce to absurdity if it were construed to mean only "without an economy, the rest of society could not exist." (The rest of society couldn't exist without oxygen, either, but no one would say that all previous history was therefore a history of oxygen.) Hence, the importance of the term "foundation." What Marx really means is not only that the economy is influential, but that its influence is like the foundation of an edifice, on which all else rests. So the real question is, What does he mean by calling the economy the "foundation"?

The difficulty of construing Marx's doctrine illustrates a common problem of philosophical interpretation. In trying to determine what he means, we are actually asking three questions at once. First, we want to determine the doctrine's exact meaning in a way that is consistent with his words. Yet we must also keep in mind a second question: Is the doctrine politically significant? After all, if the doctrine is construed in a way that makes it intelligible but devoid of any practical consequences, then why worry about it? The doctrine is largely forgettable, for example, if it means only "without economics, there would be no politics." Still, the doctrine is also intended to be believed, not merely contemplated, so we must also frame our view with an eye to a third question: Can the doctrine, as interpreted, be reasonably supported by evidence? Thus, the three questions, 1) What does it mean? 2) Why believe it? and 3) Why does it matter? all arise together, because a defensible reading needs to be intelligible, believable, and politically important all at the same time. And it is perhaps worth remembering that Marx's own frustration with the many misinterpretations of his work also drew from him (according to Engels) this haunting remark: "I am not a Marxist."[5] But to return to the doctrine itself:

---

5. Engels quotes the remark in two letters, one to Eduard Bernstein, dated November 2–3, 1882, and the other to Conrad Schmidt, August 5, 1890.

Much of the difficulty comes from the fact that Marx is using not only a metaphor, but a *vague* metaphor, meaning an implicit analogy that is not to be taken too literally. And one way to see that his metaphor *is* vague is to contrast it with the same metaphor used precisely—for example, in the work of René Descartes. Descartes uses the same metaphor (a foundation and an edifice) but in a different way. He says some of his beliefs have served as "foundations" for his other beliefs and that the others then rest on the foundations like a house. Thus, if you were to picture Descartes's view, it would look something like this:

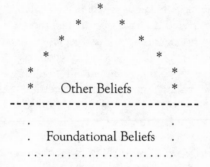

His foundations, he says, are his premises, but the other beliefs are his conclusions, and so the conclusions rest on the premises like a building.[6] Descartes's other views aside, however, his metaphor is precise in this sense: The foundations of a house can still exist without a superstructure, but a superstructure does not exist without foundations. Just so, Descartes thinks he might still entertain the beliefs he calls foundations even if he had never drawn conclusions from them, but he would never believe in the conclusions without also believing in the foundations. Thus, in Descartes's mind, the superstructure is *dependent* on the foundations, but the foundations are *independent*. Marx, however, means something quite different.

Marx *denies* that the economic foundation of a society can exist independently. Quite the reverse; legal and political institutions exist at all, he says, only because the economy needs them. But neither does he say that legal and political institutions can exist without an economy. Instead, each set of phenomena depends on the other; the superstructure needs a foundation, but the foundation also needs a superstructure. Thus, we might picture Marx's view something like this:

---

6. Descartes says this, for example, in his *Discourse on Method* (1637), Part 2, 13; and Part 3, 22 and 29; and also in the second paragraph of his *Meditations on First Philosophy* (1641).

Economic   Legal and Political

Foundations   Superstructure

In Marx's picture, you can't remove the superstructure without also disrupting the foundations. So, for Marx the metaphor is apparently only suggestive. But what, then, does historical materialism really amount to?

Seeing that the metaphor is vague is of course the first step in realizing that its logical consequences are still undetermined, yet a doctrine can be no less influential, especially among scholars, even if no one quite knows what it means. Johannes Kepler discovered the laws of planetary motion in the mistaken belief that he was confirming an insupportable theory—that all the planetary orbits could be inscribed in the five Platonic solids of geometry. Just so, a Marxist historian may well discover important economic mechanisms in the belief that he is confirming historical materialism, even if the doctrine itself is largely unintelligible to him. A similar situation may now exist in the field of sociobiology, if sociobiology is construed as a doctrine, and it supplies, I think, a useful comparison. Consider for a moment, by way of analogy, the meaning of the term "sociobiology."

The Harvard professor Edward O. Wilson, the originator of sociobiology, has defined it as the "systematic study of the biological basis of all social behavior." (I quote from chap. 1, page 4, of *Sociobiology: The New Synthesis* [Cambridge: Harvard University Press/Belknap Press, 1975], the *locus classicus* of his position.) Professor Wilson thus seems to use the same metaphor as Marx— the metaphor of a "foundation." (I assume here, of course, that a "basis" is indeed a foundation, which is the word's meaning in Latin. Elsewhere in his writings, Professor Wilson has often called biology the "foundation" of human behavior. See, for example, his *Naturalist* [Washington, D.C.: Island Press, 1994], 332 and 334.) Yet the metaphor is also vague: It would be absurd to say that human biology might exist even if human beings had *no* social behavior, as a foundation might exist without a superstructure. If human beings had *no* social behavior, most of them would be dead. Thus, the idea that biology is the "basis" of human behavior is, again, apparently only suggestive. Biology does not exist *independently* of behavior, as the base of your house, after a hurricane, might exist independently of your roof. But the key point is that the doctrine can still motivate genuine research in genetics, even if no one quite knows what it means. Even a slogan can suggest a research program (which would also explain why both marxists and sociobiologists often produce interesting results, yet sometimes become tongue-tied when asked to explain just what their philosophy is).[7] So on this view of things, Marx's doctrine is perhaps more like an incantation than an

---

7. As it turns out, a large literature has grown up around Professor Wilson's use of the foundation metaphor, but in my view, no unambiguous interpretation has yet emerged.

intelligible idea, a verbal formula that is often repeated but never really understood. Still, something more needs to be said for Marx.

In a letter he wrote while still in Brussels in 1846, Marx described his view in yet another way.

> Assume a particular state of development in the productive faculties of man and you will get a particular form of commerce and consumption. Assume particular stages of development in production, commerce and consumption and you will have a corresponding social constitution, a corresponding organization of the family, of orders or of classes, in a word, a corresponding civil society. Assume a particular civil society and you will get particular political conditions which are only the official expression of civil society.[8]

Thus, Marx thinks the economic structure of society comes in various forms (or "stages"), and for each form, there is a corresponding pattern of other institutions. Or, put another way, given any particular economic structure, certain legal and political institutions are required, and others ruled out, because everything must be compatible with everything else.

On this view, the economic structure of society is rather like a man's physique, and the legal and political superstructure like his clothing. As the man grows, some parts of his physique change inexorably, and he must then find new clothes to accommodate himself. Otherwise, his clothes, like fetters (a term Marx uses often), simply become too tight and burst apart. So, certain irresistible changes in his physique force changes in his clothing, yet the relationship is still essentially one-sided. The clothes must be changed to fit the physique, but rarely does the physique change to fit the clothes. Thus, the changes of physique are the primary cause, the changes in clothing the primary effect, and there is then a sense in which the physique is the "foundation" for the clothes it wears.

Construed in this way, historical materialism is not only intelligible; I suspect that it is probably true, and in fact Alexis de Tocqueville had already argued for a proposition of much the same sort in 1835, though with more specific content. (Tocqueville, you recall, said in Part I of *Democracy in America* that social equality, spurred by commerce and technology, would render feudal aristocracy obsolete, and he also asserted that this trend toward social equality was historically inevitable.) But the thing to notice is that Marx's general thesis, unlike Tocqueville's, is now made intelligible only at the price of depriving it of any specific consequences. And from the critic's point of view, historical materialism is now simply useless.

Consider: that *some* economic structures are incompatible with *some* political ones is obvious; to deny it is absurd. No one would deny that our politics would be

---

8. The letter is addressed to P. V. Annenkov and is dated December 28, 1846. See *The Marx-Engels Reader*, 136–37.

substantially different if we never had, say, money. On the other hand, being told only that *some* economic changes are inevitable is like being told that someday the stock market will crash. Unless you know roughly which day, the information is largely worthless. The difference between Tocqueville and Marx is that, whereas the one is talking about social equality in particular, the other is talking about economic structures in general. In a word, historical materialism is at best indefinite, whereas useful political information needs to be specific. And nothing follows from this indefinite formulation about the particular consequences of revolutionary tactics, especially ones that might undermine the rule of law.[9]

I am personally inclined to think that Marx was largely unaware of these problems. Marx read widely and was exceedingly learned in the details of economic history, but the one area in which he was particularly weak was in the study of rhetorical fallacies. The German universities of his youth were awash in bombast and imprecision (just the sort of diction later excoriated by George Orwell in his seminal essay "Politics and the English Language"), and it is, therefore, quite possible that Marx thought the metaphor of a foundation to entail particular consequences when, in fact, it did not. In any case, he seems to have left the whole question of the metaphor's vagueness or precision unexamined. He took great care in examining economics, but much less care, I suspect, in examining the meanings of his words.[10]

All the same, there is *still* a way to make Marx's historical outlook politically important once more. We can simply list the economic forms that he says are historically inevitable, and in that event we are once again confronted with the original question of capitalism's fate. As it turns out, Marx imagines no less than *five* different historical stages, all supposedly inevitable: The economic structure of ancient slavery changes inexorably into feudalism, then into capitalism, then into socialism, and finally into pure communism—with the result that Marx has a philosophy of history.

Unlike many ancient authors who imagine human history as a series of cycles, Marx pictures history as more like a story, with a beginning, a middle, and an end. He derives much of this outlook from the German philosopher G. W. F. Hegel, but his view also resembles the Christian idea that history will end in Judgment Day, with the difference that Marx substitutes pure communism for

---

9. Here, perhaps, is another way to see this problem of indeterminacy a little better. Compare Nazi Germany's "economic structure" with that of, say, Dwight Eisenhower's America. Now, were these two structures the same or different? If the same, then Marx's theory gives no way to predict significant political events such as the Holocaust, since however imperfect Eisenhower's America may have been, it involved nothing like the systematic extermination of millions of people. But if the two structures were *different*, then the very idea of economic structures is too indeterminate to be useful. After all, if the two societies weren't both capitalist, then what does the word "capitalist" mean?

10. I should add that, although some scholars will dispute my judgment on this point, the judgment is by no means original to me. This criticism of Marx's diction is quite old.

the Kingdom of God. Still, from a logical standpoint, the thing to notice is that none of the stages on this list of historical inevitabilities follows from the general doctrine of historical materialism. The doctrine is at best indefinite, whereas the list is particular. So, the argument and evidence for these changes must come from somewhere else. Where, then, is the evidence? Or put another way, why suppose that capitalism is doomed after all?

Marx's answer to this question is different from anything I have said so far; in a word, it all depends on machines.

Marx believes that the more machines a capitalist can afford, the better his chances of driving his competitors out of business. Here's the way he expresses this idea in Volume 1 of *Capital*:

> The battle of competition is fought by cheapening of commodities. The cheapness of commodities depends, *ceteris paribus*, on the productiveness of labor, and this again on the scale of production. Therefore, the larger capitals beat the smaller. It will further be remembered that, with the development of the capitalist mode of production, there is an increase in the minimum amount of individual capital necessary to carry on a business under its normal conditions. The smaller capitals, therefore, crowd into spheres of production which Modern Industry has only sporadically or incompletely got hold of. Here competition rages in direct proportion to the number, and in inverse proportion to the magnitudes, of the antagonistic capitals. It always ends in the ruin of many small capitalists, whose capitals partly pass into the hands of their conquerors, partly vanish.[11]

Large firms will drive small firms out of business, says Marx, because they can produce on an ever larger scale. And new competitors, unless they are already large, will then find it more difficult to enter the field in the first place. Marx adds that large firms also have easier access to credit, which makes it easier still for them to drive their competitors into bankruptcy. And so the result is a general tendency toward monopoly: Society's basic industries fall into fewer and fewer hands. The corps of successful capitalists grows ever smaller, because the effect of machinery is to make production more efficient as it grows ever larger.

There is another consequence of machines, too. They reduce most ordinary workers (he says) to unemployment or wage slavery. A machine, after all, is a labor-saving device. Thus, the more machines a society has, the less it needs workers. Its superfluous workers may still find employment if they can be set to providing new kinds of goods or services, but new kinds of products will sell only if there are paying customers. And with the corps of successful capitalists perpetually shrinking, most of these customers will have to be other workers. Will the one effect keep pace with the other? That is, will the prosperity of the

---

11. Karl Marx, *Capital: A Critique of Political Economy* (1867; New York: International Publishers, 1967), volume 1, part 7, chap. 25, section 2, 586–87.

workers as a whole grow at such a pace as to give each redundant worker a new
job? And can the redundant workers even be trained for new jobs? On the
whole, Marx thinks not.

> The economists tell us, it is true, that the workers rendered superfluous by
> machinery find *new* branches of employment.
>   They dare not assert directly that the same workers who are discharged find
> places in the new branches of labor. The facts cry out too loudly against this lie.
> They really only assert that new means of employment will open up for *other com-*
> *ponent sections of the working class*, for instance, for the portion of the young gen-
> eration of workers that was ready to enter the branch of industry that has just
> gone under. That is, of course, a great consolation for the disinherited workers.[12]

Instead, the whole tendency of modern machinery, says Marx, is to make
work ever simpler and more monotonous, and less muscular, so that unskilled
labor replaces skilled, and women and children enter industry in competition
with men. The effect of all these factors is to force down wages through increasing competition, and so society as a whole drifts toward crisis.

It would be absurd to expect a vast, impoverished proletariat to starve while
a tiny elite of successful capitalists enjoys what little affluence is left. In fact,
where will the capitalists find paying customers, once everyone else becomes
destitute? Instead, the more likely outcome (says Marx) is that the workers will
finally take matters into their own hands, seize the property of the capitalists and
institute a new order. Though the workers might then, in theory, simply redis-
tribute the capitalists' property to numerous private individuals, and thus start
the whole cycle over again, the more likely outcome is collective. Production is
most efficient on an ever larger scale, so the most efficient course is to keep great
factories intact, and thus turn society's basic means of production into state
property. So, in Marx's view, socialism not only is a *possible* outcome of the collapse of capitalism, it is the *necessary* outcome. And only after many further generations will the socialist state then "wither away," to become a pure communism that "inscribes on its banner: From each according to his ability, to each
according to his need."[13]

Could Marx be right? The simple answer is yes—or so I would contend.
Anyone who thinks that this scenario simply *cannot* happen is, I think, kidding
himself. History is filled with unexpected twists and turns, and some twists are far
more unexpected than Marx's. Still, the more important question is whether this
scenario is really likely. And here, of course, there are some obvious objections.

---

12. I quote from Section 5 of Marx's *Wage Labor and Capital*, first published in 1849; the
emphasis is in the original. See *The Marx-Engels Reader*, 215.
13. The phrase appears in Marx's *Critique of the Gotha Program*, first written as a letter to a fac-
tion of the German Social Democratic movement in May 1875. See *The Marx-Engels Reader*, 531.

For one thing, Marx assumes that production is most efficient on an ever larger scale. But is this really true? Some enterprises grow so large as to be unwieldy, but more crucially, new technology sometimes *destroys* the advantage of large capital over small. The invention of the automobile, for example, destroyed the monopoly over land transportation once enjoyed by the railroads; some railroads eventually went bankrupt. Put another way, Marx's assumption seems to depend on an accident of nineteenth-century technology, when bigger really *was* better. But will this assumption hold true in the future? The assumption may well have been safe in an age of coal, steam, and steel, but how does it apply to an age of gasoline, plastics, and lasers? His critics reply, to the contrary, that no one can know in advance what scale of production will be most efficient. (In Marx's defense, of course, we should note that his assumption still *might* be right; perhaps we simply cannot know.)

Marx also makes a similar assumption in discussing the effect of machines on labor. There is little doubt that machines exist to replace human labor, but it is quite another thing to say that machines must favor *unskilled* labor. Marx's opponents say, in reply, that machines now tend to eliminate unskilled labor and that, because skills take time to acquire, their overall effect is often to drive the wages of skilled laborers up. Those without skills may still fall into destitution, but it is quite another matter to say that the *majority* of workers will fall into destitution. If only some workers become destitute, why suppose they will be so numerous as to destroy capitalism? Again, say the critics, Marx's prediction looks plausible in the nineteenth century, but it is at best only a guess for the twenty-first.

Yet another attack is to ask why capitalists, reading the *Communist Manifesto* for themselves, won't simply organize relief for the workers, if not to save the workers, then to save their own skins. The *Manifesto* is addressed in part to the proletariat, but if the proletariat can understand it, so can entrepreneurs. "The executive of the modern state [says the *Manifesto*] is but a committee for managing the common affairs of the whole bourgeoisie." If so, then it should be only a small matter for this executive committee to organize sufficient concessions to forestall a revolution. (Marx writes the *Manifesto*, it should be noted, before limits on the work day, a minimum wage, occupational safety rules, unemployment insurance, or worker health coverage.) The marxist may then object that such concessions to the workers are morally inferior to socialism or communism, but this does nothing to show that capitalism will collapse. To the contrary, it might well survive indefinitely.

Apart from all this, some critics complain that no modern economy is purely "capitalistic" or "socialistic"; instead, they say, capitalism and socialism are only "ideal types" (a phrase of Max Weber's) to which real economies more or less approximate. Many countries now have a mix of both private and state enterprises, and many private enterprises are now owned partly or wholly by their workers. Thus, many countries are partly capitalistic but also partly socialistic. Though the original case for collective ownership is quite old (having been laid out, for example, in Book 5 of Plato's *Republic*) and the attack on it equally ancient (in Book 2 of Aristotle's *Politics*), the relative merits of each approach are now apt to depend on a great many technical factors, often local and impermanent, and we may, therefore, wonder whether the choice between the two systems is really as stark as Marx imagines. (As an old joke has it, "Under capitalism, man exploits man; under socialism, it is the reverse.")

In truth, marxism's historical role has been quite different from what Marx expected, and this, perhaps, is the real ideological mystery. So far, marxist socialism has functioned not as the *successor* to capitalism, but as a sort of transitional form, from medieval feudalism to the kind of mass society envisioned by Alexis de Tocqueville. And to explain this last point better, I think the easiest course is to rely once more on Tocqueville himself, who propounded this explanation even before Marx wrote.

Tocqueville (you recall) believed that the fluidity of commerce tends to generate a large middle class. That is, the instability of modern wealth makes most people *think* of themselves as middle class. But it also makes them more materialistic, and it does so because social position is now less certain than under the previous social order. Tocqueville illustrates this idea by describing what he found in America in the 1830s:

> I have never perceived among the wealthier inhabitants of the United States that proud contempt of physical gratifications which is sometimes to be met with even in the most opulent and dissolute aristocracies. Most of these wealthy persons were once poor; they have felt the sting of want; they were long a prey to adverse fortunes; and now that the victory is won, the passions which accompanied the contest have survived it; their minds are, as it were, intoxicated by the small enjoyments which they have pursued for forty years.[14]

On average, says Tocqueville, modern citizens are less capable of purely theoretical and artistic enterprises that promise no financial reward. They demand that the beautiful be useful, and they regard the useful as beautiful. On the other hand, they are also less prone to debauchery and grand personal escapades, precisely because they fear losing their resources.

Now this increasing materialism has a further, crucial effect. It makes "great" revolutions more rare. What Tocqueville means is that the more a society advances toward social equality (the condition where both rich and poor become minorities, whereas most people see themselves as falling in the middle), the less violent and abrupt will be the changes in its basic system of property. For example, the French Revolution not only overthrew a king, it

---

14. *Democracy in America*, Part 2, Book 2, chap. 10, 129–130.

aimed at a basic redistribution of wealth. But the French Revolution also embraced the revolt of a vast and impoverished peasantry. It was *not* an uprising of a middle-class majority. The middle class, once it becomes numerically dominant, resists violent commotions precisely because it fears the loss of its station. Modern citizens "desire with unexampled ardor to get rich," says Tocqueville, "but the difficulty is to know from whom riches can be taken."

> All revolutions more or less threaten the tenure of property: but most of those who live in democratic countries are possessed of property; not only are they possessed of property, but they live in a condition where men set the greatest store upon their property.[15]

He says that between wealth and poverty in a democracy,

> stands an innumerable multitude of men almost alike, who, without being exactly either rich or poor, are possessed of sufficient property to desire the maintenance of order, yet not enough to excite envy. Such men are the natural enemies of violent commotions; their stillness keeps all beneath them and above them still. (Ibid., 252)

When it comes to social revolution, no one is more conservative than the typical middle-class property owner. In Tocqueville's words, "the majority of the people do not clearly see what they have to gain by a revolution" (ibid., 253).

The perfect illustration of Tocqueville's view may well be the recent anti-Communist revolutions in Russia and Eastern Europe, which, while certainly important, have involved nothing like the class warfare of 1789 or 1917. There is now a sort of middle-class majority in these countries, a middle class developed under the former marxist regimes, and this middle class is economically conservative. It may still embrace vicious demagogues or foreign military adventures, and it may well abandon all political tradition; it may also oppress various minorities with malignant zeal. But if Tocqueville is right, the one thing we should *not* expect from it is a rapid and violent redistribution of personal possessions. The overriding concern of this middle class will be to preserve its own standing, and any wholesale attack on property would threaten this standing. Thus, if Tocqueville is right, marxist revolutions are likely to occur only where social equality is not *yet* established, and this is exactly what has happened. Except when imposed by a foreign army (as in Eastern Europe), marxist revolutions have occurred only in societies that were still essentially feudal and agrarian, and though communist revolutionaries have often proved selfless, their successors have still tended to exercise something like feudal authority over their peasant underlings. Thus, marxist socialism can be seen as a kind of

---

15. Ibid., Book 3, chap. 21, 252–53.

decaying feudalism, in which the communist cadres occupy the slots once filled by the old nobility. Once a middle class develops, however, the feudal prerogatives of these cadres seem to diminish.[16]

Still, quite apart from revolutions, cataclysms, and various historical tragedies, there are also the many smaller tragedies of ordinary people ground down by impersonal forces, often economic ones, and Marx himself was later to know this sort of tragedy firsthand.

After the *Manifesto* appeared in 1848, Marx was expelled from Brussels, then arrested in Cologne on a charge of sedition. He was eventually acquitted, but was soon expelled again, and being denied asylum in France, he finally settled in London, where he spent the rest of his life as an exile. Trained as an intellectual and devoted to agitation, he seems to have regarded menial occupations as simply beneath him. (He once applied for work as a clerk, but was told that his scrawl was illegible.) Marx never again had regular employment, except for occasional correspondence for the *New York Daily Tribune*.

Engels tried to support him through his own work in a textile firm, but Marx nevertheless fell into great poverty. He pawned most of his family's clothing, rented a two-room garret, and sometimes had nothing for his wife and children but bread and potatoes for a week. When his daughter Franziska died about a year after her birth, Marx had no money for a coffin. (A neighbor bought one.) Then, when his son Edgar died at the age of six, probably from undernourishment, Marx wrote to Engels, "I have only just learned what real unhappiness is." Yet Marx still studied most days in the British Museum, tried to organize communist agitation, and continued to work toward the publication of his ideas. He loved Shakespeare greatly, could quote long passages of Dante and Aeschylus from memory, and in his last years began to master new languages, including Russian and Turkish. Only in his last years did his financial situation ease, and when he finally died in 1883, Engels called him "the best hated and most calumniated man of his time."[17]

Marx was an irascible man, vain in his reluctance to work as a drudge, and it is only natural to want to blame him for his own misfortune. Still, his adversities and those of his family seem to illustrate at least one point with pretty fair certainty: Economic forces have no *automatic* connection to the good, and consequently the demands of the market, or those of any other economic system, are a poor excuse for failing to ask whether those around us are being treated with dignity and compassion.

---

16. On this view of things, the collapse of Soviet Communism is not the "end of history," as one writer has called it, but only Russia's final emergence from the old paternalism familiar in all feudal societies.

17. *The Marx-Engels Reader*, 682.

10.

Why Does God
Permit Evil?

IF GOD IS all powerful, all knowing, and good, then why do the innocent suffer and the wicked prosper? Just as the Book of Job sought to answer this question more than twenty-four centuries ago, so the religious and spiritual try to answer it now. The real challenge to religious faith comes not from suffering but from the apparent senselessness of suffering—an effect that struck with special force in the early life of Frederick Douglass.

Douglass was born a slave in 1818 on a plantation in Maryland, where he soon became acquainted with various murders: Bill Denby, a slave on the home plantation of Colonel Edward Lloyd (Maryland's former governor and later a U.S. senator), was shot in the face for refusing to come forward to be whipped. The cousin of Douglass's future wife, Anna Murray, was beaten to death by her mistress, Mrs. Giles Hicks, for being slow to respond to the cries of a baby. Thomas Lambdin, a ship's carpenter from a town nearby, killed two slaves, one with a hatchet, and Douglass often heard him laughing about it. John Beale Bordley Jr., a neighbor of Colonel Lloyd, killed one of the colonel's slaves for digging oysters along his own land, later apologizing to the colonel for the consequent loss of "property."

One of Douglass's earliest memories was seeing his aunt Hester hanging by her wrists from a hook in the ceiling; she had been suspended there for a whipping. Douglass, who was about six years old at the time, hid in a closet. ("I expected it would be my turn next.") Douglass usually ate cornmeal mush in a trough, but he had to fight off other children to get it. As for clothing, his only garment was a tow linen shirt that reached to his knees, and because he had neither pants nor shoes, he could keep warm at night only by sleeping in a sack used to carry grain. In winter, the frost caused deep gashes in his feet.

137

Douglass had only dim memories of his mother, who worked as a field hand on a plantation twelve miles away and could thus visit him only after walking that distance at night. He describes these visits in the first of his three autobiographies, his *Narrative of the Life of Frederick Douglass, an American Slave*:

> She was with me in the night. She would lie down with me, and get me to sleep, but long before I waked she was gone. . . . She died when I was about seven years old, on one of my master's farms, near Lee's mill. I was not allowed to be present during her illness, at her death or burial.[1]

Fifteen of Douglass's relatives were sold away ("sold South") before he was fourteen years old, and he never knew who his father was, though the man was whispered to be his master. In later years, Douglass also remembered two young women, Henrietta and Mary, who were slaves in a house across the street in Baltimore, where he was afterward sent to live. Mary's head was so covered with festering sores, caused by beatings, that she acquired the nickname "pecked." Remarking on her hunger and emaciation, Douglass writes, "I have seen Mary contending with the pigs for the offal thrown in the street" (6.59).

Douglass saw such treatment meted out to almost everyone he held dear, and all of it under the eye of a seemingly silent and seemingly indifferent God. Yet he also insisted that God's remarkable goodness saved his life. How could he believe this?

The philosophical problem of theodicy, the problem of explaining why a just god would choose to permit evil, is by no means easily resolved. Still, Douglass's own answer derived not from an abstract theory but from his personal experience. He believed that God had specially arranged for his individual deliverance. Douglass was chosen, without apparent reason when he was still seven or eight years old, to live with his master's relatives in Baltimore, an event that changed the whole direction of his life. There, his new mistress, Mrs. Sophia Auld, began to teach Douglass to read, until her husband stopped her. Her husband warned,

> If you teach that nigger how to read, there would be no keeping him. It would forever unfit him to be a slave. He would at once become unmanageable, and of no value to his master. As to himself, it could do him no good, but a great deal of harm. It would make him discontented and unhappy. (6.57)

But Douglass overheard this conversation and in a peculiar irony came to believe that Mrs. Auld's husband was actually right. The only difference was that what the husband feared, Douglass wanted.

---

1. *Narrative*, chap. 1, 40. Subsequent references are to chapter and page number.

The very decided manner with which he spoke, and strove to impress his wife with the evil consequences of giving me instruction, served to convince me that he was deeply sensible of the truths he was uttering. It gave me the best assurance that I might rely with the utmost confidence on the results which, he said, would flow from teaching me to read. What he most dreaded, that I most desired. What he most loved, that I most hated. That which to him was a great evil, to be carefully shunned, was to me a great good, to be diligently sought. (6.58)

After Mrs. Auld stopped teaching him, Douglass acquired a book:

I got hold of a book entitled "The Columbian Orator." Every opportunity I got, I used to read this book. Among much of other interesting matter, I found in it a dialogue between a master and a slave . . . the whole argument in behalf of slavery was brought forward by the master, all of which was disposed of by the slave. . . .

In the same book, I met with one of [Richard] Sheridan's mighty speeches on and in behalf of Catholic emancipation. These were choice documents to me. . . . They gave tongue to interesting thoughts of my own soul, which had frequently flashed through my mind, and died for want of utterance. The moral which I gained from the dialogue was the power of truth over the conscience of even a slaveholder. What I got from Sheridan was a bold denunciation of slavery, and a powerful vindication of human rights. The reading of these documents enabled me to utter my thoughts. (7.61)

Notice that when Douglass describes these events years later, he says not that the book *instilled* his moral ideas; instead, he implies that the book *elicited* his ideas. Its speeches, dialogues, and essays allowed him to utter "interesting thoughts of my own soul," which had previously slipped away, because they had been left inarticulate. Thus, though the words of the book allowed him to remember, the thoughts he was remembering were his own. Douglass's remarks in these passages (all taken from his *Narrative*) are at least partly suggestive of Socratic method–which is itself worth more than a moment to think about. The efficacy of Socratic method is sometimes challenged on the grounds that the questions it asks can be merely leading. The student need not *know* anything, it is said; all he has to do is answer as expected. This criticism is quite common, but it really shows much less, I think, than is often imagined. Even if the questions of Socratic method *are* leading, they still require from the student an ability to follow the lead. Thus, they still presuppose something latent in the mind. Put another way, at some point in the interrogation, the student must be genuinely ready to utter a sincere "Yes" or sincere "No" and not simply remain silent like a stone. In consequence, the method still seems to assume an innate tendency to respond in particular ways when asked to contemplate certain kinds of situations. Douglass's view is roughly similar; he asserts that *The Columbian Orator* allowed him to utter his *own* thoughts.

Douglass's outlook has a further implication. To suppose that his moral ideas were merely *elicited* by the book rather than instilled, and to suppose further that his ideas then matched those of the authors he was reading (some being ancient Greeks and Romans), is to suppose that his ideas were more than the mere whims of particular individuals or societies. Instead, it implies that certain moral ideas are culturally invariant and that they remain latent only because no one is asking the right questions. In other words, if we learn to articulate the appropriate questions, moral disagreement should recede. (Such, I think, is the implicit consequence of Douglass's opinion of the "power of truth.") As a result, Douglass's path in life soon became clear to him: He aimed above all at making himself articulate.

Douglass was only twelve years old when he acquired *The Columbian Orator*, and this fact in itself made his situation extraordinary. The book is an anthology of moral and political works intended to instill the "art of eloquence."[2] Twelve-year-olds do not always read such material to begin with, but equally important, Douglass read it while confronted by the daily spectacle of his own enslavement. Could anything be better calculated to produce a determined agitator, and perhaps also a great leader, than to enslave him as a child while at the same time giving him a book of speeches on matters of justice?

But the other half of the prediction from Sophia Auld's husband also came true. Not only did Douglass become indignant, he also became deeply unhappy. The same words that allowed him to articulate and remember his thoughts also made him feel these thoughts more intensely.

> The more I read, the more I was led to abhor and detest my enslavers. I could regard them in no other light than a band of successful robbers, who had left their homes, and gone to Africa, and stolen us from our homes, and in a strange land reduced us to slavery. . . . As I read and contemplated the subject, behold! that very discontentment which Master Hugh had predicted would follow my learning to read had already come, to torment and sting my soul to unutterable anguish. As I writhed under it, I would at times feel that learning to read had been a curse rather than a blessing. It had given me a view of my wretched condition, without the remedy. It opened my eyes to the horrible pit, but to no ladder upon which to get out. In moments of agony, I envied my fellow-slaves for their stupidity. I have often wished myself a beast. I preferred the condition of the meanest reptile to my own. Any thing, no matter what, to get rid of

---

2. Edited by Caleb Bingham and published in Boston by Manning and Loring (1797), the book includes speeches by Cicero, Cato the Younger, Socrates, Napoleon, Washington, William Pitt the Elder, and Charles James Fox, among others. The speech he remembers as the work of Richard Sheridan is actually by Daniel O'Connor.

thinking! It was this everlasting thinking of my condition that tormented me. . . . The silver trump of freedom had roused my soul to eternal wakefulness. . . . It looked from every star, it smiled in every calm, breathed in every wind, and moved in every storm. (7.61–62)

When Douglass was somewhat older but still enslaved, he passed his Sundays on bluffs overlooking the Chesapeake Bay, "whose broad bosom was ever white with sails from every quarter of the habitable globe" (10.74). And like Odysseus held captive on the island of Calypso, he cried out his sorrows to the sea and longed for a ship to carry him away. Like Odysseus again, his escape would ultimately depend on a combination of courage and cunning (on disguises, lies, and false names), but through it all he also believed that his god was watching over him, much as the goddess Athena watched over Homer's hero of old. He believed his deliverance from slavery was somehow part of a divine plan.

Going to live at Baltimore laid the foundation, and opened the gateway, to all my subsequent prosperity. I have ever regarded it as the first plain manifestation of that kind providence which has ever since attended me, and marked my life with so many favors. (5.56)

He adds,

I may be deemed superstitious, and even egotistical, in regarding this event as a special interposition of divine Providence in my favor. But I should be false to the earliest sentiments of my soul, if I suppressed the opinion . . . and in the darkest hours of my career in slavery, this living word of faith and spirit of hope departed not from me. . . . This good spirit was from God, and to him I offer thanksgiving and praise.[3]

Still, the deeper philosophical question is obvious: If God is good and chose to save Douglass, why didn't God also save others? Indeed, why did God permit slavery at all? These same questions—why a just god would permit slavery and what a just god would finally do about it—appear prominently in much nineteenth-century American thought: especially in the Second Inaugural Address of Abraham Lincoln, which Douglass attended and approved. Lincoln, like Douglass, ultimately appeals to the idea that God's intentions, though just, are largely unfathomable. Here is Lincoln brooding over this same problem of divine justice, but in a private memorandum, written somewhat earlier, probably in 1862, just after the disastrous second battle of Manassas, during the Civil War:

---

3. *Narrative*, chap. 5, 56. Considering Douglass's life as a whole, it is perhaps tempting to think also of an observation attributed to the ancient Heraclitus, "Character is fate."

The will of God prevails. In great contests each party claims to act in accordance with the will of God. Both may be, and one must be wrong. God can not
be for and against the same thing at the same time. In the present civil war it
is quite possible that God's purpose is something different from the purpose of
either party—and yet the human instrumentalities, working just as they do, are
of the best adaptation to effect His purpose. I am almost ready to say this is
probably true—that God wills this contest, and wills that it shall not end yet.
By his mere quiet power, on the minds of the now contestants, He could have
either saved or destroyed the Union without a human contest. Yet the contest
began. And having begun He could give the final victory to either side any day.
Yet the contest proceeds.[4]

Lincoln did not yet see that the war would end slavery, a point he would come back
to in his Second Inaugural. ("Each [side] looked for an easier triumph, and a result
less fundamental and astounding. . . . The Almighty has His own purposes.")[5]

Yet if God is all powerful, why must God's methods involve suffering at all?
And why does God permit wickedness? Why, in a word, is evil even needed?
And why must this evil be sometimes so unspeakable, involving (as it sometimes
does) the death of the weak and the kind in horror and fanaticism? This is the
philosophical problem of theodicy: the problem of determining whether the
existence of evil is even logically compatible with a just and powerful God.

One of the oldest and simplest answers to this problem is to deny the existence of evil outright—a solution advanced by the early Christian philosopher
Saint Augustine of Hippo, in North Africa (A.D. 354–430). Augustine says evil
is simply the absence of goodness, as darkness is the absence of light, or cold the
absence of heat—a view now called the "privative" theory of evil. Thus, evil is
merely a "privation" of goodness; not something, but only the absence of something; or, in Augustine's words, "Evil is not a substance."[6]

Augustine's theory is probably intelligible in the abstract. It is not particularly hard to conceive of God generating the goodness of creation, while at the
same time leaving various gaps or absences. These absences are what we then
call "evil." In effect, evil is neither an entity nor a quality, on this view of things;
strictly speaking, evil is nothing at all. On the other hand, Augustine's theory
gives no particular accounting of why a just god would permit these absences in
the first place. As it turns out, Augustine has a further answer for this, too. The
particular absences we call evil still contribute to the greater goodness of creation as a whole. "Though the higher things are better than the lower, the sum
of all creation is better than the higher things alone" (ibid., chap. 13, 149). Put

---

4. *Collected Works*, volume 5, 403–4.

5. *Great Speeches*, 107.

6. Augustine, *Confessions*, trans. R. S. Pine-Coffin (1961; reprint, Harmondsworth, England:
Penguin Books, 1980), Book 7, chap. 12, 148.

another way, if God had made only perfect angels and nothing more, the world as a whole would still be *less* perfect than it is now. So the appeal is once again to an architecture that is large but unfathomable.

The great weakness of Augustine's theory, I think, is not that it is necessarily false but that it is incomplete. Augustine denies the existence of evil, but he leaves suffering and wickedness intact. To be told that evil is not a "substance" is to be told about substances but not about the reason for suffering. Why is it needed at all? And to be told that suffering fits into a larger, unfathomable plan is only to be told once more that suffering's role in this plan is still beyond us. But can anything more be said? What exactly *is* the role of suffering?

One of the greatest of all meditations on the problem of suffering is actually much older than Augustine's; it is Homer's *Iliad*, which dates from about 700 B.C. and which depicts "the gods" as positively malevolent. Consider for a moment Homer's conception.

The mortal characters of Homer's *Iliad* all have various failings, none being a mere paste-up hero, but they all seem to suffer worse than they deserve. And they often receive this undeserved fate directly from the gods. The death of Hector, for example, is particularly flagrant. Hector fights through most of the poem for kith and kin, and with great courage, yet toward the end he is left all alone, trapped outside his walls, while his father, King Priam, calls down from the ramparts above. ("Back, come back! Inside the walls, my boy!")[7] Nevertheless, something holds Hector in place till his enemy, Achilles, is practically on top of him. When Hector finally decides to retreat, he starts to run wildly, but then he is suddenly brought to a stop by the appearance of what seems to be his brother Deiphobus, coming to his aid, and naturally, Hector's gratitude is immense.

> dearest of all my brothers, all these warring years
> . . . to venture out from the walls, all for *my* sake,
> while the others stay inside and cling to safety. (22.277–82)

And Deiphobus answers,

> True, dear brother—how your father and mother both
> implored me, time and again, clutching my knees,
> and comrades round me begging me to stay!
> Such was the fear that broke them, man for man,
> but the heart within me broke with grief for you. (22.284–88)

---

7. Book 22, 65. This and subsequent references are to the book and line numbers of Robert Fagles's translation, *Homer: The Iliad* (New York: Viking Penguin, 1990).

It is a touching moment, a brother offering his life to save a brother, but what Hector does not realize is that the figure he is speaking to is not really his brother at all. Instead, it is the goddess Athena in disguise, and her actual purpose is to assassinate him. When Achilles finally hurls a spear at Hector and misses, Athena, unknown to Hector, picks up the spear and tosses it back to Achilles for another throw. When Hector then turns to his brother for a spear of his own, he discovers at last that no one is there. He realizes that it has all been a trick to annihilate him. His death is still brave, but it is also unfair, and it is precisely Athena herself who makes it so.

The *Iliad* contains many such instances of divine malignity. (When Hector and Ajax resolve to fight a duel, Homer adds an exquisite touch: the gods Apollo and Athena light in a tree to watch the action in the guise of vultures.) The cruelty of the poem descends even upon the gods themselves, especially Zeus, the most human of them all. When Zeus sees his mortal son Sarpedon cornered in battle, he says to his queen, Hera,

> . . . My cruel fate. . .
> my Sarpedon, the man I love the most, my own son—
> doomed to die at the hands of Menoetius' son Patroclus.
> . . . Shall I pluck him up, now, while he's still alive
> and set him down in the rich green land of Lycia,
> far from the war at Troy and its tears? (16.514–20)

But Hera answers,

> Dread majesty, son of Cronus—what are you saying?
> A man, a mere mortal, his doom sealed long ago?
> . . . if you send Sarpedon home, living still, beware!
> Then surely some other god will want to sweep
> his own son clear of the heavy fighting too.
> . . . you will inspire lethal anger in them all. (16.523–34)

So, to preserve order in the heavens, Zeus surrenders his mortal son to his enemies, but he still weeps tears of blood, which rain upon the earth like a red flood.

The *Iliad*'s treatment of the gods, though fantastic, strikes many people as fundamentally realistic, because, they say, it expresses the true brutality of life. One could easily apply to the poem the words of Shakespeare's *King Lear*:

> As flies to wanton boys, are we to the gods;
> They kill us for their sport. (4.1.36–37)

The *Iliad*'s characters are invariably more "sinned against than sinning."

Yet many readers attack the *Iliad* for precisely this reason. Its rendering of the gods, they say, is too bleak. God is, or the gods are, fundamentally good (they say), and thus the whole theology of the *Iliad* is incorrect. The most prominent of these critics is probably Plato, who lived at a time when Homer's poems had hardened into something like Holy Writ, and who consequently argues in his *Republic* for an extensive system of state censorship (379a–392b). It is just Homer's best lines, says Plato, that ought to be banned. The better they are as poetry, the worse for the soul. And notice that if Plato is indeed right on this point, then the same criticism might also be made of much other literature—of most Greek tragedy, for example, and much of Shakespeare. The trouble with tragedy, it seems, is that it makes life as a whole look just too wretched.

Whether life really *is* wretched, is, of course, precisely the issue, but before pushing it further, there is still one remark that needs to be added in defense of the *Iliad* and, by extension, in defense of all tragic literature. The remark is Aristotle's.

Aristotle says the function of tragedy is to provoke "catharsis," but catharsis is not an attempt at laying out a correct theology. Catharsis is an emotional purge, a release of pity and fear, and as Aristotle notes, "pity is occasioned by undeserved misfortune."[8] The key word is "undeserved." Quite apart from whether God really *is* just, you will get no catharsis as a poet if your characters always suffer only what they deserve and nothing more. You may still compose a fine poem or a satisfying drama, and many of the works we now call "tragedy" result for the most part in *deserved* misfortune for the protagonist (Shakespeare's *Richard III*, for example). Still, there is a species of tragic literature that aims at a different effect, at provoking intense pity for its leading characters, and the *Iliad* belongs to this category just as *King Lear* does, or Tennessee Williams's *Glass Menagerie*, or Arthur Miller's *Death of a Salesman*. It is then essential to this effect of catharsis to make one's characters suffer undeservedly, even if the result is theologically false. Thus, the real nature of the gods has nothing to do with such literature. Put another way, even if the gods *are* good, but are nevertheless capable, somehow, of feeling emotions that can be purged, then it is entirely possible that *they* appreciate the *Iliad* as much as anyone else. But to return to the central problem: Can the existence of wickedness and suffering really be justified?

Suffering, it is said, can be beneficial. In Friedrich Nietzsche's words, "What does not destroy me makes me stronger."[9] Yet many people are indeed destroyed. How does suffering benefit them? Again, suffering is often said to be ennobling,

---

8. *Poetics*, chap. 13, 1453a5.

9. Friedrich Nietzsche, *Twilight of the Idols* (1888), "Maxims and Arrows," no. 8, in *The Portable Nietzsche*, ed. Walter Kaufmann (1954; reprint, Harmondsworth, England: Penguin Books, 1976), 467.

yet I am reminded in reply of a remark once uttered by a doctor: "Suffering isn't ennobling, recovery is."[10] And in fact, some people never recover. They die in detestable ways, in anguish, terror, confusion. Suffering can also be construed as a test of moral character, yet here the critic can be expected to ask, What would an all-knowing god need with such a test in the first place? Wouldn't God know the results of the test in advance? And even if God *doesn't* know the results, how valuable would the results be anyway? Would any compassionate being inflict intense suffering on another merely as a "test"? The biblical figure Job seems to make much the same complaint to God in verse 10, chaps. 13–14:

> . . . this was the secret purpose of
>   thy heart,
> and I know that this was thy intent:
> that, if I sinned, thou wouldst be
>   watching me . . .[11]

Is this the mercy of a forgiving god?

Again, suppose suffering is merely the necessary price that human beings pay for the development of their moral character, and suppose further that human wickedness is then only the inevitable consequence of giving these same human beings the freedom to develop that character. Still, you can always ask, Why can't an omnipotent God find a better way? Why can't an all-powerful God find means to develop moral character *without* suffering? And if not, can God's purposes, whatever they are, really justify such an awful price?

The case against God is not quite as bad as I have so far made it appear, and I shall consider the other side of the issue in a moment. But notice that to pose such questions is also to pose questions about life as a whole—whatever your opinion of religion. Your own life may well be tolerable, but you can always ask, Is everyone else's tolerable? If not, then something seems basically wrong with the universe. The essence of the problem is in fact quite simple: Either suffering is indeed evil, or it isn't; if it isn't, then why try to alleviate anyone else's suffering? But if it *is* evil, then the world as a whole seems flawed.

Friedrich Nietzsche suggests another formulation of this same question, which can be put to theists, atheists, and agnostics alike. Suppose you learned tomorrow that the whole history of the world was to be repeated in exact detail, over and over again, forever, a prospect that Nietzsche dubbed "the eternal return." All the world's beauties would recur, but also the calamities. Would you welcome this news? Or would you regard it as a great catastrophe? How you answer this question, Nietzsche thinks, throws much light on your attitude

---

10. I have been unable to trace the source of this remark, but I believe it to have been uttered in an interview by the heart surgeon Christiaan Barnard.

11. I quote from *The New English Bible* (New York: Oxford University Press, 1976).

toward life in general. (Nietzsche says for his own part that he would welcome the news "joyfully," though personally I wonder whether "joyfully" is quite the right word. I think instead of a remark by Marcus Aurelius: "Life isn't like dancing, life is like wrestling"; life has its joyful moments, but also its terrible ones).[12]

Perhaps the most powerful of all attacks on religion (and on the notion that the universe as a whole is basically good) comes from the Russian novelist Fyodor Dostoyevsky, who was nevertheless devoutly committed to the idea of a just and merciful God. But Dostoyevsky remarks, "My hosanna has come forth from the crucible of doubt." Dostoyevsky's hope ultimately is to understand God, but his method of doing so is first to see the full force of the argument against God. And he puts this argument in the mouth of his character Ivan in *The Brothers Karamazov*.

Ivan speaks to his younger brother Alyosha, a novice monk, and recounts to him a series of atrocities, apparently drawn from newspapers and history books. ("Alyosha" also happens to have been the name of Dostoyevsky's own son, who died of epilepsy at the age of three.) Ivan tells of peasants in Bulgaria being murdered by foreign soldiers. Some are nailed by their ears to fences, then hanged the next day. He also tells of a five-year-old girl in Russia who is tortured by her parents. "It's just their defenselessness that tempts the tormentor, the angelic confidence of the child who has no refuge and no appeal."[13] The girl is locked overnight in an outhouse, her face smeared with excrement; Ivan imagines her beating her "little aching heart with her tiny fist in the dark," and praying through her tears "to 'dear, kind God' to protect her" (4.124–25). He also tells of an eight-year-old serf-boy, "in the darkest days of serfdom," who accidentally injures one of his master's hunting dogs while throwing stones in play. The master, a former army general, then assembles all his serfs and retainers early the next morning.

The servants are summoned for their edification, and in front of them all stands the mother of the child. The child is brought from the lock-up. It's a gloomy, cold, foggy autumn day, a capital day for hunting. The general orders the child to be undressed; the child is stripped naked. He shivers, numb with terror, not daring to cry. . . . "Make him run," commands the general. "Run! run!" shout

---

12. Nietzsche suggests this experiment in *Thus Spoke Zarathustra* (1883–1886). Marcus's remark appears in his *Meditations*, Book 7, no. 16. Similarly, many philosophers have thought to ask whether we would consent to live our own lives over again, a question they pose as a way of determining whether we think our lives to have been worthwhile. (Hume, for example, asks this in his *Dialogues Concerning Natural Religion* [posthumous, 1779], Part 10.) Still, I am inclined to think that this further statement of the issue is misconceived. A life might well be worth living even if one would decline to repeat it; some things are perhaps worth doing only once.

13. *The Brothers Karamazov*, trans. Constance Garnett, Great Books of the Western World, volume 52 (Chicago: Encyclopaedia Britannica, 1952), Book 5, chap. 4, 124. Subsequent quotations come from the same book. References are to chapter and page number.

the dog-boys. The boy runs. . . . "At him!" yells the general, and he sets the whole pack of hounds on the child. The hounds catch him, and tear him to pieces before his mother's eyes. . . . I believe the general was afterwards declared incapable of administering his estates. (4.125)

Dostoyevsky would remind us that such incidents are not merely contrived; similar things happen somewhere in the world every day.

Then Ivan makes his point:

I am a bug and I recognize in all humility that I cannot understand why the world is arranged as it is. Men are themselves to blame, I suppose; they were given paradise, they wanted freedom, and stole fire from heaven, though they knew they would become unhappy, so there is no need to pity them. . . . But then there are the children, and what am I to do about them? . . . I've only taken the children, because in their case what I mean is so unanswerably clear. . . . If it is really true that they must share responsibility for all their fathers' crimes, such a truth is not of this world and is beyond my comprehension. Some jester will say, perhaps, that the child would have grown up and have sinned, but you see he didn't grow up, he was torn to pieces by dogs, at eight years old. Oh, Alyosha, I am not blaspheming! I understand, of course, what an upheaval of the universe it will be when everything in heaven and earth blends in one hymn of praise and everything that lives and has lived cries aloud: "Thou art just, O Lord, for Thy ways are revealed." When the mother embraces the fiend who threw her child to the dogs and all three cry aloud with tears, "Thou art just, O Lord!" then, of course, the crown of knowledge will be reached and all will be made clear. But what pulls me up here is that I can't accept that harmony . . . if the sufferings of children go to swell the sum of sufferings which was necessary to pay for truth, then I protest that the truth is not worth such a price. (4.125–26)

Ivan reduces the whole problem once more to a single question:

I challenge you—answer. Imagine that you are creating a fabric of human destiny with the object of making men happy in the end, giving them peace and rest at last, but that it was essential and inevitable to torture to death only one tiny creature—that baby beating its breast with its fist, for instance—and to found that edifice on its unavenged tears, would you consent to be the architect on those conditions? Tell me, and tell the truth. (4.126–27)

Alyosha replies no. Ivan then poses one more question:

And can you admit the idea that men for whom you are building it would agree to accept their happiness on the foundation of the unexpiated blood of a little victim? And accepting it would remain happy forever? (4.127)

Again, Alyosha says no. In Ivan's view, God's ends, whatever they are, cannot possibly justify the means. Ivan is quite willing to admit that God is working in mysterious ways to achieve a wonderful result, but he adds, "I hasten to return my ticket" (4.126). In Ivan's view, no man or woman of honor would stoop to accept it.

Ivan's complaint is not only against an omnipotent god, but even a feeble one, since no god, in his view, should have created a world in which children suffer as they do. His attack recalls, once more, the lament of King Lear, upon discovering that his daughter Cordelia has been hanged.

> Why should a dog, a horse, a rat, have life,
> And thou no breath at all? (5.3.308–9)

But consider for a moment the other side of the problem.

Suppose, for a moment, there was *no* suffering. Suppose not only that the most egregious instances of suffering were eliminated; suppose that all suffering everywhere was abolished, so that all beings felt nothing but intense and continuous joy. Is it really so obvious that the world would be better? A ridiculous question, perhaps, but how could there be courage without danger? How could there be integrity without the chance to do wrong? How could there be nobility of character without moral dilemmas and moral uncertainty? Instead, life might reduce to something very like Plato's old experiment of the oyster (the experiment suggested in his *Philebus*), in which experience is entirely blissful (the bliss of a contented oyster at the bottom of the sea) but drained of all significance. Is it really so obvious that the world as a whole would be improved? Indeed, some people argue that the whole worth of morality, as something embraced for its own sake, seems to increase with the evil to which it is opposed. Those who have endured calamity sometimes make this point: the experience, they say, has given their lives new significance, depending on how they have handled it.

A similar question might also be posed about religious doubt. If there really is a god, then why does he permit us to doubt his existence? Suppose instead that the existence of an omnipotent and benevolent god was so obvious that no human being could ever doubt it. And suppose also that it was entirely self-evident that the just would be rewarded, the wicked punished, and the good triumphant. (Of course, many people assert that such propositions already are self-evident, but I think it is possible to imagine more conspicuous proofs. God might speak to us in thunder from heaven, for example, or provide a "pillar of smoke by day and a pillar of fire by night," as in Scripture.) If the supremacy of God's justice were entirely obvious and beyond all doubt, would true integrity still be possible? Would anyone still do right because it was right, or would everything be done for the sake of rewards?

Dostoyevsky comes around to much the same point later in his novel, in a chapter titled "The Grand Inquisitor," where a cardinal in sixteenth-century

Spain believes himself to be speaking to Christ. The cardinal says, "Thou didst choose all that is exceptional, vague, enigmatic" (5.132). The cardinal believes that God has made the world deliberately ambiguous, because real morality is enacted against a background of doubt, anguish, and dread.

What, then, are we to make of such thinking? If sound, the underlying point seems simple enough: It is easy to imagine how to improve the world in small ways, but not nearly so easy to improve it in large ways. To eliminate particular instances of suffering and wickedness is an obvious duty, but to eliminate them *in general* might actually make the universe worse. Yet the trouble is neither can exist in general unless it also exists in particular. Perhaps, then, all we can do is suggest minor improvements—important but small ameliorations of our earthly condition. And thus the whole problem of theodicy, as many writers have said from the start, may well be unfathomable after all.

Suffering and wickedness lie at the heart of the problem, and I have by no means exhausted all that can be said about them. Still, the question is also connected with three other classical issues, which are also worth considering: 1) the problem of free will, 2) the problem of blind faith, and 3) the problem of divine punishment. So I shall say a word about these, too.

Many philosophers, such as Augustine, believe that morality requires free will, and what they mean is that not all our actions are determined. Instead, some of our behavior is simply chosen. So, if God is to give us the freedom to choose goodness, they say, then God must also give us the freedom to choose wickedness. The whole idea of free will is, of course, highly controversial, and many determinists not only will say that all events in the world are "necessitated" (as Thomas Hobbes puts it) but that the freedom of the will is really nothing more than "the absence of external impediments." (I use Hobbes's phrasing again [*Leviathan*, chap. 21, 261].) Thus, to call a person free is only to say that he is not in chains or at gunpoint. But can either of these views, free will or determinism, be proved? Many arguments have been offered on both sides, but probably the most subtle analysis is Kant's.

Kant insists that morality is possible only if the will is indeed free, and in calling it free, he means that your behavior cannot be entirely determined, either by heredity or environment. (Of course, *much* of your behavior is determined. Your behavior would be substantially different if you had been born, say, with the body of a dog. But your behavior cannot be *entirely* determined, says Kant—not unless a true act of conscience is then impossible.) Thus, Kant asserts that the ideas of morality and determinism are logically incompatible. And here, perhaps, is a way to test his claim.

Think for a moment about an act of conscience. Think of yourself as trying to do the right thing not merely because it is personally pleasing, but because it is right. Or put another way, imagine yourself trying to be conscientious. But then imagine yourself saying this: "I will do this thing, not because I particularly *want* to, but because I ought to, because it is right, because it is my duty—yet I realize that I will really do it only because my heredity or upbringing force me to." In Kant's view, this statement not only is false; it is incoherent, a "contradiction." Why? Because you can easily think of yourself as performing a true act of conscience, or you can think of yourself as merely reacting to biological and environmental causes. But what you *cannot* do is think of yourself in both ways at once. To act from duty is to act in the conviction that you are indeed free from impulse—at least in this one action. For Kant, the whole sense of duty carries with it the feeling that you are free to do otherwise.

Strangely, Kant never asserts that the freedom of the will can be proved. To the contrary, he says the freedom of the will can only be *assumed*, and indeed he thinks it *must* be assumed whenever we believe ourselves to be acting from conscience. On the other hand, he also says that the opposing view (causal determinism) must also be assumed, whenever we wish to understand our behavior scientifically. His doctrine is at first bewildering, but in some ways it is really quite shrewd.

Throughout, he is talking not about observed facts but about assumptions. According to Kant, the proposition that every event has a cause, or that all events are entirely determined by causal laws, is at best only an assumption necessary for scientific explanation but never physically observable. We never really *see* that every event has a cause. All we see is change. Causation in itself is entirely abstract. Causation as such has no particular color, smell, taste, feel, or sound, and it is thus completely imperceivable. Instead, we *presuppose* that every event has a cause. (It would be most odd, in asking a doctor about the cause of one's symptoms, to be told, "There is no cause; this time your symptoms are merely uncaused events.") Thus, Kant says both assumptions are necessary—causality for a scientific understanding of the world and freedom for our conduct in it—yet he also concedes that the two assumptions apparently contradict. How, then, can we "assume" both?

His answer sounds once more like an appeal to the unfathomable. He says we can never see so deeply into nature to know whether the freedom of the will is really incompatible with the apparent determinism of the physical world. All we really see are things as they appear to us ("phenomena"), but this need not be things as they really are ("noumena"). Appearance may still differ from reality. And so, things as they really are (the "noumenal world") may yet allow room for our freedom in a way that is exempt from causal law. Such is the argument in the last section of his *Groundwork of the Metaphysics of Morals*.

Thus, Kant has ended once more with something like mystery, or something like faith, or perhaps faith tinged with doubt. And maybe the whole problem of theodicy can only end in much the same way. What else can be expected from such a collection of imponderables, except mystery or faith?

Still, an appeal to faith usually raises a further, troubling question: Is it *ever* rational to believe in something merely on faith? (For example, "I believe that the planet Mars has two moons—merely on faith.") Many atrocities have been committed in the name of faith; in allowing room for faith, do we not therefore open the door to fanaticism? Let me illustrate this same question with my personal case.

However foolishly, I have long believed that I have been individually spared and unknowingly guided, on many occasions and along with many other people, by something like divine Providence. But I can give absolutely no justification for this view, and I can give no guarantee that the belief will endure. I can only say that I have had it for a long time. Is this belief irrational?

Sigmund Freud considers this same problem in his book *The Future of an Illusion*, where he says that such feelings are only the fulfillments of wishes:

> They are illusions, fulfillments of the oldest, strongest and most urgent wishes of mankind. The secret of their strength lies in the strength of those wishes. As we already know, the terrifying impression of helplessness in childhood aroused the need for protection—for protection through love—which was provided by the father, and the recognition that this helplessness lasts throughout life made it necessary to cling to the existence of a father, but this time a more powerful one. Thus the benevolent rule of a divine Providence allays our fear of the dangers of life; the establishment of a moral world-order ensures the fulfillment of the demands of justice, which have so often remained unfulfilled in human civilizations; and the prolongation of earthly existence in a future life provides the local and temporal framework in which these wish-fulfillments shall take place.[14]

In Freud's view, the god (or gods) of theism is only a projection of the loving parent upon the heavens. Religion in general is only a prolonging, in imagination, of the ordered life that one's parents supply. It is quite possible, to be sure, that the mechanism Freud identifies as the cause of religion is indeed part of the creator's plan, so that the relation between parent and child is a sort of training ground for the relation between god and mortal (and Freud implicitly concedes this point when he says, later in his book, that wish-fulfillments may yet be true). Still, Freud also supposes that once this mechanism is made known, our religious feelings will start to dissipate.

> We know approximately at what periods and by what kind of men religious doctrines were created. If in addition we discover the motives which led to this,

---

14. *The Future of an Illusion*, trans. James Strachey (New York: W. W. Norton and Company, 1989), chap. 6, 38.

our attitude to the problem of religion will undergo a marked displacement. (Chap. 6, 42)

That is, our religious feelings will diminish.

The trouble, I think, lies in this last claim. In my own case, for example, I have long been aware of Freud's explanation, yet I have never perceived in consequence the slightest diminution in my religious feelings, and I know that the same is true of many other people. More generally, Freud's account has been widely known for more than half a century, but religious sentiment as such seems to betray no worldwide decline, either among the literate or illiterate.

It can also be argued that religious faith is morally wrong on the grounds that it corrupts the intellect, or even that it is a sort of blemish on the enlightened mind, and is, therefore, as it were, aesthetically displeasing. At times, Freud seems to embrace these assertions also:

> Just as no one can be forced to believe, so no one can be forced to disbelieve. But do not let us be satisfied with deceiving ourselves that arguments like these take us along the road of correct thinking. If ever there was a case of a lame excuse we have it here. Ignorance is ignorance; no right to believe anything can be derived from it. (Chap. 6, 41)

Or again, as he remarks in his *Civilization and Its Discontents*,

> The whole thing is so patently infantile, so foreign to reality, that to anyone with a friendly attitude to humanity it is painful to think that the great majority of mortals will never be able to rise above this view of life. It is still more humiliating to discover how large a number of people living today, who cannot but see that this religion is not tenable, nevertheless try to defend it piece by piece in a series of pitiful rearguard actions.[15]

There is, I suppose, a certain intemperance in Freud's phrasing, but that aside, he expresses a common complaint against religious faith—that it is unfounded and childish. Still, the reply of his critics is not hard to see. That faith in God or in the goodness of the world is founded on "ignorance," they may readily concede; faith, by definition, is not knowledge. But why do they need a "right" to entertain it? One simply entertains faith as one entertains hope, and that is all. Put another way, why suppose that this sort of faith needs justifying in the first place? The theist can allow that his faith is unfounded, yet still ask why this circumstance should count as an intellectual defect. *Other* beliefs, if unfounded, count as defects, but this is very far from showing that *any* belief, if unfounded,

---

15. *Civilization and Its Discontents*, trans. James Strachey (New York: W. W. Norton and Company, 1961), chap. 2, 21.

is a defect.[16] Of course, there is also the issue of whether a circumspect faith damages one's intelligence, but here the appropriate question would be whether this effect can be empirically demonstrated. (If there is indeed any scientific evidence of this effect, I must say that I am personally unaware of it.) Nor does the spectacle of religious belief strike everyone as particularly ugly or humiliating, though perhaps there is no accounting for tastes.

In any event, Freud does seem to agree with many religious writers on at least one other point, and this is the last of the larger matters I mean to describe. Freud thinks the great appeal of an afterlife is that it seems to allow for a moral reckoning, to satisfy, in Freud's phrase, the "demands of justice." And many different reckonings have been imagined. How indeed *should* a merciful god punish the wicked and reward the just?

The Book of Job, it should be noted, places no special emphasis on an afterlife, and it is a misreading of the text to suppose that Job expects God to make things up to him in *Sheol*, the netherworld, which is at best only a shadowy underworld like the Greek *Hades*. Job wants justice in this world, not the next. But the demand for justice also animates many other classics, and among them is a particularly interesting meditation from the sixth century A.D., by the Roman Senator Anicius Boethius, called *The Consolation of Philosophy*. Let me say a word about this old and passionate discourse.

Boethius had been a child prodigy in Rome in an age of great turmoil and disaster, and he eventually became one of the ancient world's leading scholars. He produced Latin translations of Aristotle, Porphyry, Euclid, and Archimedes; coined the term "quadrivium"; wrote five works of his own on logic; and composed a treatise on music that was still in use at Oxford University as late as the eighteenth century. His great ambition was to demonstrate the essential harmony of the philosophies of Plato and Aristotle, but shortly before the age of thirty, he was called by his king to serve the state.

Theodoric, king of the Ostrogoths, appointed Boethius to a series of important posts. He rose to become Roman consul, then head of the civil service. Finally, his happiest day came at the age of forty-two, when both of his sons were made consuls jointly, and Boethius himself then delivered an address to the king before the Roman Senate. Soon afterward, however, he was arrested on a charge of treason. Though Boethius was Roman by birth, the military regime he served consisted of Germanic Goths, who had only recently conquered the Western Roman Empire. And Boethius was also an orthodox Christian, like most Romans of his time, whereas most Goths were Arian Christians (a difference that is now nearly impossible to explain). And to a king growing increasingly paranoid, these facts made Boethius automatically suspect. Boethius was impris-

---

16. Another way to put this reply is to say that Freud assumes a conception of rationality that some theists will dispute from the start.

oned at Pavia, near Milan, and he probably knew early on that he would never leave prison alive. Nevertheless, where other men might only have bewailed such a fate, Boethius chose instead to make art of it, and the result, his *Consolation*, tries to consider his predicament from several points of view.

He imagines that he is visited in prison by the "goddess of philosophy."[17] She is immensely tall and appears before him in an imperishable robe, though of fabric "obscured by the dust of long neglect." Small bits of fabric have also been torn from her garment in several places, and she explains to him that, after the days of Socrates and Plato, various philosophical schools, like "mobs," had each torn off little pieces of the cloth in the mistaken belief that they had thereby obtained "the whole of philosophy." She comes to his cell, she says, because she has heard that one of her true servants (Boethius himself) is in trouble. And so he pours out his sorrows to her.

He had taken philosophy seriously, he tells her, and believed in the warning of Plato's *Republic* that the penalty for good men and women who refuse to participate in government is to be ruled by people worse than themselves. When only a scholar, he had been happy, and he and the goddess had often traced together the paths of the planets and had discussed numerous philosophical mysteries. But once in government, his honesty was rewarded with hatred. Evil men conspired against him. And ultimately even the Senate had left him to die, though most of the senators knew perfectly well that he was innocent. Boethius remarks, "I seem to see the wicked haunts of criminals overflowing with happiness and joy" (Book 1, 46).

The goddess replies, if he dies, he will not be the first of her martyrs. Socrates faced death bravely, as did Seneca, who was ordered by the Emperor Nero to commit suicide. (Today, we might also think once more of Thomas More, or again, of Cicero, whose head and hands were cut off on the order of the Roman general Marc Antony.) The goddess reminds Boethius of the many blessings in his life: his wife, his sons, his once splendid position. "There is no one who would not have called you the luckiest man in the world," she says. "In my opinion, you beguiled Fortune." Indeed, he has achieved more in a few brief years than nearly anyone else achieves in a lifetime. How, then, can he complain now? Fortune is like a wheel, she explains, and those who ride this wheel to the top must also be ready to ride it to the bottom. Yes, says Boethius, all this is true. And yet, "In all adversity of fortune, the most wretched kind is once to have been happy" (Book 2, 59–61).

The goddess finally takes Boethius through a long series of complicated proofs (the exact logic of which I shall not try to analyze), but she eventually convinces him that evil is only the absence of goodness, that wickedness is a

---

17. *The Consolation of Philosophy*, trans. V. E. Watts (1969; reprint, Harmondsworth, England: Penguin Books, 1984), Book 1, 36–39.

kind of nothingness, and that consequently the souls of the wicked tend toward nonexistence. (This last doctrine may sound bizarre, but it expresses an old and recurring theme in moral philosophy—that one's sense of self is strongest when one acts from conscience; to act from appetite, and only from appetite, is to feel less like a person, more like a thing.) Among the wise, says the goddess, there is no place for hatred, and she ultimately leads Boethius to feel pity for his betrayers instead of despising them.

Boethius was executed in prison about a year after his arrest, and King Theodoric, embittered, died about two years later, after first executing the Pope.

The desire for a moral reckoning is strong, widespread, and perhaps automatic, and the great challenge, of course, is to prevent it from degenerating into mere bitterness. Yet there is one further vision of divine justice that I would also like to mention, because I find it especially interesting, and because personally I happen to like it best. It comes from Charles Dickens's charming little meditation on the meaning of a holiday, A Christmas Carol.

Christianity, like any other religion, can be exceedingly pedantic and exceedingly cruel, and Dickens knew this danger well. Just as patriotism is the last refuge of a scoundrel, so piety can be the special guise of brutality, venom, and deceit. Dickens makes this point with particular force in David Copperfield, where two adults, Edward and Jane Murdstone, abuse a young boy and rob his mother, while all the time enforcing the steely "Murdstone religion." The boy recalls the Murdstones at a church service:

> I listen to Miss Murdstone mumbling the responses, and emphasizing all the dread words with a cruel relish. Again, I see her dark eyes roll round the church when she says "miserable sinners," as if she were calling all the congregation names. Again, I catch rare glimpses of my mother, moving her lips timidly between the two, with one of them muttering at each ear like low thunder.[18]

They beat the boy mercilessly, inherit his mother's property when she dies in childbirth, and then cut the boy adrift. The Murdstones call themselves Christians, but, of course, they are really just bullies.

Like all religions, however, Christianity doesn't need to be brutal at all, so Dickens set himself the task of finding its "real meaning," and the result is his tender little story about Christmas. Christianity contains many doctrines and elaborations, some quite complicated, and the same can be said of almost any other creed. But you can also ask, among all the complexities, what is most important? The question is much like the one posed to Jesus: Which of God's commandments is greatest? Just so, you can always ask, which tenets of Judaism are most important, which of Islam, which of Buddhism, and which of Hinduism?

---

18. David Copperfield (New York: New American Library, Signet, 1980), chap. 4, 62.

Dickens's *Christmas Carol* involves a similar question, because the whole effect of the story is to underscore some themes while discounting others. And two principal ideas then stand out. The first is compassion, which the story advances through the fate of a small crippled boy and the parents who struggle to save his life; the second is redemption, the faith that even a bad man, even an iniquitous one, can yet become good, and all in one night.

Yet Dickens has a vision of a moral reckoning, too—though a peculiar one. The ghost of Jacob Marley appears to his erstwhile business partner, Ebenezer Scrooge, and, of course, Marley carries about him a ponderous chain, "forged in life." But at another point in the story Marley suggests something quite different.[19] He opens a window and invites Scrooge to look out, where, in the swirling mist, Scrooge sees a woman without a home, who is struggling to shield her baby from the cold. Around her there is a swarm of phantoms, invisible to the woman herself, but plainly seen by Scrooge and Marley. And both Scrooge and Marley realize that some of the phantoms were once "men of business" like themselves. One phantom is still tied to a safe that it had owned in life. Others, perhaps "guilty governments," seem to be chained together. But all the phantoms are now in utter misery as they swarm about the woman, and Scrooge wonders why. Because, he soon discovers, the phantoms "seek at last to interfere for good in human matters, but have lost the power forever." And so Dickens's hell is really quite simple. Hell, in this sense, is nothing more than moral enlightenment, combined with the loss of our power to do anything with it. This is the sort of hell I would fancy, I suppose—moral enlightenment. But, of course, the whole point of the story is to remind us that, unlike the phantoms, we have not yet lost our power.

19. *A Christmas Carol* (New York: Simon and Schuster, Washington Square Press, 1970), Stave One, 56–57.

Appendix

Suggestions for Further Reading

FOR ANYONE SEEKING a further acquaintance with influential works of moral and political thought, I list, chronologically, some suggested readings. Most classics in the field are available in many good editions.

Thucydides, *History of the Peloponnesian War*, trans. Rex Warner (1954; reprint, London: Penguin Books, 1986). This detailed history can be condensed into the following abridgement: Book 1, 1–88, 118–25, and 139–46; Book 2, 1–65; Book 3, 1–85; Book 5, 84–116; Book 6, 8–52; Book 7, 59–87. (Selections are identified by the scholarly reference numbers that appear in the margins.)

Four of Plato's early dialogues, the *Euthyphro*, the *Apology*, the *Crito*, and the *Phaedo*, in *The Last Days of Socrates*, trans. Hugh Tredennick and Harold Tarrant (1954; reprint, New York: Penguin USA, 1995).

Plato, *The Republic*, trans. Richard W. Sterling and William C. Scott (New York: W. W. Norton, 1996).

Aristotle, *The Nicomachean Ethics*, trans. J. E. C. Welldon (Amherst, N.Y.: Prometheus Books, 1987); and the *Politics*, trans. T. A. Sinclair (1962; revised, reprint, New York: Penguin USA, Viking, 1992), especially Books 1 through 3. Because Aristotle's treatises seem to derive from mere lecture notes, a commentary is often useful, such as Sir David Ross's *Aristotle*, 6th ed. (New York: Routledge, 1995).

Epictetus, *Encheiridion* in *Epictetus*, volume 2, trans. W. A. Oldfather (1928; reprint, Loeb Classical Library, 1996); or Marcus Aurelius, *Meditations*, trans. Maxwell Staniforth (1964; reprint, New York: Penguin, USA, Viking, 1987).

Aquinas, whose ethical and political views are often available in separate collections, such as *St. Thomas Aquinas on Politics and Ethics*, ed. Paul E. Sigmund (New York: W. W. Norton and Company, 1988).

Machiavelli, *The Prince* in *The Prince and the Discourses*, trans. Luigi Ricci (New York: Modern Library, 1950).

More, Thomas, *Utopia*, trans. Robert M. Adams (New York: W. W. Norton and Company, 1975).

Hobbes, *Leviathan*, ed. C. B. Macpherson (1968; reprint, New York: Penguin USA, Viking, 1982), Parts 1 and 2.

Locke, *The Second Treatise of Government*, ed. C. B. Macpherson (Indianapolis: Hackett, 1980).

Rousseau, *The Social Contract*, trans. Maurice Cranston (1968; reprint, New York: Penguin USA, 1987).

Smith, Adam, *An Inquiry into the Nature and Causes of the Wealth of Nations*, ed. Edwin Cannan (New York: Modern Library, 1937), Book 1, chaps. 1 through 9 and the conclusion of 11; Book 4, chap. 2.

Paine, Thomas, *Common Sense*, ed. Isaac Kramnick (1976; reprint, London: Penguin Books, 1986).

Kant, *Foundations of the Metaphysics of Morals*, trans. Lewis White Beck, 2nd ed. (New York: Macmillan, 1989), also known as the *Groundwork of the Metaphysics of Morals*.

Burke, Edmund, *Reflections on the Revolution in France*, ed. Conor Cruise O'Brien (1968; reprint, London: Penguin Books, 1986).

Tocqueville, *Democracy in America*, ed. Phillips Bradley (1945, reprint, New York: Alfred A. Knopf, 1993). Also available in useful abridgements, such as *Democracy in America*, ed. Richard Heffner (New York: Penguin Books, Mentor, 1984).

Narrative of the Life of Frederick Douglass: An American Slave, Written by Himself, ed. David W. Blight (New York: St. Martin's Press, Bedford Books, 1993).

Marx and Engels, whose works appear in many anthologies, such as Robert Tucker, ed., *The Marx-Engels Reader*, 2nd ed. (New York: W. W. Norton and Company, 1978).

Mill, John Stuart, *On Liberty*, ed. Gertrude Himmelfarb (1974; reprint, London: Penguin Books, 1985).

King, Martin Luther Jr., *Letter from Birmingham Jail* in *Why We Can't Wait* (1964; reprint, New York: New American Library, 1991).

The reader interested in the connection between morality and clear expression may also wish to consult George Orwell's seminal essay, "Politics and the English Language," included in his *Collection of Essays* (1953; reprint, New York: Harcourt Brace Jovanovich, 1970).

Index

Panzón levantó un pequeño tubo° dorado.°

—¡Caramba, Panzón!— replicó Pepino. —Te he dicho mil veces que no se debe tocar nada. A lo mejor ' huellas digitales,° pero si metes tus mano⁵ borrarás todo.

—Perdóneme jefe.— Panzón parecía com a llorar.

—Bueno, no importa. Búscame mi lupa y unos . Los dejé por allá, cerca del esqueleto del dinosaur Y diciendo esto Pepino tomó el objeto que Panzón había recogido, manchándolo aún más. Lo examinó.

—Miremos. ¿Qué es lo que tenemos aquí? Parece ser un estuche. Pero qué cosa más rara. Adentro hay otro tubito, sólo que éste es rojo y pegajoso.° ¿Será sangre? ¿O tinta mágica? ¿O quizá es una carta secreta?

—No, jefe— explicó Panzón, regresando con la lupa.

—Eso es lo que usan las mujeres para pintarse los labios. Se llama un lápiz labial.°

—Ah sí. Claro. (Pepino estaba un poco avergonzado de haber olvidado algo tan típicamente femenino.) Ya puedo imaginarme a la mujer que usaba este lápiz labial. Una mujer bella, joven, una de esas mujeres que siempre se enamoran de mí y . . .

—Sí, jefe, ¿pero qué tiene eso que ver con el robo de la momia?

—Pues eso es lo que tenemos que averiguar. ¿Para qué crees que somos investigadores privados? Bueno, a trabajar. Vete por ese lado, por donde queda la pirámide en miniatura, y ve si los ladrones dejaron otra cosa. Yo te esperaré aquí. Tengo que pensar. Es muy importante pensar. Sherlock Holmes decía siempre que . . .

—Sí, jefe, ya voy— dijo Panzón muy acostumbrado a lo que dijo Sherlock Holmes.

Mientras que Panzón buscaba detrás de los mapas y los cuadros° del antiguo México y mientras que buscaba bajo las vidrieras llenas de trajes típicos y artefactos primitivos, Pepino se paró en el centro

tubo, ' *do* ·

pegajoso, sticky

lápiz labial, lipstick

cuadros, pictures

15

del museo. Estaba pensando. El museo quedó en silencio· Pero era un silencio extraño. Pepino no se sentía bien. Miró alrededor de la sala, pero sólo vio a Panzón arrodillado° bajo una mesa cubierta con adornos y jarros de plata.

arrodillado, on his knees

—¡Qué extraño! Estoy seguro de que alguien nos está observando— pensó Pepino. —¿Quién puede ser? El señor Delgado nos dijo que habían cerrado esta sala después del robo y que nadie podía entrar sin la llave especial.

Pepino estaba perdido en sus pensamientos. No se dio cuenta de que Panzón había terminado de revisar la sala y que ahora estaba parado detrás de él.

—No encontré nada jefe— dijo con una voz resonante.°

resonante, loud

—¡Ay!— exclamó Pepino, brincando del susto al oír la voz de Panzón tan cerca. —Te he dicho mil veces que no debes venir a la sordina.° Bueno, vámonos de aquí. Esta sala me pone nervioso. Además creo que hemos hecho todo lo que hay que hacer.

a la sordina, without noise

16

5. ¡Ayúdame por favor!

Pepino y su ayudante fiel salieron del gran Museo de Antropología. Era una tarde hermosa. Los pájaros cantaban y el sol brillaba. Sin embargo° Pepino continuó con la impresión de que todo no estaba bien.

—Oye, Panzón— dijo en voz baja. —Creo que nos siguen.

—¿Quién, jefe? ¿La momia?— dijo **Panzón** sorprendido y un poco confuso.

—¡No seas tonto! ¿Cómo nos va a seguir la momia de alguien que murió hace siglos? Tengo una idea. Entremos al zoológico aquí enfrente y veremos si nos siguen allí también.

En la Avenida de la Reforma entre los turistas y un grupo de estudiantes Pepino y Panzón esperaban poder cruzar la calle. Los automóviles y los camiones pasaban a toda prisa. Era la hora de mayor tránsito en la ciudad de México. Esto significa que todo el mundo conduce a velocidades de 100 kilómetros por hora. De repente° Panzón recibió un violento empujón° que casi lo tira a media calle, en pleno camino de los coches. Pepino lo agarró en el último momento.

—¿Pero, qué haces? ¡Te has vuelto loco!— le gritó.

—No, jefe— dijo Panzón temblando —alguien me empujó.

Los dos investigadores miraron por todos lados. No vieron nada sospechoso. Sólo estaban los turistas y los

sin embargo, nevertheless

de repente, all of a sudden
empujón, push

17

estudiantes inocentes.

—No entiendo por qué me empujaron— dijo Panzón, con voz todavía llena de miedo. —¡Alguien trató de matarme!

Cruzaron la calle con mucho cuidado y entraron al zoológico. Panzón temblaba menos, pero los dos hombres no estaban tranquilos. Miraron a los pájaros exóticos y a los leones sin mucho interés. Panzón compró una bolsa de cacahuates,° luego fueron a ver a los osos. Comenzaba a sentirse mejor, pero Pepino pensaba todavía en la escapada difícil:°

—¡De milagro que te agarré! Si yo no hubiera estado allí . . . .Claro— continuó, súbitamente dándose cuenta de su heroísmo, —yo estoy siempre alerta. Pero qué lástima que no hubiera un fotógrafo para que todo el mundo pudiera darse cuenta de mi valor y mi . . .

—Mira a esos monos jugando en la jaula ° —dijo Panzón entre risas. —¡Y qué chistoso° se ve el elefante!

Caminaron un rato más hasta que Pepino estaba seguro de que nadie les seguía. Hacía calor y Panzón tenía sed.°

—Tengo sed, jefe. Conozco un café donde podemos tomar un refresco. Sólo queda a dos pasos del parque de Chapultepec.

Llegando al café los dos hombres se sentaron en la sombra. Eran los únicos allí, algo que satisfizo a Pepino ahora que se daba cuenta de que el trabajo que hacían era peligroso. Vino el mesero.

—Una Carta Blanca por favor — pidió Pepino.

—Y yo — dijo Panzón, —quiero dos refrescos, uno de naranja, el otro de uva y un pan dulce y unos chocolates y unas papas fritas. ¡Tengo mucha hambre!

Pasaron unos momentos serenos. Oían las voces alegres de los niños jugando en la distancia y el sonido musical de la fuente cercana.° Pepino, pensando siempre en lo ocurrido, tuvo una inspiración:

—Oye Panzón. ¿Crees que quien te empujó tiene algo que ver con el robo de la momia? A lo mejor alguien

cacahuates, peanuts

escapada difícil, narrow escape

jaula, cage
chistoso, funny

sed, thirst

cercana, nearby

18

no quiere que busquemos a la momia. ¿Pero por qué? ¡Este caso es muy complicado!

—Y no olvide lo del lápiz labial— añadió Panzón, siempre muy astuto.

—Sí— dijo Pepino pensativo. —No sé por qué pero me dice mi nariz que allí está el secreto de todo. Cuando averigüemos a quien pertenece sabremos la verdad.

Pepino siguió hablando y Panzón siguió comiendo. Ninguno se dio cuenta de que ya no estaban solos. Alguien se acercaba sin hacer el menor ruido. Apareció una bella mujer, caminando muy de prisa. Estaba vestida de negro. Un sombrero ancho escondía su cara.

—Señor Pepino— dijo la señorita misteriosa con una voz dulce pero inquieta.° —¡Tiene que ayudarme!

Pepino se levantó con sorpresa:

—Con mucho gusto, señorita, con mucho gusto. ¿Qué es lo que podemos hacer?

La señorita miraba por todos lados, como si tuviera miedo de algo. En la distancia se oían unos pasos acercándose. La señorita misteriosa se puso más nerviosa.

—Nadie debe saber que estaba aquí. Tengo que irme. ¡Les ruego° no decir que me han visto!

Sin decir otra palabra la señorita misteriosa entregó un pedazo de papel a Pepino y caminó hacia el parque donde los árboles pronto la escondieron. Al instante en que desapareció, dos hombres entraron en el café. Vestidos con impermeables° y lentes oscuros y con un cigarro entre los dientes, no parecían muy amables.° Echaron una mirada rápida a Pepino y a Panzón y salieron sin decir ni una palabra.

—¡Chihuahua, jefe! ¿Se fijó en esos tipos? ¡Me dio miedo sólo verlos!

Pepino no le hizo mucho caso. Todavía pensaba en la señorita misteriosa. Estaba orgulloso. Se imaginaba que eran unos caballeros andantes° de los días anti-

inquieta, uneasy

les ruego, I beg you

impermeables, raincoats

amables, friendly

caballeros andantes, knights

19

guos que salvaban a las damas en peligro:

—Soy exactamente como ese Lancelot — dijo, —sólo que mejor. Soy audaz, valiente. Hasta te salvé la vida. ¡Y ahora esta señorita me escogió a mí, a Pepino González, para ayudarla! Vas a ver, Panzón, voy a llegar a ser tan famoso . . .

—¡Eh! Jefe, ¿qué fue lo que le dio la señorita?

—¡Ah sí! (Pepino regresó bruscamente de las nubes°.) Abrió el pedazo de papel. —Pero qué raro, son dos boletos para la corrida y una nota que dice solamente: "esta tarde en la plaza de toros".

nubes, clouds

6. A las cuatro de la tarde

Eran casi las cuatro de la tarde, hora en que empiezan siempre las corridas de toros. La calle frente a la Plaza de Toros se llenaba de aficionados, turistas, niños, vendedores, coches y camiones. Estaba tan llena que ni Pepino ni Panzón pudieron acercarse a la entrada. Todos empujaban en diferentes direcciones. Todos querían ver la corrida.

—¡Jefe! (La gente hacía tanta bulla° que Panzón tuvo que gritar.) ¿Por qué estamos aquí? ¿Qué tiene esto que ver con la momia que se robaron del museo?— Panzón se rascó la nariz, no entendía nada.

bulla, noise

—No seas tonto—contestó Pepino —ya te dije. Vamos a ayudar a la señorita misteriosa, la que . . . .— Pero el resto de su explicación se perdió en las exclamaciones del gentío:°

gentío, crowd

—¡Quiero cinco boletos!

—¡Helados! ¡Refrescos! ¡Tortas! ¡Cerveza!°

cerveza, beer

—¡Compre su programa! ¡Compre su programa!

—¡Mamá, mamá!— lloraban los niños perdidos.

—¡Cuánta confusión!— pensó Pepino.

Una señora muy gorda le pisó el pie a Panzón.

—¡¡Ay!!— gritó, enojadísimo.° —¡Es la tercera vez que me pisan el pie!°

enojadísimo, furious
me pisan el pie, they step on my foot

—¿Pero por qué habrá tanta gente hoy?— dijo Pepino. —Yo creía que sólo se iba a las corridas los domingos.

Un muchacho joven miró hacia ellos. Estaba vestido

muy a la moda,° con una corbata° ancha, pantalones rayados° y una camisa floreada.°

—¿No saben? ¡Hoy torea "el Valiente"!

—¿El quién?— preguntaron Pepino y Panzón a la vez.

—¡Pero cómo es que no han oído de él!— El joven de la camisa floreada los miró como si acabaran de llegar de otro mundo. —Es el torero más famoso de España y hoy es su última corrida, regresa esta noche a Madrid.

—Pues, qué bien que la señorita nos dio los boletos, si no, nunca hubiéramos entrado —dijo Panzón, siempre el más práctico.

Todos empujaban para adelante, hacia la entrada principal. Los que no consiguieron° boletos trataban de entrar secretamente, mientras otros, más astutos, vendían boletos ilegalmente a diez veces el precio original. Por fin los dos investigadores llegaron a sus a-sientos. Habían subido las escaleras hasta lo más alto. Los asientos estaban en pleno sol, al lado de una familia grande; la mamá, el papá, la abuela, cuatro hijos y un bebé que lloraba sin parar. La familia había traído un almuerzo enorme. Todos comían. Panzón miró con envidia a la torta del niño sentado junto a él.

—Jefe, tengo una hambre espantosa.° Voy a com-prarme algo para comer.

—Tú te vas a callar y te vas a quedar aquí. A lo mejor esa señorita nos está buscando. Le prometí que le ayudaríamos y no podemos romper nuestra promesa.

La corrida iba a empezar. Por el altavoz° se oía la música tradicional. Los toreros, vestidos del traje de luces,° los ayudantes y los picadores montados a caballo salieron en fila.° El público aplaudió con en-tusiasmo. En el centro de la arena estaba "el Valiente". Se inclinaba hacia la derecha y hacia la izquierda, saludando a los aficionados con la montera.° Era un

a la moda, stylishly
corbata, tie
rayados, striped
floreada, flowered

consiguieron, obtained

espantosa, frightful

altavoz, loudspeaker
traje de luces, the elaborate costume a bullfighter traditionally wears
en fila, in a row

montera, the bullfighter's hat

22

hombre presuntuoso. Tenía la mirada de alguien que no sabe sonreír. No parecía simpático. Al ver a los dos hombres que le seguían Panzón se quedó perplejo.

—Oye, jefe, creo que los vi en algún lado, hace muy poco. Sólo que no me acuerdo en dónde fue.

Pero Pepino no le había oído. Pensaba en otras cosas:

—¡Qué bonito ser famoso! Veremos si un día todos me aplaudirán así. Quizá cuando me elijan° el investigador del año . . .

Un toro entró corriendo en la arena. La corrida había comenzado. El primer torero no era muy diestro, movía la capa, pero el toro no hacía nada. El público chiflaba.° Algunos hasta echaron sombreros, cojines° y botellas para mostrar su disgusto. Todos esperaban a "el Valiente", todos menos Panzón. Panzón estaba aburrido.° Hacía calor y tenía ganas de dormir. Poco a poco sus ojos iban cerrándose. Pronto comenzó a roncar.°

elijan, elect

chiflaba, whistled

cojines, cushions

aburrido, bored

roncar, snore

7. El picador tiene miedo

Mientras Panzón tenía bellos sueños de pasteles, caramelos, helados y otras delicias, Pepino buscaba con los ojos a la señorita que necesitaba ayuda, la señorita tan bonita pero tan misteriosa. Estaban sentados en lo más alto y había mucha gente. ¡Sería difícil encontrar a su propia madre allí, mucho menos a una señorita que apenas° había visto una vez! Comenzó a pensar sobre el caso en que trabajaban:

apenas, scarcely

—Primero desaparece la momia del museo. Luego encontramos el lápiz labial y alguien trata de matar a Panzón. Después esta señorita nos pide ayuda. Y ahora estamos aquí. No sé por qué pero algo me huele° mal. A lo mejor todo fue un truco° para que no encontráramos a la momia. Tendremos que proseguir° con mucho cuidado.

huele, smells
truco, trick
proseguir, advance

Pepino iba a despertar a Panzón y contarle su nueva idea cuando fijó la mirada en la primera fila. Allá abajo estaba sentada la señorita. La distancia entre ellos era bastante grande y Pepino no podía verla muy bien. Pero estaba seguro de que era ella. Se levantó. Sacudió° a Panzón:

sacudió, shook

—Ahora regreso. Voy en busca de la señorita.

Pero Panzón siguió durmiendo. ¡Era necesario hacer más que sacudir a Panzón para despertarlo!

La primera corrida terminó. No había sido buena. El torero era demasiado inexperto y el toro demasiado tranquilo. El público esperaba con impaciencia. Pronto iba a salir "el Valiente".

Pepino bajó las escaleras de dos en dos, tropezando°

tropezando, tripping

24

varias veces con los vendedores de cerveza y tamales.
Llegó a la primera fila° pero no podía encontrar a la *fila*, row
señorita. Ya no estaba allí. Pepino iba a regresar a su
asiento cuando un hombre lo agarró° del brazo: *agarró,* grabbed
—¿Dónde andabas Manuel?— dijo con una voz ame- *amenazadora,* threatening
nazadora.° Ya es hora de que te vistas. Ven, te estába-
mos esperando.
    Pepino lo miró con asombro:° *asombro,* astonishment
—¿Cómo? Pero yo no soy. . . .
    Pero el hombre no le dejó terminar. Sin soltarle° el *sin soltarle,* without letting go of him
brazo halaba al pobre de Pepino hacia la empalizada° *empalizada,* fence
que rodeaba la arena.
—Anda, apúrate— decía el hombre feroz. —Se nos
hace tarde.
    Y los dos hombres entraron por una puerta cerca del
toril.° *toril,* where the bulls are kept
    Varios minutos habían pasado. El sol era menos
fuerte y la gente más animada. "El Valiente" domina-
ba la arena y todos gritaban "¡olé!". Era el momento
de los picadores. Panzón seguía durmiendo. De repente el público comenzó a reir. Todos fijaban su
atención en la arena riéndose más y más. El niño al
lado de Panzón le dio un codazo:° *codazo,* elbow
—¡Eh señor! ¡Mire!
    Panzón abrió un ojo. Había olvidado donde estaba,
hasta había olvidado quien era. Pero el niño siguió
hablando y señalando hacia la arena:
—¡Mire! Allí está su amigo. ¡Qué chistoso se ve!
    Ahora Panzón estaba bien despierto. Se dio cuenta
de que su jefe ya no estaba a su lado y que el público
no se había dejado de reir. Al mirar hacia donde el
niño señalaba, abrió los ojos más. Allí a un lado de la
arena estaba Pepino, pero un Pepino muy asustado° *asustado,* frightened
y muy diferente. Vestido de picador, con una lanza
en la mano, estaba montado a caballo. Al otro lado
de la arena estaba el toro. Era obvio que ni Pepino
ni el toro sabían que ocurría y que dentro de unos
instantes el toro iba a investigar.

8. El coche azul

Pepino temblaba en el centro de la arena. El pobre trataba de no resbalarse° del caballo pero el esfuerzo° de mantener la lanza larga, guiar al caballo y estar lo más lejos posible del toro era demasiado, y cuando más se reía el público, se cayó del caballo dándose un golpe fuerte. El toro, muy curioso, se acercó para mejor observar a este señor tan extraño.

resbalarse, to slip
esfuerzo, effort

Pepino, al ver al toro tan cerca, dio un grito de alarma y se levantó de un solo brinco. El público se moría de risa. Era muy cómico ver a Pepino, con su traje de picador hecho pedazos,° corriendo en círculos mientras el toro, divirtiéndose enormemente, correteaba tras él. Panzón se tapó° los ojos. No quería ver más. Pero en ese momento el altavoz interrumpió:

hecho pedazos, in shreads

tapó, covered

—Señores y señoras, parece que hay una pequeña dificultad. Les rogamos° su paciencia. Dentro de unos instantes la corrida continuará.

les rogamos, we beg you

Varios empleados entraron a distraer° al toro. Alguien ayudó a Pepino a caminar hacia la salida. Salió el verdadero picador y la corrida recomenzó.

distraer, to distract

Minutos después Pepino, pálido y vestido otra vez de su ropa ordinaria, regresó a su asiento. Panzón, muy alegre de ver a su jefe sano° y salvo,° trató de averiguar lo que había pasado:

sano, healthy
salvo, safe

—¿Qué pasó? ¿Cómo llegó allí? ¿Por qué estaba vestido de picador? ¿Quién le hizo hacer eso? ¿Qué pasó?

—¡Qué miedo! ¡Qué miedo!— fue lo único que Pepino pudo responder. Pero al fin Pepino explicó:

—No sé mucho, sólo que un hombre me agarró y me llevó al cuarto de los toreros bajo las escaleras. Allí estaba "el Valiente" y dos otros. ¡Tenían pistolas! Me hicieron vestirme del traje de picador y después me montaron a caballo y después el toro y . . . .

Panzón estaba pensando:

—Jefe, yo creo que lo hicieron a propósito.° ¿No ve? Alguien quiso matarme y ahora le echan a usted frente a un toro. Todo eso de la señorita que necesita ayuda sólo fue una trampa.° *a propósito*, on purpose / *trampa*, trick

Pepino pensaba la misma cosa, sólo que no quería admitir que esa señorita tan bonita le había engañado. Pero sí admitió que algo muy raro estaba sucediendo. "El Valiente" acabó de torear. Había tenido mucho éxito, logrando las dos orejas y el rabo° del toro, uno de los honores más altos. Caminaba por la arena con las manos en alto. El público, loco de alegría, aplaudía y gritaba sin parar. Todos se habían olvidado del pequeño episodio del picador extraño, todos menos Pepino. El todavía sentía miedo de pensar en lo ocurrido. Tenía muchas ganas de estar lo más lejos posible de los toros. *rabo*, tail

—Vamos a la oficina— dijo. —Estoy bien cansado.

Los dos investigadores dejaron sus asientos. Salieron afuera a esperar el camión que pasaba frente a la Plaza. Pepino hablaba para sí:

—Pues en fin, no fui tan malo como picador. Ese traje me quedaba muy bien y tuve bastante destreza. ¿Te fijaste como mantuve la lanza? ¡A lo mejor me he equivocado de carrera!

—Pero jefe. . . .— Panzón iba a recordarle que un picador no debe tener miedo, cuando hubo un disturbio. Dos hombres con expresiones crueles arrastraban° a una mujer hacia un coche azul que esperaba enfrente de la salida. En el coche estaba otro hombre. *arrastraban*, dragged

—¡Ese es el hombre que me agarró!— dijo Pepino.

27

—¡Son los mismos tipos del café!— dijo **Panzón**.

—¡Esa es la señorita misteriosa!— dijeron los dos.

Tan preocupados estaban sosteniendo a la señorita que nadie había observado a Pepino y Panzón. La señorita comenzó a gritar:

—¡Suéltenme! No, no, yo no he hecho nada. Déjenme. ¡Auxilio!° ¡Auxilio!   *auxilio,* help

Los hombres la empujaron en el coche y en el momento en que cerraron la puerta el coche arrancó.°   *arrancó,* took off

—¿Qué vamos a hacer?— dijo Pepino, cuando llegó un taxi. Pepino y Panzón saltaron adentro:

—Siga ese coche azul. Es urgente.

El chofer volvió a mirarlos. Tenía una expresión aburridísima:

—¿Se cree el James Bond, eh?

—No. Hablamos en serio. —Pepino sacó su cartera.°   *cartera,* wallet

—¡Ah bueno, en ese caso vamos!

El taxi correteó tras el coche azul. Los dos coches iban muy de prisa. Pepino y Panzón estaban sentados a la orilla del asiento. Estaban demasiado preocupados para tener miedo. Se preguntaban con ansia:°   *con ansia,* anxiously

—¿Pero qué pasa? ¿Por qué la secuestran?° ¿Dónde   *secuestran,* kidnap
la llevan? ¿Podremos salvarla a tiempo?

9. La bella señorita misteriosa

Panzón se mordía las uñas.° Diez minutos habían ⟶ *uñas, fingernails*
pasado desde que la señorita misteriosa gritó "auxilio".
No había pasado nada. Los dos coches subían la
Avenida de los Insurgentes. Era difícil seguir el coche
azul. Insurgentes es una calle principal con mucho
tránsito y mucha policía. El chofer del taxi estaba
impaciente:

—Miren señores, no sé lo que ocurre, pero se acabó
el juego. Si continuamos a esta velocidad o me agarra° ⟶ *agarra, catch*
la policía o acabamos todos en el hospital. Además
hemos perdido el otro coche.

Era cierto. Había desaparecido. Pasaban coches por
todos lados pero el coche azul no estaba. Pepino estaba preocupado:

—Bueno, nos bajaremos aquí en la esquina.— Su voz
era triste.— ¡Tanto que quería ayudar a aquella señorita!
Es tan bonita, se decía y además estoy seguro de que
ella nos puede decir algo del robo del museo.

—¡Cómo, jefe! ¿Usted cree que ella se robó a la
momia?— Panzón le miró con curiosidad.

—No sé todavía— dijo Pepino. —Me gustaría pre-
guntarle algunas cosas. ¿Te has fijado° que cada vez ⟶ *fijado, noticed*
que la hemos encontrado, algo nos ha pasado?— Y
Pepino tembló. Todavía se acordaba del encuentro
con el toro.

El taxi los dejó en la Avenida de la Reforma

frente al monumento a Cuauhtémoc. Pepino estaba cansado y enojado. El taxi le había costado veinticinco pesos y no le quedaba ni un centavo. Todo había sido en vano. Ya era tarde y la calle estaba llena de gente que regresaba del trabajo. Panzón también estaba cansado. Tenía mucha hambre. Sólo quería ir a casa a descansar y a comer uno de los platos sabrosos que prepara su esposa. Caminaban lentamente en dirección de la oficina. Pepino tenía que cerrar las puertas y apagar° la luz. Pasaban hoteles, restaurantes, tiendas llenas de joyas y ropa elegante. Pero fue frente a una agencia de viajes que Pepino se paró. Miraba por la ventana de la agencia.

apagar, turn off

—¡Mira Panzón! Allí está el señor Delgado. ¿Pero qué hace dentro de una agencia de viajes?

Panzón le miró con asombro. Le parecía obvio:

—Pues está comprando un boleto de avión, jefe.

Pero Pepino movió la cabeza.

—Algo no me parece bien. El nos ha empleado° para encontrar a la momia, pero cada vez que he tratado de llamarle por teléfono nunca ha estado en el museo. Me parece que no le importa mucho si la encontramos o no.

empleado, hired

El señor Delgado venía hacia la puerta. Pepino y Panzón le esperaban afuera. En la mano llevaba un boleto de avión. Abrió la puerta y al ver a los dos investigadores dio un salto° hacia atrás. Se puso pálido.

salto, jump

—Pero ¿qué hacen ustedes aquí?— les preguntó con una voz nerviosa. Trataba de esconder el boleto de avión.

—Buenas tardes, señor— dijo Pepino. —Le vimos aquí adentro y como hemos tratado de llamarle toda la tarde pensábamos que sería bueno hablar con usted.

El señor Delgado había sacado su pañuelo perfumado. Se frotaba la frente. Estaba sudando° mucho.

sudando, perspiring

—Están equivocados.° Yo he estado en mi oficina todo el día y nadie me ha llamado.

equivocados, mistaken

Pepino estaba muy confuso. ¿Por qué le mentía el señor Delgado? El señor Delgado siguió frotándose° la frente y miró a Pepino con una expresión extraña:

—¿Han encontrado a la momia?

—No, todavía no— contestó Pepino. —Aunque sí hemos encontrado algunas huellas. En el museo encontramos un lápiz labial y . . .

Al oír esto el señor Delgado se puso muy animado. Hablaba para sí mismo:

—¡Lo sabía! Ella conoce el secreto de la momia. Si sólo pudiera encontrarla. En Madrid, sí, en Madrid todo se resolverá, fue allí donde comenzó.

Miró el boleto de avión y sin decir otra palabra comenzó a caminar en dirección contraria. Pepino y Panzón se miraron. ¿De qué hablaba el señor Delgado? ¡Qué señor más raro! Panzón se rascó la nariz:

—Oye, jefe, ¿cree que todos los funcionarios de los museos están locos como él?

—¿Quién sabe? Pero creo que hay muchas cosas que no nos ha dicho. Bueno— siguió Pepino. —Hemos tenido un día largo. Vete a tu casa y yo cerraré todo en la oficina.

—Gracias, jefe, y hasta mañana.— Panzón estaba muy feliz porque ya no tenía que trabajar más.

Cinco minutos más tarde Pepino llegó a la oficina. Subió las escaleras hasta el piso más alto donde estaba el pequeño despacho° y la placa sobre la puerta de la entrada anunciaba: "Investigaciones Privadas, S.A." Iba a abrir la puerta cuando vio una silueta. ¡Alguien estaba sentado adentro! ¿Sería un ladrón?° Pepino abrió la puerta con mucho cuidado. Pero al ver quien estaba allí se quedó con la boca abierta. Era ella, la señorita misteriosa. Vestida siempre de negro estaba más bella que nunca. Al ver a Pepino se levantó.

—¡Gracias a Dios que ha venido! No sé lo que debo hacer. Todos quieren matarme porque soy la única que sabe lo que le pasó a la momia. Sólo usted me puede ayudar.

frotando, wiping

despacho, office

ladrón, thief

31

Pepino estaba tan sorprendido de verla que todavía no se había enterado de lo que ella le decía.

—Siéntese, señorita, y cálmese. Le haré un poco de café y me lo puede contar todo.

—No tengo mucho tiempo— dijo la señorita con voz agitada.— Pronto se va a dar cuenta de que me escapé y mandará a sus hombres a buscarme. Pero antes le debo decir que me llamo Carmen del Valle. Soy de Madrid. Allí conocí al "Valiente". Fue él quien me obligó a participar en el robo de la momia.

Pepino se quedó mirándola. Aquellos ojos dramáticos y el perfume exótico le habían hipnotizado. Se había olvidado de todo, hasta de su promesa de preparar el café. Tan hipnotizado estaba que no había oído los pasos° en la escalera.° Alguien llegaba. Pero Pepino sólo tenía ojos para la señorita Carmen:

—No se preocupe señorita. Yo la ayudaré. Soy muy fuerte, soy audaz. No tenga miedo de nada y . . . .

La puerta se abrió con un ruido fuerte. Dos hombres entraron, uno de ellos apuntaba a° Pepino con una pistola. Pepino los reconoció.° Eran los mismos hombres feroces que Panzón había visto en el café y los mismos que habían llevado a la señorita Carmen en el coche azul. Al verlos Carmen dio un grito de susto° y se desmayó.° Pepino no sabía qué hacer. Trató de asistir a Carmen cuando sintió un golpe fuerte. Todo se volvió oscuro. La última cosa que recordó fue que unos toros, muchos toros venían corriendo hacia él.

pasos, footsteps
escalera, staircase

apuntaba a, pointed at

los reconoció, recognized them

susto, fright
se desmayó, fainted

32

10. Los investigadores van a Madrid

Era una mañana hermosa. Apenas° eran las ocho y ya brillaba el sol. El aire era fresco y dulce y Panzón, caminando las últimas cuadras hacia la oficina, se sentía feliz. Había dormido bien, había comido un enorme desayuno y ahora estaba silbando.° Miraba a unos niños jugando en la banqueta° con una pelota y pensó:

—¡Qué bonito ser joven y poder jugar todo el día!

El día anterior había sido un día muy largo y complicado. Panzón esperaba que el día de hoy no tendría que trabajar tanto.

—A lo mejor ya han encontrado a la momia— se dijo.—Y entonces podremos regresar a lo que hacíamos antes: buscar a los perros perdidos y ayudar a los turistas. En fin — admitió —no me gusta el trabajo, sobre todo el trabajo que suele ser° peligroso.

Panzón llegó a la oficina. En frente Lupe, una señora gorda y vieja, barría° las escaleras. Cada mañana Lupe limpiaba el edificio. Lupe estaba vestida con el mismo delantal° verde que había llevado desde que Panzón la conoció. Aunque no trabajaba muy rápidamente ni limpiaba muy bien, era bastante inteligente. Había ayudado a los investigadores varias veces en el pasado. Sonrió a Panzón, mostrando que le faltaban algunos dientes, y le saludó:

apenas, hardly

silbando, whistling

banqueta, sidewalk

suele ser, tends to be

barría, was sweeping

delantal, apron

33

—Buenos días, señor Panzón. ¡Estaría trabajando sobre un caso muy importante porque las luces todavía están prendidas en su oficina! ¿De qué se trata esta vez?

—Luego te cuento todo, Lupe— dijo Panzón y subió las escaleras de dos en dos. Panzón estaba sorprendido. El jefe nunca se olvida de apagar las luces.

—A lo mejor se levantó temprano— pensó Panzón. Pero eso también sería curioso. El jefe nunca se despierta antes de las diez. ¿Pasará algo?— Llegando al piso más alto trató de abrir la puerta. Estaba cerrada.° Buscaba su llave cuando oyó un ruido extraño. Panzón pausó.

cerrada, closed

—¡Qué fue eso! ¿Quién estaba allí?

Abrió la puerta y cuidadosamente entró. No vio a nadie. Pero otra vez oyó el ruido tan extraño. Venía desde el otro lado de la oficina cerca del escritorio de Pepino. Las piernas de Panzón comenzaron a temblar. Iba a salir cuando vio a su jefe. Estaba tirado en el suelo. Parecía que estaba durmiendo, o ¡qué horror! ¿podía estar muerto? Panzón corrió a su lado.

—Jefe, jefe. ¡Hábleme! ¿Está muerto? ¿Qué hace en el suelo?

En ese instante Pepino abrió los ojos. Miró a Panzón vagamente° como si se estuviera despertando de un sueño. Al tratar de levantarse dio una exclamación de dolor y se llevó las manos a la cabeza:

vagamente, vaguely

—¡Ay! Mi pobre cabeza. ¡Cuánto me duele!

—Pero jefe, no entiendo.— Panzón estaba algo confuso pero alegre de ver que su jefe no estaba muerto.

—¿Por qué no fue a dormir a su casa? No puede ser muy cómodo° dormirse sobre el piso de la oficina.

cómodo, comfortable

—¡Tonto! ¿Crees que me dormí aquí porque me dio la gana?° Pues no, unos hombres . . .—Y Pepino dejó de hablar. Se había recordado de la señorita Carmen. Miró por la oficina:

me dio la gana, I felt like it

—¿Dónde está? ¡Se la llevaron!

Panzón le miró con preocupación. ¿De qué hablaba

34

el jefe? ¡A lo mejor la noche que pasó en el suelo le
había afectado el juicio!° Pero Pepino, ya más des- *juicio,* intelligence
pertado, le contó todo, desde el momento en que en-
contró a Carmen en la oficina hasta que los dos
hombres con pistola entraron. Al oir esto Panzón se
puso muy serio:
—Jefe, tenemos que llamar a la policía. Si esos hombres llevaron a la señorita y si tenían pistolas—¡son
peligrosos! Usted tuvo suerte que no le dieron un
balazo.° *balazo,* bullet
wound
Pepino no estaba de acuerdo. Estaba enojado y un
poco desanimado.° Le dolía la cabeza, tenía ham- *desanimado,*
discouraged
bre y lo más importante—no había podido ayudar a
Carmen.
—No he sido un buen investigador. Sherlock Holmes
estaría muy enojado conmigo— dijo en una voz triste.
Sonó el teléfono. Panzón fue a contestarlo:
—Buenos días, Investigaciones privadas, S.A. Paco
Panzón a sus órdenes.— Panzón volvió hacia Pepino.
—Jefe, es para usted. Habla el director del museo, el
señor Muñoz. Dice que el señor Delgado ha desapare-
cido y que si nosotros sabemos dónde pudiera estar.
También quiere saber si hemos encontrado a la momia.
Pepino movió la cabeza.
—Dile que no sabemos nada. Ah . . . espera. ¿Te
acuerdas como se portó ayer? Dile que quizá Delgado
se ha ido a Madrid.
Panzón repitió esto en el teléfono y luego escuchó° *escuchó,* listened
por un largo rato. El señor Muñoz estaba hablando.
Panzón colgó° el teléfono y miró a su jefe con ojos *colgó,* hung up
grandes:
—El señor Muñoz quiere que vayamos a Madrid.
¡Hoy! Esta tarde. Dice que recibió una carta anónima° *anónima,* anonymous
diciendo que la momia está allá. Nosotros tenemos
que ir a recogerla y regresar con la momia antes de la
exposición que tendrá lugar° pasado mañana. *tendrá lugar,* will
take place
—Todo eso en 24 horas— contestó Pepino. —¡Es
imposible!

—Iremos por avión— explicó Panzón. —El señor Muñoz nos ha comprado boletos en un nuevo 747. Tenemos que estar en el aeropuerto a las cuatro.

—Pero la señorita Carmen, ¿qué le pasará a ella si yo no la ayudo?— dijo Pepino.

—No se preocupe, jefe. Mi primo vive en Madrid y dice que allá todas las chicas son bonitas, ¡tan bonitas como aquí!

—¿Ah sí?— Y por primera vez en ese día Pepino comenzó a sentirse mejor.

A las cuatro en punto los dos investigadores bajaron del taxi frente al aeropuerto grande de México. Cada uno llevaba una pequeña maleta° con una camisa limpia, unos pañuelos y un cepillo de dientes.° En la maleta de Pepino también había una pistola, algo que afirmaba que éste no iba a ser un viaje de placer. Entraron en la sala del aeropuerto y recogieron sus boletos. Todo estaba en orden. El avión iba a salir dentro de media hora. Pepino compró un periódico y varias novelas policiacas para leer durante el viaje. Panzón se compró una bolsa grande de dulces y chocolates, por si acaso° no hubiera suficiente comida en el avión. Entraron en la sala 4. Por la ventana se veía el avión. Era enorme. Brillaba como una joya preciosa con el sol de la tarde. Pepino y Panzón, con los demás pasajeros salieron afuera y subieron las escaleras del avión. Una muchacha vestida en minifalda roja les llevó a sus asientos.

—Abrochen sus cinturones° por favor— dijo con una sonrisa.

Panzón, sentado al lado de la ventana, miraba hacia afuera. Estaba un poco aprehensivo. Sabía que dentro de unas horas estarían en un país desconocido,° lejos de México. ¡Quién sabe lo que les espera allá!

—Oye jefe, ¿qué cree que encontraremos en Madrid? ¿Cree que todo saldrá bien?

Pero Pepino no le había oído. Sus ojos todavía seguían la minifalda de la camarera° atractiva.

maleta, suitcase

cepillo de dientes, toothbrush

por si acaso, in case

abrochen sus cinturones, fasten your seatbelts

desconocido, unknown

camarera, stewardess

36

11. Bienvenidos

El altavoz de Barajas, el aeropuerto de Madrid, anunció la llegada del 747 de México. En la sala de espera° un hombre se levantó. Era bajito y gordo y estaba vestido de uniforme de sargento de policía. Era un guardia civil° español. El sargento miró a todos los pasajeros que bajaron del avión de México y al ver a Pepino y a Panzón se dirigió rápidamente hacia ellos.

sala de espera, waiting room

guardia civil, Spanish police

—¡Panzón!— gritó el sargento.

—¡Sanzón!— contestó Panzón y se dieron un fuerte abrazo.°

abrazo, embrace

Pepino estaba asombrado.° ¿Qué hacía la policía aquí? ¿Panzón ha cometido algún crimen? Panzón pronto le explicó:

asombrado, astonished

—Jefe, le presento a mi primo,° el sargento Sanzón. El trabaja aquí en Madrid, quizá nos puede ayudar a encontrar a la momia.

primo, cousin

—Bienvenidos° a Madrid— dijo el sargento dándole la mano a Pepino. —¡Qué bueno que han venido a visitarnos!

bienvenidos, welcome

Sanzón se parecía tanto a Panzón que casi hubieran podido pasar por gemelos.° Tenía la misma forma de cara con la misma sonrisa. Usaba el mismo peinado, hasta tenía el mismo estómago grande. La única diferencia era en la manera de hablar. El sargento hablaba español con un acento castellano, mientras

gemelos, twins

37

que Pepino y Panzón hablaban con acento mexicano. Los tres hombres se encaminaron hacia afuera. Todavía era muy temprano y Pepino y Panzón estaban cansados. Habían pasado la noche en el vuelo y la ropa que llevaban estaba arrugada.° Panzón tenía hambre. Subieron al coche negro del sargento.

—Primero daremos un paseo por la ciudad—dijo Sanzón. —Luego comeremos. Conozco un café donde hacen unos huevos rancheros° sabrosísimos.

—¡A él le gusta comer tanto como a Panzón!— pensó Pepino.

El coche cruzaba las calles principales de Madrid. Era una mañana agradable. El sol apenas salía y la ciudad parecía bella y tranquila. Pepino miraba hacia afuera por la ventana. Sanzón, muy orgulloso de poder enseñarles su ciudad, no había dejado de hablar ni un solo minuto:

— . . . y aquí a la derecha — decía, —está el célebre Museo del Prado. Adentro se encuentran obras de todos los pintores españoles; Goya, el Greco, Velázquez. Desde el museo se ve el hermoso Parque del Retiro donde hay jardines botánicos, un estanque° y un jardín sólo de rosas. Pronto llegaremos a la Puerta del Sol. Es el centro de la capital y también es el puerto más importante. Desde allí comienzan todas las carreteras principales de España. . .

—Sí, pero ¿cuándo comeremos?— interrumpió Panzón, ya hambriento.

Momentos después estaban sentados en el café La Madrileña, cerca de la Plaza Mayor. Todos estaban bebiendo café con leche y comiendo unas rebanadas° de pan tostado con mermelada de fresa. Sanzón les había preguntado lo que hacían en Madrid y Pepino por fin tuvo la oportunidad de hablar. Le contó todo.

— . . . y así es que venimos en busca de una momia que fue robada del museo de México— concluyó Pepino. —También tenemos que encontrar al señor Delgado y a Carmen del Valle.

arrugada, wrinkled

huevos rancheros, scrambled eggs with hot sauce

estanque, pond

rebanadas, slices

38

El sargento se rascó la nariz. Estaba pensando. Tomó el último pedazo de pan y dijo:

—No sé si la policía de Madrid les pueda ayudar. Ahora estamos preocupados buscando a unos ladrones° internacionales que acaban de robar una gran cantidad de joyas preciosas.° Pero ya he oído hablar de esa señorita Carmen.

ladrones, thieves

joyas preciosas, precious jewels

Pepino dejó de comer. Su corazón palpitaba fuertemente.

—Antes trabajaba en un museo de Madrid — dijo Sanzón. —Pero un día desapareció. Algunos piensan que ella tuvo algo que ver con esos ladrones internacionales. La policía quiso hacerle algunas preguntas pero no pudieron encontrarla. Quizás ustedes tendrán mejor suerte. ¿Por qué no preguntan por el Rastro?° Ella tenía unos amigos que trabajaban allí.

el Rastro, Madrid's fleamarket, open mainly on weekends

—El Rastro — dijo Panzón. —¿Qué es eso?

—Es un gran mercado en donde venden de todo. Queda aquí cerca en la Plaza de Cascorro. Allí se pueden comprar muebles viejos, ropa del siglo pasado, botellas usadas, monedas antiguas, relojes.

—¡Ah,qué bonito! A lo mejor encontraré un regalo de cumpleaños° para mi hijo — dijo Panzón, muy contento.

regalo de cumpleaños, birthday present

—¡Caramba Panzón! — Pepino le reprendió. —¿Qué crees? ¿Que venimos a divertirnos? Estamos aquí para salvar la reputación de nuestro país. Nuestro trabajo es importantísimo. Un día seremos famosos. El presidente nos invitará a cenar.° Saldremos en la televisión. Hasta en España todo el mundo conocerá nuestros nombres y vendrán a . . .

cenar, to dine

—Sí jefe — interrumpió Panzón, —pero primero tenemos que encontrar a la momia.

12. En la tienda del gitano viejo

Sanzón tenía que ir a la prefectura° de policía a
trabajar. Dejó a los dos investigadores en la entrada
del mercado. Antes de despedirse les dio un consejo.°
—Tengan mucho cuidado. Madrid puede ser un lugar
muy peligroso. Y no se olviden de hablarme por teléfono
si deciden hacer algo.

Pero ni Pepino ni Panzón le hicieron mucho caso.
Ya caminaban por el Rastro. Habían tiendas a cada
lado de la calle, pero casi todas estaban cerradas. La
calle estaba desierta. Eran los únicos allí. No había
ni un sonido, sólo se oía el ruido de sus pasos sobre
el pavimiento. Era un silencio extraño y Panzón sentía
escalofríos en la espalda.

—Oiga jefe — dijo en voz baja, —mejor que nos
vayamos de aquí.

Pepino también estaba un poco nervioso pero no
quería admitirlo. Trató de demostrar que él era el
más audaz.

—¡Caramba Panzón!— contestó Pepino. —Los investigadores nunca tienen miedo. ¡Oh mira!— dijo,
señalando con el dedo. —Aquella tienda, la que se
llama La Navaja,° parece abierta. Vamos a preguntar
allá.

Panzón no quería ir, pero su jefe ya había cruzado
la calle y entraba en La Navaja. Dentro, la tienda

prefectura, headquarters

consejo, advice

audaz, brave

navaja, switchblade, razor

40

era muy curiosa. No había mucha luz pero podían ver que la tienda estaba llena de toda clase de armas: pistolas y cuchillos amontonados sobre muchas mesas: rifles y espadas° viejas apoyadas° contra las paredes. Hasta en un rincón vieron un enorme cañón de artillería. También había polvo por todos lados. Parecía como si nadie hubiera estado allí en algunos años. Panzón estornudó° varias veces. Por ningún lado vieron al dueño de la tienda.

espadas, swords
apoyadas, leaning

estornudó, sneezed

—Buenos días— dijo Pepino en voz muy alta. —¿Hay alguien aquí?

En la parte de atrás había una puerta cubierta con una cortina° roja. Los investigadores vieron que la cortina se movía. ¡Alguien estaba escondido mirándolos! Al fin salió un gitano° viejo. Tenía el pelo blanco y la piel arrugada como una pasa, pero aunque era anciano había algo diabólico en su mirada.

cortina, curtain

gitano, gypsy

—¿Quieren comprar un cuchillo?— preguntó. —¿O quizá una pistola? Vendo balas° también.— Después con una risa horrible añadió —les aseguro que el que dispara con una de mis pistolas nunca falla.°

balas, bullets

falla, misses

—¡No!— contestó Pepino, algo escandalizado por la oferta. —Venimos en busca de información.

Al oír esto el viejo se asustó:

—¿Son de la policía?

—No— dijo Pepino, —sólo queremos saber algo acerca de la señorita Carmen del Valle.

Era evidente que el gitano viejo no quería hablar sobre ese tema. Pepino estaba confundido. ¿Qué haría su héroe, Sherlock Holmes, en una situación semejante? De pronto encontró la respuesta.°

respuesta, answer

—Si Ud. nos dice donde podemos encontrar a la señorita le daremos un regalito.— Diciendo esto Pepino sacó su cartera.

Los ojos del viejo se abrieron. Miraba la cartera de Pepino con envidia.

—Bueno— dijo, —pero le va a costar 1.500 pesetas.°

1.500 pesetas, approx.
10 dollars

Pepino hizo una pausa, pero finalmente le dio el

dinero. Sabía que era importante encontrar primero a Carmen para poder averiguar dónde estaba la momia. También sabía que el señor Muñoz le devolvería el dinero. El viejo tomó las mil pesetas. Las contó cuidadosamente. Cuando estuvo satisfecho abrió la cortina roja y los invitó a pasar al cuarto del fondo. El cuarto era aún más pequeño. Todo estaba muy sucio. Había una mesa y algunas cajas que servían de sillas. El viejo buscó bajo la mesa y sacó una botella y unos vasos no muy limpios.

—Siéntense y beban un poco de vino— dijo a media voz. —Sólo sé que la señorita a quien se refieren llegó ayer a Madrid acompañada de tres tipos. Mi informador me ha dicho que la llevaron a las cuevas° °cuevas, caves y que nunca saldrá viva de allá.

13. Una copita de vino

Pepino le miró con la boca abierta. ¡Qué terrible! pensó. ¡La pobre señorita! Quería saber más pero el viejo se negó a hablar° hasta que le entregaran otras mil pesetas. Discutieron un rato hasta que el viejo dijo que tomaría 700 pesetas. Parecía preocupado. Miraba su reloj a cada rato como si tuviera una cita importante que temiera perder.

°negó a hablar, refused to speak

—Las cuevas son de unos gitanos— dijo rápidamente. —Quedan a una hora de Madrid por la carretera que va a Valencia. Ahora tengo que irme por un momento. Si quieren saber más, espérenme aquí. Regreso dentro de unos diez minutos.

El viejo caminó hacia la puerta. La cerró de un golpe. Pepino y Panzón quedaron solos otra vez. Panzón caminaba por la tienda mirando a todas las armas. Pepino se quedó sentado en el cuarto de atrás. Pensaba en Carmen. Estaba triste. Las cosas no les iban bien. Miró a la botella de vino que todavía estaba sobre la mesa. Se sirvió una copita.° La bebió y pronto se sintió mejor. Se sirvió otra vez y comenzó a olvidarse de sus problemas. Varios minutos pasaron. Panzón había encontrado una espada llena de adornos como las que usaban los piratas y los generales. Estaba pensando como le gustaría a su hijito, cuando recordó la hora.

°copita, a little drink

—Oiga jefe — dijo. —Ha pasado más de media hora.

A lo mejor el viejo no va a regresar. Mejor que nos vayamos.

Cuando Pepino no contestó, Panzón fue a buscarlo. ¡Qué sorpresa! Pepino estaba sentado frente a la mesa, parecía que estaba durmiéndose. . Panzón lo sacudió pero Pepino no se despertó. Quedaba muy poco vino en la botella. Panzón pensó que su jefe había bebido demasiado cuando notó que algo olía raro. ¿Podía ser el vino? Panzón lo miró con más cuidado. ¿Por qué tenía ese color oscuro?, se preguntaba. Lo iba a probar° cuando vio un frasco° bajo la mesa. Panzón lo recogió. Era un frasco de medicina, con una inscripción: *pastillas para dormir.°* Estaba completamente vacío. ¡Pepino estaba endrogado!°

—¡Ay! ¿Ahora qué hago?— se dijo, retorciéndose las manos. Fue hacia Pepino. —¡Pronto! Levántese jefe— le rogó. —Tenemos que salir de aquí antes de que regrese ese viejo malo.

Agarró a Pepino y lo arrastró hacia la salida. Pepino pesaba mucho y era difícil sostenerlo.° Hicieron mucho ruido cuando tropezaron con una mesa y tiraron todas las pistolas que estaban encima. Afuera, la calle seguía desierta. Sólo un coche estaba estacionado frente a la tienda. Panzón se alegró cuando vio que era un taxi libre. Abrió la puerta del coche y empujando a su jefe hacia adentro se subió. Panzón estaba demasiado preocupado para pensar lo raro que era encontrar un taxi esperando en una calle tan desierta como aquella.

—¿Adónde van?— preguntó el chofer, mirándolos con ojos maliciosos.

Panzón le iba a decir a la prefectura de policía cuando tuvo una idea. En lugar de eso° dijo:

—Por la carretera a Valencia, como a una hora de Madrid. Buscamos unas cuevas de gitanos.

El coche arrancó. Panzón miró a su jefe. Estaba bien dormido. Esperaba que Pepino se despertara pronto. El taxi iba muy de prisa.° Panzón miró por la ventana. Las bellas calles de Madrid pasaban, pero

probar, to taste

frasco, small container

pastillas para dormir, sleeping pills

endrogado, drugged

sostenerlo, support him

en lugar de eso, instead of that

de prisa, fast

44

Panzón no las miraba. Se estaba recordando° de lo   *recordando, remembering*
que le había dicho su primo. —A lo mejor le debo
avisar lo que nos ha pasado — pensó.

—¡Eh chofer!— ordenó: —pare el coche un momento, quiero hacer una llamada telefónica.

El chofer hizo como si no oyera. Panzón repitió
sus palabras. Pero otra vez el chofer no le hizo caso.
El coche iba más rápido. Habían salido de Madrid.

—¡Qué nos va a pasar!— dijo Panzón angustiado.

—¡Ah! ¿Por qué no presté más atención a lo que nos
dijo Sanzón?

14. Peligro en las cuevas

El taxi dejó la carretera principal. Ahora iba por un camino poco transitado° que corría a la orilla de una montaña. Una hora había pasado desde que Panzón y Pepino salieron de la tienda del gitano viejo. Panzón trató de nuevo de despertar a su jefe, pero era inútil.° Pepino seguía endrogado. El coche se paró frente a unas cuevas. Era un lugar triste, árido. Habían algunos gitanos afuera sentados en el suelo, y varios perros descarriados° buscaban comida entre las rocas y la tierra. Alguien tocaba la guitarra. Era una melodía lenta, melancólica que dio a Panzón un presentimiento° de que algo muy mal les iba a pasar. El chofer se había bajado del taxi. Era joven y feroz. Vestía de. pantalones y camisa negros. Sacó un enorme cuchillo del bolsillo.

—¡Salgan del coche!— les ordenó, mostrando el cuchillo puntiagudo,° —¡o les corto las orejas!

Al oír esto Panzón se puso palidísimo.—¡Qué horror quedarse sin orejas!—pensó. Pepino había comenzado a despertarse. Estaba asustado de encontrarse en un lugar desconocido. Panzón le explicó rápidamente lo que había pasado. El chofer indicó que debían entrar en la cueva. Estaba muy oscuro adentro y Panzón casi no podía caminar del miedo. Pero el chofer seguía tras ellos con el cuchillo. Pepino estaba demasiado

poco transitado,
little used

inútil, useless

perros descarriados,
stray dogs

presentimiento, feeling

puntiagudo, pointed

46